Praise for the Book

Anil Khandelwal offers unique insights about the transition of the financial services sector and evolution of industrial relations to human resources. He provides a unique insider perspective having first-hand experience in these remarkable evolutions. Even more, he brings the rigour of his academic training to observe, codify, and convert generalization insights into actions. A wonderful narrative from a truly exceptional CEO.

Dave Ulrich,
Rensis Likert Professor, Ross School of Business,
University of Michigan; Partner, The RBL Group

Dr Anil Khandelwal's book reflects his temperament, and more important, his background as a trainer, a teacher, an executive, a chief executive of a bank, a thinker, and finally a writer. It is of extraordinary value because it contains the distilled wisdom narrated through personal experience and episodes without losing sight of theory and the big picture. It describes the remarkable journey of our finance from static control system to pervasive confusion and finally to consolidation into a modern bank.

The book is both a record of institutional history and an evaluation of financial sector in general and banking in particular. I have no doubt that the book is of great value not only for HR professionals, but also for practitioners of management and academics.

Y.V. Reddy,
Former Governor, Reserve Bank of India

CEO—*Chess Master or Gardener?* is a brilliant blend of management theory and executive experience. As usual, Anil Khandelwal is a master storyteller and narrates his own lessons in leadership related to transforming the culture of state-owned enterprises.

Jagdish Sheth,
Charles H. Kellstadt Professor of Business,
Goizueta Business School, Emory University, USA

(*Continued*)

An engaging, timeless, and timely reminder that employee relations is strategic and a key driver of firm performance. The lessons from a master practitioner are both fascinating and useful for the CEOs.

Ravi Venkatesan,
Non-executive Chairman, Bank of Baroda

This book, based on the involved experiences of a participant–researcher, is a kaleidoscope of organizational learning. It brings together the perspectives of a CEO, an HR leader, and an intense professional, giving it many flavours picked up through one's career journey. The metaphors in the title of the book simply reflect Dr Khandelwal's unique style of storytelling.

Santrupt B. Misra,
CEO, Carbon Black Business,
Director, Group Human Resources,
Aditya Birla Group

This is a remarkable saga of how empirical research findings on the IR culture of a large public sector bank evolved into a massive business transformation of the organization.… It is a remarkable story of how the courage and commitment of one man could use 'intangibles' like authenticity, empowerment, engagement, and dialogue to create the trust and passion which, combined with long-term strategy, processes, and metrics, produced powerful tangible business outcomes.… This is a story of creative destruction with two areas of focus: engaging directly with employees and developing capabilities. It shows the path we must all tread if we are to be successful in this Age of Disruption.

Rajeev Dubey,
Group President (HR & Corporate Services),
CEO (After-Market Sector),
Member of the Group Executive Board, Mahindra & Mahindra Limited

CEO
Chess Master or Gardener?

CEO

Chess Master or Gardener?

How Game-Changing HR
Reforms Created a New Future for
Bank of Baroda

ANIL K. KHANDELWAL

OXFORD
UNIVERSITY PRESS

OXFORD
UNIVERSITY PRESS

Oxford University Press is a department of the University of Oxford.
It furthers the University's objective of excellence in research, scholarship,
and education by publishing worldwide. Oxford is a registered trademark of
Oxford University Press in the UK and in certain other countries.

Published in India by
Oxford University Press
2/11 Ground Floor, Ansari Road, Daryaganj, New Delhi 110 002, India

ISBN-13 (print edition): 978-0-19-948564-2
ISBN-10 (print edition): 0-19-948564-X

ISBN-13 (eBook): 978-0-19-909204-8
ISBN-10 (eBook): 0-19-909204-4

Typeset in Arno Pro 10.5/14
by Tranistics Data Technologies, New Delhi 110 044
Printed in India by Replika Press Pvt. Ltd

Disclaimer: Tables, figures, and boxes that do not mention any specific
source are author's own works.

*Dedicated to the individuals who sharpened my ideas and enriched
my professional journey in countless ways:*

N.R. Sheth • Late L.B. Bhide • Late Udai Pareek • Late S.P. Talwar •
T.V Rao • Vinod Rai • Dwijendra Tripathy • P.C. Sharma •
Pradip Khandwala • Sid Khanna • Rajen K. Gupta •
Late Harish Chandra Sharma

CONTENTS

TABLES, FIGURES, AND BOXES

Tables

Figures

Boxes

ACKNOWLEDGEMENTS

Rajen K. Gupta, professor, Management Development Institute, has been a gravitational pull in nudging me to write this book. He and his wife, Indu, endured my countless visits to their home and affectionately extended every courtesy. Rajen travelled at least four times to Mumbai only for this project, so that we could sit together to plan and discuss the various chapters in detail. We had many hours of stimulating conversations together. Being an avid reader, thinker, and researcher, he helped me in developing an academic perspective in putting the research and practice together. Also, his deep insights helped to improve the substance and style of the book. Thank you, Rajen! This book exists because of you.

I am grateful to my research guide, Professor N.R. Sheth, former Director, Indian Institute of Management (IIM) Ahmedabad, who read the first draft and made some very useful suggestions. Also, thanks are due in an equal measure to Professor Dwijendra Tripathi, former Dean IIM Ahmedabad and an eminent business historian, who provided useful insights. Jyoti Jumani gave some important editorial help in the initial phase. Thank you, Jyoti.

I would also like to thank my friend, B.P. Vijayendra (who recently retired as Principal Chief General Manager of Reserve Bank of India), for reading the final draft word by word and offering many editorial corrections. He got passionately involved with the project and spent several days working with me during the final phase of completion of the book. His inputs, especially from the perspective of a reader, were very useful. Dhwani provided excellent secretarial help in typing the manuscript.

C.V. Chandrashekhar (Chandra), former Deputy General Manager, Human Resources, in Bank of Baroda helped me with important materials like union circulars and in recapitulating important events during the transformation. Thank you, Chandra, for your help. The inputs from two reviewers were also very useful in shaping the book into its present form.

My wife, Vandna, has always stood by me and been my rock-solid support in moments of anxiety. She has been a wonderful host to many friends with whom we had discussions and conversations while preparing the book. She also made sure that I remain committed to the project and was not bothered on the home front. Manoj, our domestic help, would happily run around to maintain a constant supply of tea/coffee, an essential stimulant to keep the work going. His culinary skills made him popular with Rajen and Vijayendra.

I am particularly grateful to Oxford University Press India team for encouraging the publication of this book and for their cooperation at every stage of the publication process.

ABBREVIATIONS

AIBEA	All India Bank Employees Association
AIBOA	All India Bank Officers' Association
AIBOBECC	All India Bank of Baroda Employees Coordination Committee
AIBOBEF	All India Bank of Baroda Employees Federation
AIBOBOA	All India Bank of Baroda Officers' Association
AIBOC	All India Bank Officers' Congress
AICOBO	All India Confederation of Bank Officers
ATM	Automated Teller Machine
BDC	Business Development Committee
BEFI	Bank Employees Federation of India
BoB/the Bank	Bank of Baroda
BOBETUC	Bank of Baroda Employees Trade Union Congress
BPS	Bipartite Settlement
BSRB	Banking Service Recruitment Board
CBS	Core Banking Solutions
CEO	Chief Executive Officer
CoE	Committee of Executives
DAW	Disciplinary Action Wing
EMC	Executive Management Committee
ERC	Eastern Regional Council
HP	Hewlett-Packard
HR	Human Resource/s
HRD	Human Resource Development
HRM	Human Resource Management
HRnes	Human Resource Network for Employee Services
IBA	Indian Banks' Association

IIM	Indian Institute of Management
INTUC	Indian National Trade Union Congress
IR	Industrial Relations
IT	Information Technology
KRA	Key Responsibility Area
LTC	Leave Travel Concession
LWOs	Labour Welfare Officers
MDI	Management Development Institute (Gurgaon)
MoU	Memorandum of Understanding
MPs	Members of Parliament
MSA	Multi Service Agency
MSCs	Multi-service Centres
NABOBO	National Association of Bank of Baroda Officers
NCR	National Capital Region
NIBM	National Institute of Bank Management
OBC	Oriental Bank of Commerce
PC	Personnel Committee
PSBs	Public Sector Banks
RBI	Reserve Bank of India
RRB	Regional Rural Bank
SC	Scheduled Caste
SMEs	Small and Medium-sized Enterprises
ST	Scheduled Tribe
UAE	United Arab Emirates
UFBU	United Forum of Bank Unions
UP	Uttar Pradesh
USA	United States of America
VDC	Village Development Centre
VRS	Voluntary Retirement Scheme

PREFACE

This book is about my research study and about two decades of executive roles at the Bank of Baroda (BoB). The inspiration to publish this work came from more than one source. For quite some time, my academic friends have been encouraging me to publish my research work because they saw the merit of my work in the context of the continued paucity of research endeavours in the messy domain of industrial relations (IR), and more particularly in the study of 'management' as an important actor in IR.

I have often heard scholars point out that there is a gap between those who conduct research and those who are in a position to implement research findings (Rynes et al., 2007). Connectedness between research and practice is now a popular subject in many academic conferences. This is perhaps the single-most common reason why management practitioners have not shown much interest in research either by way of supporting academics with research grants or by sparing time to engage with researchers to jointly identify research problems or allow them access to the strategic level of management.

Originally, I undertook research on managerial strategies in IR in BoB, one of the largest public sector banks in India, between 1984 and 1988. I was then working as a senior core faculty member at the Bank of Baroda Staff College in Ahmedabad, where part of my role was to undertake organisationally relevant research. Batch after batch of senior managers who came to attend the programme, 'Managing IR at the Branches', which I had initiated in the context of the difficult IR situation at the branch level, revealed their helplessness in tackling IR at their respective branches. They uniformly pointed to the intransigence of the trade unions and lack of support from the management in addressing the various IR issues. Industrial relations was considered no one's problem even though it was one of the foremost obstacles in business development and delivering good customer service.

Against this background, as part of my research, I decided to investigate the Bank's management strategies in IR to gain further insights into the problem. One of the key considerations of the Bank's management in allowing me to do research on this sensitive topic was the possibility of my research findings contributing to helping it design a better IR policy.

I received some useful insights as an outcome of my research, which had the potential to bring about qualitative change in IR at the Bank. But, by the time I had finished with my research, the key actors in the management had changed and initiating change in IR was no longer a priority. I myself was not senior enough to trigger the necessary changes.

As I moved ahead in my career, the time came when I knew I could influence policy changes in the Bank's IR management. The year was 2000 and I had just been elevated to a board-level position as an Executive Director (I was later to become Chief Executive Officer [CEO] of BoB). Both the setting and the time were right. Liberalisation had left public sector banks experiencing major aftershocks from the competition posed by two newly formed private sector banks with state-of-the-art technology and from the demands thrown up by the retail revolution in the country. Public sector banks had to change, and quickly, to adopt modern technology and transform their customer service orientation; and BoB was no exception. The prevailing pattern of IR at the Bank, however, posed a major challenge in undertaking any transformational programme, and this had to change if the Bank was to use technology to move forward.

This book describes the history of BoB's IR, characterised as it was by informal and ad hoc responses to problems, and then comprehensively charts the major changes in IR strategies that I initiated: first, in my two operational roles at the zonal level; and later, in my two strategic roles as an Executive Director and as the Bank's CEO. We managed much of the transition and associated tensions and turbulence based on my understanding and insights about the unions and their functioning, which I had gained during my fieldwork.

Although some scholars (Blake and Mouton, 1976; Pettigrew, 1985; Schein, 2003) have provided a detailed account of organisational changes as a consultant or researcher over a long period of time, it is rare that a trainer-researcher comes to occupy the position of CEO in the same business organisation and is able to attempt a major organisational change based on research insights and inferences. I dare say that but for these insights, I would have not attempted the changes in IR strategies that I did, or been successful in effecting them, as the situation was complicated.

In view of the unique opportunity I had as a researcher–practitioner, I hope this book will prove to be a valuable contribution in bridging the gap between theory and practice in the field of IR.

Finally, I want to say that many individuals like past CEOs and others have been mentioned in the book in a particular context. The intention has been to describe them in a role without meaning any ill will to anyone personally.

INTRODUCTION

In organisations, as also in the realm of management science, there has been an increase in dissatisfaction with the relevance of management theories to management practices (Ghoshal, 2005; Tushman and O' Reilly, 2007; Van de Ven, 2007). The much-professed gap between theory and practice, which has been a persistent concern in applied social sciences (Argyris and Schön, 1974; Lindblom and Cohen, 1979; Lupton, 1983; Shapiro and Wagner DeCew, 1995; Lawler et al., 1999), was the key reason for me to seriously consider crafting this book to record how I shaped a new industrial relations (IR) policy framework in my executive role at the Bank of Baroda (BoB).

During the 1980s, public sector banks (PSBs) were in the grip of militant trade unionism which severely affected their business levels and the quality of customer service they offered. In spite of industry-level wage settlements and service conditions, individual PSBs constantly experienced IR trouble. For too long, IR was considered, at best, a nuisance to deal with or to live with, and managerial initiatives were few in terms of strategic planning for effective management of IR. Initially, I was quite stumped to be part of a system where the managerial initiatives were far too few to improve the dynamics of IR and where operating managers often felt themselves to be victims of a system over which they felt they had no control.

It was around this time that a chance perusal of the *British Journal of Industrial Relations* brought out, for me, an altogether new perspective. In an article, 'The Management of Industrial Relations in the Modern Corporation: Agenda for Research', Purcell (1983) stressed the significant role of the management in influencing many facets of IR, which was a healthy departure from the hitherto observed obsession with the role of trade unions in IR. Purcell observed that very little was known, however, about the process of management and the way managerial initiatives were formulated and carried through. He called for a study of the higher echelons of management to understand their strategy and structure in managing IR.

* * *

A sensitive and complex subject like IR, which involved the top management's strategies and also the dynamic interplay of the various factors that shaped the relationship between management and trade unions, was a difficult undertaking. However, BoB's General Manager, Personnel, at that time, L.B. Bhide, was both progressive and proactive, and he encouraged me. One of the key reasons for the theory–practice gap seems to be methodological weaknesses. As access to top management echelons is not always easy, most researchers tend to be driven by a positivist paradigm and to rely on questionnaire-based surveys or arm's-length interviews and case studies. Such research, in spite of best intentions, fails to capture the subtleties of daily organisational life. I have been fortunate on two counts. As an officer of a progressive organisation, I had access to the top echelons of management. More importantly, the Bank had a progressive tradition of supporting academic work. Bhide was an extraordinary professional who looked positively at academic endeavours; he had himself obtained a one-year full-time diploma in Human Relations and Labour Welfare from the London School of Economics in 1965 on the Bank's nomination. On the academic side, I was lucky to meet up with N.R. Sheth, Director of the Indian Institute of Management (IIM) in Ahmedabad, a leading academic in IR, whose classic research study, *Social Framework of an Indian Factory* was a landmark ethnographical account of workers in a manufacturing industry. Sheth's association with BoB in a consulting assignment had provided him deep insights into the workings of a bank. He readily agreed to guide me through my research.

* * *

My research study focused on examining the strategies and policies of chief executive officers (CEOs) in IR and covered the tenures of six of them from 1956 to 1988 (excluding Goipuria, who was CEO for just three months).

The key finding of my research was that the CEO was the key designer of IR strategy and that decision-making in IR was highly centralised in the CEO. It was revealing to observe:

1. How top management strategies were shaped, what organisational and environmental factors dictated changes in policies and strategies, how policies and strategies were implemented, what difficulties were encountered in the process of implementation, and what were the intended and unintended consequences of implementation of strategies.
   - How some CEOs manipulated the IR agenda to their advantage, sometimes to seek business results and at other times to enhance their personal power.
2. How some CEOs created company unions and carefully nurtured them to ensure industrial peace in the Bank to seek competitive advantage in conducting day-to-day business in a hostile IR environment in the banking industry.
3. How CEOs and key leaders of unions created a surrogate collaborative relationship, using it to enhance their own power.
   - How, within the rungs of the top management in a PSB context, unions were manipulated and occasionally enticed to play into the management's hands in their pursuit of personal ambitions of promotions.
   - How key union leaders enhanced their own power by seeking favours and concessions and exploited this by browbeating operating managers.
4. How, despite specialisation of the personnel function, personnel specialists were used and abused (by playing with structure, location, and processes) to gain personal power by some CEOs, even at the cost of derailing personnel administration; and how some personnel functionaries who did not kowtow to the CEOs and become part of this manipulated agenda, were sidelined.
5. How high centralisation of personnel decision-making and alienation of personnel specialists led to bureaucratisation of personnel decision-making, inconsistencies in implementation of rules at operating levels, loss of corporate control in personnel matters, and an increasing tendency at the operating level to make compromises with unions under pressure to maintain business levels.

6. How oscillation in management policy in IR from occasional confrontation to mollycoddling obstructed a policy framework for the effective conduct of IR and created various patterns of IR at different times; and how an IR pattern based primarily on CEOs' strategies was inherently unstable and unable to cope with an increasingly complex market and political and social environment; and how the IR pattern oscillated between collaboration and classical conflict.

7. How, in a multiple union situation, favouring one union under pressure from its leaders gave rise to problems with the other unions, which led to turbulence in IR and managerial control at the operating level.

8. How IR based on a relationship between the CEO and top union leaders created a disconnect between top management and operating managers, and between senior trade union leaders and their members; and how this led to dilution of authority of operating managers in the workplace (in this case, the Bank branches).

9. How swings in management strategies in dealing with various leaders in trade unions sent conflicting signals to operating managers about the importance and priority accorded by the top management to dealing with the critical and sensitive issue of IR, including discipline and productivity.

10. How, in the entire dynamics, operating managers lost control and experienced difficulty in managing workplace conflicts and in dealing with restrictive practices and customer service; and how operating managers avoided accepting any responsibility for IR.

* * *

After the completion of my research in 1991 and a stint as the principal of the Bank of Baroda Staff College in Ahmedabad, I moved to the Personnel Department in the Bank's corporate office in Mumbai, and in 1994, I was appointed Deputy General Manager of Human Resources (HR). Subsequently, I had two tenures in banking operations (as zonal manager) in two challenging territories in India: the Western Uttar Pradesh Zone, headquartered in Meerut; and the Eastern Zone, headquartered at Kolkata. Later, in 2000, I moved to a board position as executive director and in 2005, as CEO of the Bank.

In my field operations (see Part II of the book), I experienced the impact of the IR strategies of the CEOs in the working of the Bank and closely observed top management responses on a day-to-day basis.

Subsequently, as executive director (2000–03) and later as CEO (2005–08) (from February 2004 to February 2005, I was appointed CEO of Dena Bank, a mid-sized PSB), in my policy-making role, I initiated a series of IR reforms in the context of the many changes that the banking industry experienced post-liberalisation. The core of the new strategy was to move from an essentially informal and accommodative mode of IR to a more orderly and formalised mode to develop consistency in policy-making and its implementation. The changeover from an essentially unstructured relationship based on personal relations to an institutionalised framework which had fairness at its core was not without its problems.

In Part III of this book, I have elaborated upon the initiatives that were undertaken, the experience of undertaking these initiatives, and their outcomes.

In spite of the many hiccups and turbulence we faced in shaping the new IR framework, it was possible to redefine the role of the unions and streamline the hitherto prevailing unstructured pattern that was mainly supported by favours and concessions extended to the unions. The transition was facilitated by certain insights I had gained during my fieldwork. Some of my specific learning points are outlined next:

1. Management is an active actor in IR and plays an important role in creating a congenial climate in the organisation in relation to its overall objectives.
2. An IR that is based essentially on personal relations between key personalities on both sides may prove to be unstable and lead to conflict, as the favours and concessions granted by each party to the other have no rational basis, and change in leadership on either side could disturb the existing relations.
3. Mere strengthening or weakening of unions at the corporate level does not help in improving the IR climate at the operating level. Such a strategy needs to be accompanied by improvement in personnel decision-making and the installation of an effective and consistent system in dealing with people's issues at all levels.

4. An effective approach to IR must take into account all aspects of relationships between employers and employees. A relevant and comprehensive corporate policy must be framed, covering relationships with unions, collective bargaining, arrangements for consultation, union recognition, facilities for union functionaries, methods of conflict resolution, and the broad range of personnel decision-making, all of which have an impact on IR. Once an organisation adopts the view that IR policy should be an integral part of the overall management policy, there are obvious advantages in defining its IR policy formally.

A well-defined policy is likely to promote consistency in management and enables all operating managers, as well as union representatives, to know where they stand in relation to the overall intentions and objectives. It further encourages the orderly and equitable conduct of IR by enabling the management to plan ahead by anticipating events and taking the initiative to deal with changing situations.

Analysis of management strategies over a long period reveals that despite the external environment, which is common to all banks, it is the management of internal environmental pressures within a bank that is of crucial importance in managing IR.

* * *

Methodology

This was a longitudinal study of top management policies and strategies at BoB for the period from 1956, when the Bank had its first Indian CEO, to 1988. The focus of the investigation was the strategy of the top management in relation to IR management. Although the area of investigation was relatively new and sensitive, my acquaintance with the Bank and both my professional and academic interest in IR were major factors in guiding my decision to choose the Bank for the purpose of my investigations. The study was exploratory in nature. Considering the nature of the investigation, that is, studying managerial strategies in IR in a large bank, I chose the case study method for, as Dalton (1961) rightly said, '[t]he method of enquiry should be functional to the world being studied.'

In order to analyse the top management strategy for various periods, a combination of techniques was used. These included: interviews with former CEOs and other key members of the top management team, such as general managers and deputy general managers; interviews with functionaries of the Personnel Department during each period; interviews with union leaders who had dealt with the top management during different periods; and interviews with critical outsiders, such as officials of the Indian Banks' Association (IBA), the government, and ex-consultants who possessed special knowledge about a particular incident/episode in IR at a given point of time.

For each period, circulars on IR issued by the management, the workmen's unions, and the officers' associations were studied. These circulars provided useful insights into the attitudes of both the management and the unions, as well as the quality of the relationship between them.

In all, 31 interviews were conducted with top and senior management personnel: the current CEO (1985–88); 3 general managers (out of a total of 6); 5 deputy general managers (total 12), 5 zonal managers (total 9); and 17 regional managers (total 52). Interviews were also conducted with 25 personnel specialists. Besides this, interviews were conducted with 4 former CEOs, 3 former executive directors, and 5 former general managers/deputy general managers.

Interviews with trade union leaders, including the general secretaries of both workmen's unions (the All India Bank of Baroda Employees Federation [AIBOBEF] and the All India Bank of Baroda Employees Coordination Committee [AIBOBECC]), and the general secretaries of the officers' associations (the All India Bank of Baroda Officers' Association [AIBOBOA] and the National Association of Bank of Baroda Officers [NABOBO]) were also conducted. Apart from these, interviews were conducted with 5 zonal secretaries and 13 office-bearers of the various unions.

Other sources of data were documentary material, inter-office memoranda, correspondence with the unions, union settlements, minutes of meetings with the unions, and minutes of meetings of the Personnel Committee, Committees of Executives, and the Executive Management Committee.

In order to understand the operational reality of IR during 1987–88, interviews were conducted with 95 branch managers of urban and metropolitan branches who attended training programmes at the Bank's Staff College.

Attempts were also made to understand the operational reality of IR by attending a number of meetings between the management and the trade unions, meetings of the Personnel Committee, conferences of personnel managers, among others. In all, I attended 8 management–union meetings at the central office, 3 conferences of personnel managers, 1 Personnel Committee meeting, and 8 management–union meetings at the zonal level.

Lastly, a survey covering 250 branch managers of large urban and metropolitan branches on various aspects of the IR climate as perceived by them during 1987–88 was undertaken.

Part I

RESEARCHING INDUSTRIAL RELATIONS

This section delves into the author's research about the managerial strategies in IR of six CEOs between 1956 and 1988. This research eventually earned me a PhD degree. While the empirical work with regard to managerial strategy has been retained in substance, only some introductory context-setting chapters have been substantially edited. The chapters provide, in a chronological sequence, the development of IR strategies by different CEOs during their tenures. Five CEOs' IR strategies have been studied through personal interview and archival material, and the strategies of sixth CEO have been studied during actual fieldwork and through the methodology of participant observation, interviews, survey of 250 branch managers, and study of documented material.

Additionally, this section also covers the managerial strategies of three more CEOs, as observed and experienced by me during my various executive roles in the field and in the corporate office.

Chapter 1
SETTING OF THE RESEARCH AGENDA

This chapter examines the contextual setting of the research study—IR in the banking sector—the BoB, and IR and trade unionism at the Bank.

IR in the Banking Sector

Overview of the Banking Industry

Banking is one of the basic instruments of economic growth. Since it is considered the backbone of economic development, the development of the sector assumes crucial importance. The Indian banking system operated primarily in the private sector till the passing of the Banking Laws (Amendment) Act of 1968 by the Parliament, consequent to which 14 large commercial banks were nationalised in July 1969, followed by nationalisation of six more banks in 1980, thereby bringing a major segment of the banking system under the direct control of the government. Post nationalisation, banking services were made available to larger segments of society through rapid expansion of bank branches, as a result of which several million people in agriculture and in small-scale industries, who had been denied access to the banking system till then, started receiving benefits from the industry. With expansion and rapid growth, the banking industry faced problems of efficiency, productivity, and profitability. Post liberalisation in 1991, a committee appointed by the government, popularly known as the Narasimham Committee, under former Reserve Bank of India (RBI) Governor, M. Narasimham, recommended seminal changes, including restructuring of banks, bringing transparency to balance sheets, liberal branch licensing, and improved IR and human resource management (HRM).

The period after 1991 saw the advent of private banks which used the latest technology in their operations, offering customers a completely new banking experience. This had an adverse effect on PSBs. After dilly-dallying about the use of technology in PSBs, the bank unions accepted the introduction of new technology, popularly known as core banking, in the banks, and this heralded a major phase of transformation in PSBs, including the retail banking revolution.

In recent years, technological developments are changing the way in which banks and their customers interact. Digitalisation and fintech are driving new possibilities in the field of finance as never before.

The PSBs account for about 70 per cent of the assets of the Indian banking system and contribute significantly to the country's economic development, in particular to the rural, agriculture, small-scale industries, and export sectors (Reserve Bank of India, 2017). As at present, the deposits and outstanding credit of the PSBs aggregate about Rs 75,000 billion and over Rs 50,000 billion, respectively. The PSBs provide services through a network of nearly 100,000 branches and over 200,000 automated teller machines (ATMs). Going forward, PSBs are expected to play a major role in the financing of infrastructure and new economy sectors, in addition to the traditional sectors. Another emerging imperative for PSBs is to aggressively participate in financial inclusion.

With the onset of the retail revolution, PSBs have launched many customer-centric innovations. Practically all banks have rolled out core banking and provide Internet and mobile banking services. The quality and range of services have improved considerably, but so have the risks.

IR

Industrial relations in the banking industry have had a chequered history. The trade union movement evolved in the 1950s and the mid-1960s against the background of a litigatory and exploitative culture in the banks. A major breakthrough took place in 1966 with the signing of the first bipartite settlement (BPS) at the industry level between the Indian Banks' Association (IBA) (representing the employers) and the majority trade union, the All India Bank Employees Association (AIBEA), in matters of wages and service conditions of workmen staff. This system of bipartism continued even after nationalisation of banks. Subsequently, the wages and the service conditions of the officer staff were also brought under the purview of industry-level negotiations between the association of officers and the IBA. Table 1.1 illustrates the kind of employee issues discussed and resolved at the various levels

TABLE 1.1   Employee Issues Discussed and Resolved at Various Levels in the Banking Industry

Level	Parties	Issues	Personnel/IR Competence
Apex	IBA and central organisation of bank employees.	Salary scales, allowances, service conditions, issues of industry-level importance like automation.	IBA's Personnel Department consultations with solicitors/use of competence of specialists from banks.
Bank	Bank management and bank-wise unions.	Promotion policy, bonus, staff loan schemes, interpretations of service conditions, staff welfare and amenities, facilities to unions.	Personnel executives at central/head office level, IR advisors/solicitors' advice from IBA.
Zonal/Regional	Zonal/regional management and zonal units of bank-wise unions.	Premises, staff shortages, staff amenities, interpretation of bipartite settlement (BPS), unresolved issues at branch level.	Senior operating managers like zonal and regional managers and officers/staff officers.
Branch	Branch manager and branch secretaries/representatives of branch-level units of bank-wise unions.	Work allocation, overtime, implementation of awards/settlements, job rotation, interpersonal problems, inter-union/intra-union rivalry, discipline management to some extent.	No specialised knowledge in personnel/IR.

Post standardisation of wages and service conditions as a result of collective bargaining process at the industry level, the litigatory culture in IR has virtually ended. Over a period of time, bank employees have achieved reasonably better service conditions than their counterparts elsewhere. In this scenario, the relevance of any central labour laws has become almost non-existent, except for the application of the Industrial Disputes Act, 1947 which provides the mechanism for dispute resolution.

Although the bipartite mechanism has provided some stability in IR in banking by saving individual banks from separately pursuing wage negotiations, it has also led to many problems, such as restrictive practices, rigidities in deployment of staff, and lack of motivation on account of uniform wages irrespective of productivity and performance levels. It has also led to united trade union movements, often hijacking the reforms in the banking industry.

Absolved from direct responsibility for negotiations with employees on wages and service conditions, many managements have paid much less attention to IR issues than they would have had they acted in their individual capacities. The growth in the size of banks has led to increasingly impersonal relations between the top management and their workforce; and this lack of engagement with the staff has been a key reason for trade unions to militantly articulate employee grievances.

Harmonious IR are sine qua non for creating a climate of effective service. The nature of banking makes it imperative for a bank to develop a committed workforce. This makes IR management central to the survival of banking itself.

Despite liberalisation and competition, the concomitant reforms in the IR mechanism have not taken place, except for the introduction of new technology. The uniformity of compensation across PSBs, irrespective of capacity to pay or profitability and productivity benchmarks, has stunted the motivation of employees and officers. The current system of industry-level wage settlement is not in sync with the aspirations of the employees or the needs of the banks.

Wages for the executive cadres[1] are grossly inadequate when compared to their private sector counterparts, which causes problems in hiring talented

---

[1] Officers in the senior management and top management cadre are referred to as executives.

executives at the senior levels in highly specialised areas such as technology. Lack of professionalisation of the human resource (HR) function and initiatives by individual bank managements and the government to reform the pattern of IR has been the key reason for many problems afflicting the banking industry today. Many banks have learned to live with current practices, among them inflexibility in redeployment of staff, rigidities in utilisation of staff, and antiquated settlements with trade unions. Most banks have not undertaken any worthwhile reforms in IR. Nor have they initiated any progressive HR policies.

A report on HR by a government-appointed committee, which I had the privilege to chair (Khandelwal Committee, 2010), cautioned about the lack of professionalisation of HR, prevailing rigidities in policies, and the demotivating impact of the industry-level wage settlements, which cumulatively are not in sync with the new order of banking. Status-quoist policies in the IR/HR domain could hamper the growth process of the traditional banking sector in India.

It is contended that unless HR issues, including the current arrangements for wage settlements, are reviewed and faced head on, they may well end up proving to be the Achilles' heel that could topple banking sector reforms.

The BoB[2]

Founded in 1908 under the patronage of the princely state of Baroda in western India, the BoB has made rapid strides over the years to achieve top position in the Indian banking sector. For the first 40 years of its operations, the Bank's progress was rather slow as compared to its peers, although few others enjoyed the kind of security BoB enjoyed under state patronage.

World War II gave a much-needed fillip to the Indian economy and the banking industry benefited immensely. After Independence, state control over the BoB was removed to put it on the path of progress. It improved its ranking from the fifth to the fourth-largest commercial bank in the country. Around 1956, the Bank initiated an aggressive strategy in business development and expansion. The business-minded attitude of the second-generation leaders was convincingly reflected in the Bank's domestic and

[2] This section draws heavily from Tripathi (2007).

overseas expansion. The Bank opened several overseas branches in the 1950s. This marked the beginning of its foreign exchange business and its exposure to banking in affluent societies. The Bank also simultaneously expanded its Indian operations in various states, among them West Bengal and Maharashtra. In an effort to galvanise its operations, the Bank paid considerable attention to the professionalisation of its management by establishing new departments such as Economic Research, Agricultural Finance, and Personnel Management.

The Bank carefully diversified the pattern of its services during the 1960s and introduced a number of attractive deposit schemes. Its innovations included launching mobile branches in and outside India. The BoB was also the first Indian bank to introduce credit cards in 1964.

Nationalisation of Banks

The nationalisation of 14 commercial banks in 1969, BoB among them, was an important milestone in the history of Indian banking. Although banks were brought under a common ownership, they were expected to continue to compete in various areas of business in almost the same manner as before. The BoB's growth acquired a strong impetus after nationalisation. To meet the objectives of nationalisation as well as strengthen its commercial base, the Bank brought in necessary changes in its organisational set-up.

Under the Lead Bank Scheme[3] formulated soon after nationalisation, the BoB expanded at a phenomenal rate in the states of Uttar Pradesh (UP), Rajasthan, and Gujarat, where it was allotted lead districts for intensive development. In the first five years after nationalisation, the Bank set up substantial infrastructure to serve the weaker sections and rural population, and its relative ranking in the league of nationalised banks went up from fourth position in 1969 to third in 1975. The BoB pioneered an innovative scheme called Multi Service Agency (MSA) to meet the financial and

---

[3] Lead Bank Scheme's origin lay in the recommendation of a committee headed by D.R. Gadgil, a well-known economist, which submitted its report just a few months before nationalisation. It was suggested by the committee that each commercial bank should be allotted specific number of districts where it could act as a pace setter or leader in providing integrated banking services.

non-financial requirements of a vast multitude of self-employed persons with modest incomes, not only in rural and semi-urban areas but also in metropolitan cities and towns. Under this scheme, the Bank made finance available to self-employed artisans, small traders, cobblers, rickshaw pullers, among others. Similarly, in 1977, the Bank pioneered the concept of village development centres (VDCs) by identifying a number of branches in rural and semi-urban areas and encouraging them to focus their attention on rural development. The Bank has registered steady progress on various fronts over the years as may be seen from Table 1.2.

The most distinctive feature of the BoB, however, was its emphasis on overseas expansion. This was the outcome of the Bank's visionary management which took the lead in initiating overseas operations in the early 1950s. Over the years, the Bank expanded its overseas operations to many advanced countries. According to Bank's Annual Report at the end of 1985, BoB had 54 branches abroad, spread over 11 countries (Tripathi, 2007). In 1985, the Bank's operations were spread over 1,900 branches managed through a decentralised zonal and regional structure.

Post liberalisation and the opening up of the Indian economy in 1991, the Bank implemented new norms with regard to capital adequacy, asset classification, and provisioning as per the guidelines of the RBI. It also responded effectively to competition provided by new private sector banks with innovative initiatives, such as opening specialised corporate banking branches to cater exclusively to big corporate clients, and new services, such as a subsidiary each for mutual funds, capital markets, and credit cards. The Bank also had a public issue in 1996, when its shares were listed on the stock exchange. The follow-on public issue was brought out in 2006.

TABLE 1.2 The Bank's Progress on Various Fronts (Rs Million)

Year	Net Profit	Deposits	Advances	Branches
1969	5.60	3,549.10	2,338.10	433
1979	43.00	24,234.10	14,285.10	1,460
1989	232.00	107,348.40	62,914.30	2,154
1999	4,214.40	446,140.40	210,915.30	2,561

Source: Tripathi (2007).

The BoB underwent a major transformation in 2005 on my assumption of responsibilities as CEO with the introduction of several seminal and customer-centric initiatives, such as core banking, ATM expansion, rebranding and logo change, groundwork for new subsidiaries for mutual funds and life insurance, aggressive expansion of overseas operations, and establishing a presence in new territories. The Bank also introduced pioneering initiatives in the area of human resource development (HRD), readying itself for future growth.

Currently, its corporate functions are managed from two locations: the head office in Vadodara (earlier known as Baroda, where the Bank was established in 1908); and the corporate office in Mumbai (earlier known as Bombay). The top management operates from Mumbai, that is, the CEO, executive director, and a majority of general managers operate from the corporate office. In Vadodara, three general managers handle the three important functions of operations and services, audit, and HR operations. The BoB's inherent strength and resilience have helped it to weather storms and cope with multiple vicissitudes in its long history. In the 100 years since its inception, it has posted profits uninterruptedly. Its financial fundamentals, too, continue to be strong and sound. Many leaders have brought their own distinctive styles and ethical values to their work, which got enmeshed in the Bank's psyche. Many employees, through their exemplary conduct and integrity, have strengthened the underlying fabric of the Bank. Financial integrity, business prudence, and an abiding care for the hard-earned savings of the customer continue to shine as the hallmarks of the Bank's cardinal philosophy.

According to the Bank's Annual Report, today, BoB has a total business of about Rs 10 trillion and ranks amongst the top three PSBs in India. The Bank has become a multi-specialist bank with huge corporate, small and medium-sized enterprises (SMEs), and retail portfolios, with more than 40 per cent of its credit deployed in priority sectors, including agriculture. The Bank is technologically savvy with anytime–anywhere banking services, mobile banking, and a network of over 5,000 branches and about 10,000 ATMs. It has over 100 offices abroad, including in Europe, the United States of America (USA), Africa, the United Arab Emirates (UAE), Australia, New Zealand, Fiji, Singapore, China, and Hong Kong. Overseas business contributes over 20 per cent to its total business. In recent years, BoB has become a valuable banking brand.

The Personnel and IR Functions

In the early years after its establishment, the personnel function at BoB was handled by the Staff Department at the head office in Vadodara. This department mainly looked after recruitment, salary administration, and terminal benefits. The recruitment function was limited to recruiting people from known sources, like customers, relatives, and friends of executives. In the early 1940s, the Bank introduced a written test in arithmetic and English for new entrants, thus introducing an element of objectivity into the recruitment process.

In response to the litigatory battles that took place between bank managements and trade unions at the industry level in the late 1940s and 1950s, the Bank recruited a labour welfare officer (LWO) in 1956, primarily to represent its case in tribunals, attend to employee grievances, and deal with the workmen staff unions.

The Bank built a sound culture of collective bargaining. The BoB was the only bank at the time which recruited specialists to perform the personnel function, which demonstrated that it valued professionalisation in this vital sphere of work

Fast expansion and government control following the nationalisation of banks in 1969 created some strain between the Bank's management and its majority trade union. In order to cope with the demands of rapid expansion, the BoB handed over its recruitment function to the National Institute of Bank Management (NIBM), which undertook recruitment along scientific lines. Subsequently, the Banking Service Recruitment Board (BSRB) was established in 1977 by the Government of India to handle all recruitments in clerical positions and officers' cadre at the entry level. In view of its rapid development, the Bank paid increasing attention to the training and development of its employees. It started a training college in Mumbai in 1962 jointly with another major bank; later, in 1965, it set up its own college in Ahmedabad. In 1978, the Bank converted its training college into a full-fledged staff college, called the Bank of Baroda Staff College, with provision for training, research, and in-house consultancy. In 1978, BoB set up a formal HRD department under a personnel specialist to focus on the nurturing of its human resources through training and development. The personnel and IR functions were mostly handled by trained personnel

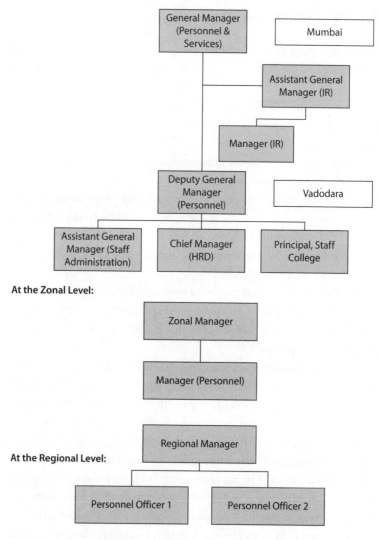

FIGURE 1.1   Structure of Personnel Function in 1985

specialists. In 1985, when this research study was undertaken, the senior personnel staff were all specialists, except the deputy general manager, who was an operational banker. At the zonal and regional levels too, the personnel staff were all specialists. The structure of the personnel function was as given in Figure 1.1.

Unionism at the BoB

The Workmen's Unions

Although the first trade union in BoB was formed in Mumbai in 1946 and was headed by an outsider trade union leader, between 1946 and 1956, union activities were confined to large cities such as Mumbai, Bengaluru (earlier Bangalore), Kolkata (earlier Calcutta), and Delhi. The Government of India had a policy to discourage strikes and lockouts during the World War years and had taken powers to refer any industrial dispute to compulsory adjudication under the Defence of India Rules. Thus, many disputes in different banks were referred to adjudicators. During the period of implementation of the all-India tribunal awards, the unions in various places decided to form an all-India union for proper implementation of the awards using a coordinated approach. This lead to the formation of the AIBEA in 1946 at the industry level, which remains a majority union of employees till date at this level.

The ideological differences among the key leaders of the union in the Bank's Mumbai unit created a split in the union, with a powerful group led by the Mumbai unit breaking away to form the All India Bank of Baroda Employees Federation or AIBOBEF (hereinafter called the Federation). The formation of the Federation was supported by the management in a clever move to keep BoB away from the militant postures of the AIBEA. The remaining union members formed the All India Bank of Baroda Employees Coordination Committee or AIBOBCC (hereinafter called the Coordination Committee), which was affiliated to the AIBEA. But it was the Federation that held a clear sway over the employees.

The Bank maintained a durable and cordial relationship with the Federation for about two decades from 1956 to 1970 and during that period, entered into a number of agreements with the Federation on various matters relating to the employees and extended to its participation in various committees. Subsequently, the Federation had a chequered relationship with the Bank, especially in the post-nationalisation phase. In 1973, the Bank recognised the Federation as the sole collective bargaining agent for all policy matters and the Coordination Committee was accorded consultative status. As a recognised union, the Federation has been the key union in championing matters relating to employees. Through a system of periodical meetings between the Bank and the Federation, issues relating to individual member grievances are discussed at the regional, zonal, and corporate levels. As a majority and recognised union of workmen, the Federation has its representatives on the Welfare Committee at the corporate level, and on the Committee for Allotment of Flats of Subordinate Staff in Mumbai. Over the years, the Federation has maintained its independent character, except for a brief period during the Emergency (1975–77) when it sought affiliation with the Indian National Trade Union Congress (INTUC), the labour wing of the Congress Party, which was in power during that time.

Apart from the Federation, the Bank also had to deal with the Coordination Committee, affiliated to the AIBEA, the majority organisation of bank employees at the industry level. Despite its minority status in the Bank, over the years, the Coordination Committee has maintained a highly militant posture and has, from time to time, organised a number of agitations on various policy matters, such as promotions, right of consultation, and special allowances for employees. The Bank holds discussions on policy matters with the Federation, but also consults the Coordination Committee before the final settlement is signed with the Federation.

On account of the split in the AIBEA, the majority union at the industry level in 1980, a new union was formed which was known as the Bank Employees Federation of India (BEFI). This union was ideologically affiliated to the Communist Party of India (Marxist) and had a presence mostly in eastern India, that is, in West Bengal and the North-East. As a result of this split, the BoB Eastern Regional Council (ERC) was formed in Kolkata which was affiliated with the BEFI.

In addition, the Bank had another small trade union, the Bank of Baroda Employees Trade Union Congress (BOBETUC), which was affiliated to the INTUC. The BOBETUC functioned mainly in Mumbai.

The Bank experienced intense inter-union rivalry at the operating level on account of the presence of the two major unions, the Federation and the Coordination Committee, and the intensity of this rivalry was exacerbated by the presence of the BEFI in states such as West Bengal.

At the time of research, the position of workmen's unions in BoB is shown in the Figure 1.2.

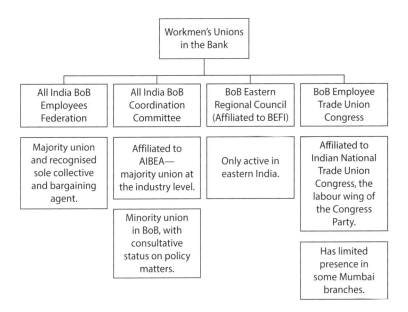

FIGURE 1.2 Workmen's Unions at BoB

The Officers' Unions

After the nationalisation of banks in 1969, and the consequent expansion of the Bank in rural areas, a number of problems arose with regard to transfers and promotions of officers. Further, the increasing militancy of the workmen's unions and the indiscipline of the staff created a feeling of frustration amongst the officers, who had to work long hours and face restrictive practices from the workmen cadres. Moreover, there was no forum to represent the grievances of the officers to management. This provided the impetus for the formation of an officers' association at the Bank. The initiative to form such an association was taken by the general secretary of the Federation (with the support of the management) and one of its joint secretaries took over as secretary of the officers' association.

The first officers' union, the All India Bank of Baroda Officers' Association or AIBOBOA (hereinafter called the Association), was established in 1964. For about 10 years after its formation, the relationship between the management and the Association remained extremely cordial and the Bank had little difficulty in dealing with it. The Association too has a chequered history in its relations with the management, with many ups and downs over the years.

Bitter conflict between the old Association and the Federation (once the biggest allies) led to the formation of a rival association by the Federation leader in 1974 under the title National Association of Bank of Baroda Officers (NABOBO). The NABOBO was affiliated to All India Confederation of Bank Officers (AICOBO)—an industry-level majority organisation of bank officers. The management supported NABOBO and extended it the facility of structured meetings and full-time association work during working hours to its general secretary, especially during 1978–81, during its conflict with the old Association. For more than a decade, the Bank experienced bitter inter-association rivalry. Fed up with the internal leadership struggles (often instigated by the management) and changing attitudes of the management, it finally merged with the old Association in 1987.

At the time of research, the position of officers' unions in BoB is shown in the Figure 1.3.

The Employee Director Scheme

After the nationalisation of banks in 1969, the Nationalised Banks (Management and Miscellaneous Provisions) Scheme, 1970 contained a provision for the representation of employees on nationalised bank boards, one each from the 'employee' (clerical and subordinate staff) and 'officer'

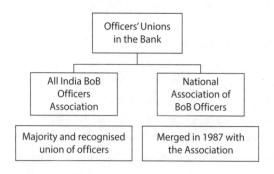

FIGURE 1.3   Officers' Unions at BoB

categories. This not only gave legitimacy to employees as important stakeholders but also heightened the trade union movement in the banking industry.

Scheduled Caste (SC) and Scheduled Tribe (ST) Welfare Associations

With the introduction of a reservation policy[4] in PSBs post nationalisation, there has been an increasing intake of SC and ST employees in the Bank. This has led to the formation of separate pressure groups in the form of SC/ST welfare associations in the banking industry, including BoB. Although these associations do not enjoy the status of trade unions in the strict legal sense, for all practical purposes, they act as powerful and vociferous groups to articulate the grievances of these categories of employees. The SC/ST employees have their own specific problems of social acceptance, interpersonal relations, mobility, and issues relating to training and development. Apart from this, SC/ST employees often feel that all the benefits detailed in the reservation policy are not accorded to them. These associations therefore act as a watchdog to ensure the implementation of the reservation policy in both letter and spirit, and also to ensure equality, justice, and dignity to their members. The BoB bears a sympathetic attitude towards the issues raised by SC/ST employees. It periodically discusses issues relating to their grievances with the welfare associations. The Bank has always enjoyed cordial relations with the SC/ST welfare associations on account of its proactive and empathetic policies towards its community.

---

[4] As per the reservation policy applicable to PSBs, in all recruitments in the workmen and officer cadres, 15 per cent reservation for SCs and 7.5 per cent reservation for STs must be ensured. This is a statutory provision.

Chapter 2

PRAGMATIC PATERNALISM (1956–68)

The BoB was decidedly conservative in its policies until 1956, under the leadership of the British CEO, William G. Groundwater. In the decade after Independence, the Bank opened only 40 new branches. The first Indian CEO, N.M. Choksi, was appointed in 1956. Choksi had been the manager of the Bombay main office[1] and was an astute banker with a special aptitude for international banking. Before joining BoB, he had worked in Hind Bank, Kolkata—which was later merged with BoB—where he had supervised its international operations. Choksi's leadership prompted the management to spread its wings and follow an aggressive policy of expansion and growth. Choksi was also anxious to cover ground lost by the conservative policies of the past.

After half a century of conventional banking since its inception in 1908, the Bank appeared poised for development and growth when it celebrated with élan its golden jubilee in 1958 under the leadership of a professional banker of eminence (Tripathi, 2007)

The upsurge of the trade union movement in the banking sector in the 1950s, however, posed a major challenge to the Bank's efforts to develop and grow. The IR climate in the banking industry was considered to be a major problem in the process of growth at that time.

Despite the general militancy of bank unions and the culture of agitations at other banks, the BoB was able to maintain a comparatively peaceful internal climate, which gave it an edge over the other banks in business development. During this period, the Bank made rapid strides in domestic

---

[1] Bombay underwent name change to Mumbai in the year 1995. I have throughout used Mumbai in the text.

business and expanded its business abroad. There was complete rapport and trust between the management and the two main trade unions—the Federation and the Association.

It is important to understand the factors that contributed to the shaping of the IR policy and strategy of that time. The new CEO, Choksi, was anxious to spread the Bank's presence and shift focus from traditional profit orientation to enable the Bank to move towards more aggressive growth-oriented strategies. It was felt that industrial peace in the Bank held the key to growth and development, considering the IR environment prevailing in the banking industry at that time.

As mentioned earlier, the first trade union of the BoB employees was formed in 1946 and was affiliated to the AIBEA. While union activity was conducted at various centres, the hub of such activities was Mumbai, where more than 50 per cent of the Bank's business was concentrated. The Bank often had to face problems arising out of intra-union tangles as two strong pressure groups within the union tried to overpower each other.

The split within the union and the consequent emergence of the Federation provided an opportunity for the Bank to counter the influence of the AIBEA, a militant union backed by the Communist Party of India. According to L.B. Bhide, LWO at that time and later General Manager, Personnel (1983–86):

> The Bank's preference was obviously for the Federation whose leadership was from within. The sober and intelligent leadership of the Federation against the rustic and rowdy behaviour of AIBEA leaders helped us in establishing a rapport with the Federation. The management obviously wanted a union that understood the problems of the management and believed in negotiations and discussions.

Later events showed that the BoB management was able to ensure a peaceful IR climate at the Bank through a strategy of informal recognition of the Federation.

Mutual Cooperation

As mentioned earlier, the process of implementation of the all-India tribunal awards provided legitimacy and strength to union activity in banks. There was, therefore, considerable give-and-take in the relationship between the management and the Federation. It was common for the senior executives of the Bank to spend a lot of time in settling employees' grievances as represented by the Federation. A senior executive at that time observed:

> The Federation would raise technical and legal issues requiring a lawyer's skill to convince them. Obviously it took up a lot of our time at the cost of business. We had also to bear the heavy cost of lawyers' fees for advice on legal issues.

Against this background, in 1956, the Bank recruited a legal specialist, designated as the LWO. His primary responsibility was to prepare the briefs for national tribunals, liaise with the IBA, and deal with the Federation in matters of interpretation of service conditions and employee grievances. The role of the LWO was purely advisory and he was not expected to take decisions; the decision-making function was strictly retained by the top management.

The recruitment of the LWO did not help much. 'Problems kept cropping up with the Federation becoming militant,' said a senior executive. According to the general secretary of the Federation:

> The LWO was a typical lawyer: rigid, inflexible, argumentative and a stickler for rules. He was by temperament a negative person who believed that unions existed only to destroy the organisation.

Under pressure from and persistent attack by the Federation, the LWO left and the Bank recruited another LWO, L.B. Bhide, who had a legal background and experience in adjudication. The new LWO was regarded as mature and humane in his approach. He played an important role in turning around the IR climate at BoB. Describing the change in the Bank's IR scenario after Bhide's induction, the Federation leader[2] of the time observed:

> In contrast to his predecessor, the new LWO was quite understanding, a good listener and very objective in his judgement. He would take immense pains to understand problems and explain to us the logic of a decision if it was not in our favour. Though he was a firm believer in rules, he did not attempt to use rules against the interest of employees

---

[2] Throughout the subsequent discussions, I have used the word 'Federation leader' for the general secretary of the Federation.

and advocated a liberal interpretation of rules whenever it was possible. He did not twist facts. He always explained our viewpoint to [the] top management. For us, convincing the LWO was as good as convincing the 'Management'.

The Federation leader supplemented his statement with this example:

We had made a demand that in small branches having only one manager and one cashier, the cashier may be authorised to sign jointly the Bank's instruments like demand draft, mail transfer, and telegraphic transfer and be paid an allowance for this additional work. There was no provision of such an allowance in any award or settlement. We were able to convince the LWO that if a small allowance is given to cashiers, the Bank can be saved from the problem of providing for a second officer in small branches for signing the instruments. We were able to convince the LWO about our logic and later the Federation signed a settlement with the Bank on this issue. Many other banks subsequently followed this practice.

Most of the issues raised during this period by the Federation were settled through negotiation. Before any decision was taken on any matter by Choksi, he consulted the LWO and gave his opinion due weight. When agitations were launched in branches, it was common for the Bank to depute the LWO for an on-the-spot study of the matter. When employees' grievances were in question, normally the Federation first discussed the matter with Bhide and only then was it taken up to the CEO.

The trust reposed by Choksi in Bhide and the good rapport between Bhide and the Federation leader saw the resolution of many pending matters during that time. Some of the important settlements signed with the Federation through mutual negotiations were:

1. An agreement in the matter of fixing the proportion between the direct recruitment of officers and internal promotions to officers' cadres.
2. An agreement regarding payment of a special allowance to cashiers entrusted with the work of signing demand drafts, mail transfers, fixed deposit receipts, in addition to the cashiers' routine work.
3. Absorption of *ramoshi* (retired policemen), who were working as temporary watchmen, in the regular service of the Bank.
4. An agreement on promotion from the clerical to the supervisory cadre.

Discussions with personnel functionaries of that time revealed that not a single case was referred by the Federation either for conciliation or for adjudication during the entire decade. An atmosphere of mutual understanding and across-the-table problem-solving characterised union–management relations during this period.

Staff Welfare

Apart from its policy of settling IR issues and disputes bilaterally, the Bank also encouraged participation of the Federation leader in dealing with managerial tasks and the problems of the Bank. For example, Choksi often shared information regarding profits and performance with the Federation. He sometimes invited the Federation leader to the annual general meetings of shareholders to help him understand the concerns and problems of the shareholders.

The spirit of consultation was extended to cover areas of improvement in the Bank's systems and procedures. A representative of the Federation was nominated to the Standing Committee on Organisation and Methods. As the Federation leader observed: 'We were consulted on anything that affected the employees and also in matters of common good.' For example, the Federation was involved, at the request of the Bank, in mobilising contributions from employees towards famine relief efforts in Bihar.

A factor of strategic significance that later became a major contributory factor to a trustful relationship between the Bank and the Federation was Choksi's humanistic orientation. A number of examples were cited by both management and union officials, as well as by individual employees, to illustrate this. A Federation official remarked:

> On our demand for housing accommodation for subordinate staff in Mumbai, there were two proposals: one for building chawls with provision of rooms and common toilets and the other for flats with independent self-contained rooms and attached toilet facilities. Choksi approved the proposal for the flats and remarked that he wanted his subordinate staff to live comfortably in flats with attached toilet facilities.

A chief manager who was a clerk at that time observed:

> I secured admission for higher studies in one of the US universities. I was earlier refused permission to have a lien on my service. Later, I

approached Choksi who, after being convinced about my sincerity, granted me two years' leave for going to the US and also a lien on my service. He also gave me a letter of introduction to a senior executive of an American bank to give me a part-time job in his bank while pursuing higher studies.

About Choksi's compassion and breaking the barriers of rules, Bhide gave an example:

> Once, an employee disappeared from the Bank and was not traceable for about six months. Choksi gave employment to his wife purely on compassionate grounds when no rules or conventions on such matters existed.

A retired peon said:

> I had requested the Bank to give me reimbursement of expenses for replacement of my dentures. This was refused by the administration on the grounds that there were no rules in this regard. Even the union had shown its inability to pursue my case, as the rules did not provide for the same. I hesitatingly approached the boss [Choksi] who allowed reimbursement to me.

About Choksi's sense of justice, an ex-manager stated:

> I was dismissed for some bad advances which resulted in some financial loss to the Bank. I was, therefore, not paid gratuity as per the rules. After the advances were recovered, I was paid gratuity on the personal instructions of Choksi, even though the rules did not provide for it.

About staff welfare, the Federation leader remarked:

> He encouraged formation of staff housing cooperative societies by giving loans to these societies when such facilities did not exist in any other bank. He also introduced a system of paying additional ex-gratia gratuity to those who retired after 30 years of service.

It was this humane approach that made Choksi popular with the staff and the Federation.

A Spirit of Accommodation

It is not that there were no tensions ever between the management and the Federation during this period. But whenever tensions arose, the issues were sorted out in a spirit of mutual accommodation. Each party demonstrated flexibility in accommodating the viewpoint of the other. In 1966, the Bank decided to implement the provisions of the first BPS reached at the industry level between the AIBEA and the IBA. The Federation, which was not a party to this industry-level settlement, protested against its implementation in the Bank. The Federation contended that a settlement signed by its rivals could not govern the service conditions of the employees in the Bank, a majority of who were its members. According to the Federation, it was a matter of its prestige and identity. If the industry-level settlement was implemented in the Bank, it could reduce the Federation's influence and give the rival union a special advantage.

The Bank salvaged the pride of the Federation by granting one additional increment to employees with certain years of service over and above the industry-level settlement and persuaded the Federation to accept the BPS. Thus, the Bank was able to resolve the crisis even at the cost of inviting criticism from the AIBEA.

The Coordination Committee, the BoB trade union that was affiliated to AIBEA and the Federation's rival union, would often create problems on some issue or the other and launch agitations in the Bank's branches in north India and in Gujarat, where it had majority membership. According to an executive in the Personnel Department, the Coordination Committee started taking even small problems to the streets and launched violent agitations involving harassment of managers and executives. At that time, BoB started supporting the Federation more openly to reduce the influence of the militant Coordination Committee.

The Bank extended a number of concessions to the Federation leader, such as allowing him to do union work during working hours and to use the Bank's phones for union work. A liberal view was also taken of his travel to various parts of the country. This was apparently to enable him to canvass for membership and reduce the influence of the Coordination Committee. The Bank also promoted the Federation leader to the officers' cadre and allowed him to lead a workmen's union even as an officer.

An Association for the Officers

Despite the cordiality that existed at the top level between the Bank and the Federation, the scenario in the branches was quite different, especially in the western region, which comprised Mumbai and Gujarat. Due to an upsurge of the union movement, the indiscipline amongst the workmen staff members was on the rise and increasing incidents of harassment of officers by workmen staff were reported. The management could do little to curb the growing indiscipline of the workmen staff and the officers had to suffer the harassment. The officers also felt discriminated against vis-à-vis the workmen staff, as the salary differential between the two categories had reduced and the commitment of the workmen staff to work had shrunk considerably. As one executive who was an officer at that time put it:

> It was common for the officers to sit late beyond working hours and complete the work left uncompleted by the workmen staff. There were no forums for resolving the grievances of officers who were expected to show results. Many other policies of the Bank had created frustration among the officers. There was a general desire among the officers to unite and get a better deal from the management.

In response to the prevailing frustration among the officers, an effort was made by some officers to form an association. The effort, however, fizzled out due to general apprehension about how the management would react to such a move. The management, however, encouraged the Federation leader to create a forum of officers. An activist of the Federation, who was an officer, took the initiative to form an officers' association in 1964 under the guidance of the Federation leader; this was the AIBOBOA or the Association. The promotion of the Association by an activist of the Federation did not pose a problem for the management, which had an excellent rapport with the Federation. Apparently, the management strategy was to be sympathetic to the rising grievances amongst the officers, but it wanted to ensure that the officers' association was led by an internal leader who had an understanding with the Bank. While, on the one hand, the management response to the prevailing dissatisfaction amongst the officers was pragmatic rather than the usual antagonistic response, on the other, the management manoeuvred the situation to ensure that the officers' issues were also managed under the aegis of the Federation leader. Immediately after the formation of the Association, the management appointed a joint committee consisting of some executives and office-bearers of the Association to look into the grievances of the officers and submit a proposal. Simultaneously, the management granted an interim relief of Rs 50 to every officer, indicating its willingness to enhance the wages of the officers. This action immediately soothed the distressed feelings of the officers.

The joint committee eventually submitted a report to Choksi, which provided the basis for improvement in the service conditions of officers at the Bank. Choksi then began to periodically discuss officers' grievances with the Association. The Bank thus displayed a responsive and cooperative attitude to the emerging unionism amongst its officers.

Throughout this period, both the organisations, namely, the Federation and the Association, worked together in complete understanding. Their leaders visited the branches together and canvassed membership for the Association. Often, both organisations issued joint circulars in various matters of common interest. Each pleaded the case of the other with the management. For example, in 1968, when the management did not invite the Association for discussions on the bonus issue, the Federation refused to enter the discussions until the Association was also invited. The management accepted this demand. The management supported the Federation–Association combine in order to maintain a peaceful IR climate and to dilute the influence of the militant AIBEA.

The prevailing peaceful IR environment helped the Bank make spectacular progress through aggressive expansion and multiplication of branches through mergers with four smaller banks. It achieved a four-fold increase in number of branches from 82 in 1956 to 302 in 1968. Apart from this, the BoB made impressive progress in overseas operations by opening branches in various countries. Thus, the management succeeded in transforming a regional institution into a national, and to some extent an international, institution by adopting innovative and aggressive business strategies. The Bank's performance during this period was better than the average performance of other banks in the country in terms of deposits and advances. Table 2.1 shows the progress made by the Bank during the period 1956–68.

* * *

In the prevailing scenario of IR marked by militant unionism and litigatory culture in the banking industry, the CEO, who had an ambitious agenda for growth and development, chose to encourage and support an internal

TABLE 2.1 Growth of BoB (1956–68)

	1956	1968
Number of branches	82	333
Number of foreign branches	5	17
Deposits	Rs 600 million	Rs 3,130 million
Advances	Rs 360 million	Rs 1,960 million
Number of staff members	2,735	9,893
Credit deposit ratio	60%	62.61%
Representation of the Bank	9 states	14 states

Source: Tripathi (2007).

union, the Federation (a breakaway group of the AIBEA), to contain the adverse effects of industry-level militant union, the AIBEA.

He extended all encouragement to the Federation to establish a hold over the employees by providing organisational support, including favours and concessions to its general secretary (the Federation leader) and facilities to employees over and above the industry-level BPS (signed between the AIBEA and the IBA, the latter representing the bank management) governing the service conditions of bank employees. The strategy was clearly to develop the Federation as a 'company union'. The cooperative relationship between the two important figures on the management and the union side set the tone of IR. Both sides ensured that there was no embarrassment to either side and ensured restrained behaviour.

Some of the actions of the management, such as promotion of the Federation leader to the officers' cadre and still allowing him to represent the workmen, could be interpreted as a ploy to buy the support of the Federation leader. The CEO's subsequent move to ask the Federation leader to organise an officers' forum to contain the growing frustration in that cadre and create the AIBOBOA under his guidance was clearly a clever strategy to contain any IR problems from the officers' cadre. The move might have helped the Bank at that time, but it was to have serious repercussions for the Bank's IR subsequently, as later events showed.

This strategy helped management to receive all the support from the Federation leader and resolution of problems in a cordial manner. The atmosphere of understanding gave an edge to the Bank compared to its peers in containing the militant influence and litigatory culture adopted by the AIBEA in other banks. This helped the Bank to grow at a faster pace than its peers and undertake many new initiatives, including starting operations abroad.

A key factor that apparently contributed to the long duration of peace and an environment of business growth at the Bank was the professionalisation of the personnel/IR function, which meant recognising personnel management and IR as specialised managerial functions.

Choksi's support and confidence in Bhide (the LWO) and his positive orientation towards the Federation created a culture of trust and bipartitism between the Federation and the management. It is to be noted that the CEO developed a strong working relationship with the Federation leader, both directly in regular meetings and through his open-door policy and indirectly via the LWO, who worked closely with him. The positive chemistry among Choksi, Bhide, and the Federation leader helped create a trustful IR environment and enabled problems to be solved with empathy and understanding.

A factor of significant influence in the IR of that time was Choksi's humanitarian attitude towards employee problems. This, with his professional approach towards the IR function and his astute strategy of building, encouraging, and supporting an internal union, created a cordial IR environment in the Bank that helped it achieve growth in business. Undoubtedly, Choksi managed to gain the confidence and trust of the Federation and the Association both at the personal as well as institutional level.

In sum, it can be seen that a concrete IR strategy emerged at the Bank in response to various environmental and organisational forces, as also the belief system of the CEO. The management was successful in maintaining industrial peace and in dealing with IR problems in a mutually satisfactory manner. Flanders (1970: 96) suggests that 'management must share control to regain control'. In this case, the variety of strategies adopted by the Bank, such as sharing information with the trade unions about the various aspects of business, including profitability, and enabling employee participation in important areas, including reforms in the systems and procedures of the Bank, goes to demonstrate that the management shared its power, which in turn helped to increase its power.

The quality of IR at the Bank during 1956–68 fits the 'adaptive cooperative pattern' as described by Purcell (1981: 66):

> The dominant characteristics in this pattern are high trust and cooperation between negotiators, which extend institutional trust and are bound up with the personal relationship between a few key people on either side, supported by their advisors. There are few, if any, formal written agreements, especially of a procedural nature, and if there are any, they are largely ignored.

Chapter 3

A TESTING TIME (1969–70)

The year 1969 was a very critical and significant year for the BoB. First, the sudden death of CEO Choksi after a massive heart attack deprived the banking industry—and the Bank—of one of its most dynamic and charismatic leaders. Although Choksi was due to retire within a fortnight, his sudden death plunged the entire BoB organisation into uncertainty. Second, 1969 witnessed the nationalisation of banks in India, marking the beginning of a new era and necessitating a major strategic shift in the objectives of commercial banking in the country. One of the key objectives of nationalisation was to spread banking services to rural areas and make bank credit available to agriculture and other priority sectors such as small-scale industries, small business, and retail trade.

The new CEO, M.G. Parekh, had worked as general manager under Choksi, and since he had grown with the Bank, he symbolised continuity. As an insider, he was no stranger to the Bank's traditions, strategies, and areas of concern. Taking over the reins of the Bank from a dynamic and popular predecessor was, however, both a challenge as well as a handicap for Parekh—a challenge because he needed to maintain the tempo of business development that Choksi had begun as well as meet the new challenges posed by nationalisation, and a handicap because he had already reached the age of superannuation and it was not certain how long he would remain CEO.

Parekh was known to be rule oriented and a strict disciplinarian. Hence, many people in management were concerned about the possible negative impact of his image on the IR climate in the Bank. Describing the contrast in the personalities of Parekh and Choksi, Personnel Manager L.B. Bhide, who had worked with both, said: 'Choksi was large-hearted and democratic, but Parekh was rule-oriented and a hard-core disciplinarian.'

The leader of the Federation agreed with Bhide, saying:

> Parekh was a stickler for rules and believed in the management's right to manage, as against Choksi who did not allow rules to come in the way of his concern for employees. Choksi also believed in managing through collaboration with unions and employees.

Many others in the management at that time had also predicted new problems in IR because of Parekh's formal and disciplinarian approach. Their apprehension was not unfounded. An unintended consequence of the IR strategy of Choksi, which focused on favours and concessions to the Federation leader, was that this accommodative stance was perceived as leniency and indulgence by the Federation and the employees. For the Federation, this yielded an excellent opportunity to strengthen their power and control by raising new demands on the management on the employees' behalf. This new power dynamic in IR became a decisive factor in the management of IR and business over succeeding periods, as we shall see later.

Apart from the differences in personality between the two CEOs, Parekh did not endorse certain aspects of the IR policy pursued by his predecessor, especially the concessions granted to the top Federation and the Association leader. He told me:

> The management under my predecessor had been extravagant in giving concessions to the Federation and to the officers' association. For example, promoting the general secretary of the Federation and allowing him to do union work as an officer was a wrong decision and the Bank had to pay for it by agreeing to allow the same privilege to a member of the rival union.

Nevertheless, during 1969–70, the BoB continued to pursue its earlier strategy of supporting the Federation by extending concessions and favours mainly on account of environmental pressures and Parekh's limited and uncertain tenure post nationalisation. Thus, status quo in IR strategies needs to be understood in the context of various external and internal pressures faced by the management at that time.

Nationalisation of Banks

The nationalisation of banks had brought about a major reorientation in the objectives of banking in terms of change of focus from class banking to mass banking. Banks were now expected to channel their resources for intensive rural development by expanding their branches in rural areas. One of the principal mechanisms by which the new objectives of social transformation through rural development were sought to be achieved was through the Lead Bank Scheme. Under the same, each bank was allotted certain districts for which it acted as a consortium leader to expand and popularise banking. The BoB was allotted 35 districts—12 in UP, 10 in Rajasthan, seven in Gujarat, two in Karnataka, and four in Maharashtra—and was expected to open some 100 new branches every year. Except Maharashtra and Gujarat, the Bank did not have much presence in the regions where it was allotted lead districts.

The change of ownership after nationalisation brought with it increasing control by the government in the form of exclusive authority to appoint chief executives and close monitoring of development and expansion through a newly created Banking Department in the Ministry of Finance. The RBI acquired increasing control over the credit policy and branch expansion programmes of the nationalised banks. In short, nationalised banks came more and more under the control of the RBI and the Ministry of Finance, and their authority in matters of business and expansion were curtailed to a great degree.

In the area of personnel management, the government imposed no major changes initially. However, it was understood that banks would no longer enjoy the freedom that they had in the past in matters of personnel management and IR, and that they would now have to operate within the overall framework of the industry-level bipartite agreements.

Nationalisation also provided a shot in the arm to the AIBEA, which had long been demanding the nationalisation of banks. The leaders of the Coordination Committee, the AIBEA's affiliate trade union at the BoB, nursed a grievance against the Bank because of the management's policy of supporting the Federation and discouraging its activities. It was, therefore, apprehended that the Coordination Committee would increase pressure on the management to gain acceptance and might even launch an agitation to draw public attention, especially in the northern region where it had a firmer base and where the Bank had been given lead bank responsibilities.

Apart from these external pressures, the BoB also had to deal with a variety of pressures from within. For example, the continuance of Parekh as CEO even after superannuation was seen as an ad hoc arrangement by two ambitious top executives who began vying for the top position. This posed a problem in creating a cohesive management team at the top. It was no secret that both these executives were liaising with government officials as well as with the leaders of the Federation and the Association to boost their chances in the CEO race.

Another factor that caused considerable anxiety at that time was the attitude of the two key leaders of the Federation and the Association, who had acquired tremendous power during the tenure of the previous CEO, N.M. Choksi. The two leaders interfered frequently in various personnel management functions. Although the leaders were cooperative through-out and espoused the resolution of problems through peaceful means, they expected favours and special treatment from the management. Many senior executives resented the power wielded by these leaders, but few of them stood up to challenge their interference in the day-to-day management of the Bank. One senior executive, R.C. Shah, who later became the CEO of the Bank, told me:

> The management had all along pampered the leaders and they had emerged as a parallel management. They interfered in day-to-day management and they did not hesitate to blackmail the executives who questioned their interference.

Problems of Sudden Growth

The nationalisation of banks had two major implications for personnel policies. First, in the area of personnel administration, it opened up a need for massive recruitment in the clerical and officer cadres, accelerated promotions, and training of existing personnel as well as new recruits. The second was to ensure smooth opening of new branches in lead districts allotted by the government by maintaining a conducive IR climate.

In order to meet the growing pressure on the personnel function, the BoB recruited professional personnel specialists for each region. These specialists were expected to lend support to regional managers in all aspects of personnel administration and IR.

At the corporate level, too, the Personnel Department was strengthened with more specialists. A new Management Services Department was established to design induction and training policies. The department was expected to arrange for the expansion of in-house training infrastructure by opening training centres to train employees to man the new branches and prepare existing employees to take up new roles as 'social bankers' in the changing context of banking.

During this period of transition, the Bank had to undertake massive recruitment and promotion exercises to provide manpower for the newly opened branches, deal with the issues raised by the Federation and the Coordination Committee in matters of payment of new allowances, and resolve issues raised by the Association regarding problems encountered by officers on account of transfers.

The sudden growth in manpower aggravated the problem of union rivalries as each union tried to co-opt the new recruits as their members. The task of personnel function thus became more difficult. While the Personnel Department was bogged down with routine personnel administration chores, the unions, especially the Federation, wanted a greater say in almost all aspects of personnel management. Accustomed to special treatment by the management, it frequently pressurised the management to grant special concessions so that it could maintain its hold over employees to checkmate the rise of the Coordination Committee (AIBEA).

During this period of transition, the management continued with its earlier strategy of supporting the Federation and the Association. Although Parekh did not favour union interference in the administration, he had seen the positive results of the cooperation received from both these organisations in the past in return for concessions and favours. He was also constrained by his uncertain tenure. He, therefore, continued with Choksi's policy of allowing the formal participation of the Federation and the Association leaders in important business meetings. The management also allowed several other concessions to the Federation, such as giving them the results of the promotion tests from the clerical to the officer cadre a day in advance of the declaration of the result, sanctioning about

25 posts of daftary (a post carrying a special allowance in the subordinate staff cadre) at the Mumbai main branch, and so on.

The special attention accorded to the Federation and the Association reinforced the power of their leaders. Officers and executives approached them seeking favours in matters of transfers and postings. According to a close aide of Parekh, the leaders would ask for transfers and postings of officers and Parekh often obliged them. To illustrate the growing clout of the Association: a specialist officer was transferred in 1970 from Mumbai to Chennai (then Madras). His representation against the transfer and the recommendations by his immediate superior, who was a senior executive, were rejected by Parekh. The transfer, according to this officer, was cancelled only when the activist of the Association intervened in the matter.

Apart from extending favours in terms of transfers and promotions, the management also obliged an important Federation leader in matters of recruitment of subordinate staff. According to a senior official of the Personnel Department, a number of candidates belonging to the Federation leader's hometown were recruited in the subordinate cadre during that time. This is substantiated by the fact that there were internal squabbles later on this issue, ultimately creating two groups within the Federation. Resentment levels on this issue became so grave that some members of one group eventually left the Federation and organised an agitation demanding recruitment of only locals in the subordinate cadre.

It is thus apparent that the personnel function at the Bank, which the management aimed to professionalise, was simultaneously being eroded by union interference. The lines between the union and management roles had become blurred. The CEO, despite his initial reluctance to continue his predecessor's policy, was forced by the reality of circumstances to toe the same line.

The Federation Goes on Strike

Despite every effort by the BoB to help the Federation maintain its distinct identity by extending various concessions even under the changed circumstances, there were times when the Bank just could not accommodate the Federation's demands. For example, in 1970, the Federation refused to accept the implementation of the second industry-level BPS on wages and service conditions signed between the IBA and the AIBEA. The Federation's plea was that it was not a party to the settlement. Accustomed to special favours and concessions over and above the industry-level settlements, and with a view to maintaining its unique identity, the Federation demanded a separate settlement on the wages and service conditions of the Bank staff.

The Bank knew very well that as a member of the IBA and as a nationalised bank, it was duty-bound to implement the settlement. So, it could not accommodate the Federation on this issue as might have been done earlier when it was in the private sector. The Federation too was aware of the limitations and constraints faced by the Bank. At the same time, it did not want to sign the settlement arrived at by its rival, the AIBEA, without any additional benefits. This would have meant loss of its credibility.

Consequently, for the first time ever since its inception, the Federation called a strike against the implementation of the second BPS. It was unusual for the Bank to face a strike, but it knew that the strike was not against the management. In fact, the Federation's rival union, the Coordination Committee, claimed that the top management had helped the Federation to disrupt clearing in different metropolitan centres to bring pressure on the government for some understanding on the issue in favour of the Federation. The Federation leader conceded that the strike had, in fact, been called to put pressure on the central government to intervene and it was not against any policy of the Bank as such.

The strike continued for 14 days and business suffered considerably. The government advised BoB to consider some additional demands in the nature of welfare measures raised by the Federation. The Federation called off the strike and an understanding was reached that certain concessions would be granted as a welfare measure, including subsidised quarters to subordinate staff residing in Mumbai, reduction in interest rates on housing loans, and a welfare fund for employees. As expected, the Coordination Committee protested, but did not get very far because it involved benefits for all the employees of the Bank, including their members. The IBA resented the behaviour of the Bank in extending concessions beyond the industry-level agreement. The BoB, however, had pursued its own logic. As Bhide put it:

> No union worth its name would sign on the dotted lines of the settlement signed by rival union. The Bank had a stake in the Federation, which had throughout maintained industrial peace in the Bank.

Isolating the Federation would have meant going closer to the Coordination Committee, whose militant and agitating methods would have cost the Bank a lot more in terms of industrial unrest.

It is evident from the given analysis that both at the time of the first BPS in 1966 as well as the second BPS in 1970, the BoB management took pains to protect the identity of the Federation and gave additional benefits to employees over and above the industry-level agreements. The management and the Federation thus maintained their relationship of mutual accommodation, leading to industrial peace.

The satisfactory progress made by the Bank both in business and expansion of branches in lead districts in the two years under Parekh suggests that the management successfully achieved the objective of settling down in the period of transition from the pre-nationalisation to the post-nationalisation stage and achieved success in specific areas of its operation. During the period 1969–70, the Bank opened more than 150 branches and achieved a deposit growth better than the average of the countrywide banking industry due to industrial peace ensured by the Federation and the Association.

* * *

The period under discussion was marked by the pressures and exigencies faced by the banking industry in the period immediately after the nationalisation of banks. A long-time votary of nationalisation, the Coordination Committee (AIBEA) received a shot in the arm from the move. Massive expansion and the concomitant pressures of recruitment and transfer created anxiety in the employees, who had generally stayed at their original place of posting until then. Trade unions too faced pressure from their members to maintain the status quo as there was reluctance to move to rural areas when branches were opened there. Increasing rivalry between the two rival BoB trade unions, the Federation and the

Coordination Committee, created more complexity in managing IR at the workplace. This rivalry increasingly showed up in the placement and promotion of their members, which was necessitated on account of massive expansion.

In the surcharged environment of inter-union rivalry and the pressures of expansion, as also the new responsibilities to achieve the government-set goals of developmental banking, the management opted for disruption-free IR and adopted an accommodative stance in dealing with the unions despite CEO Parekh's personality as a tough and unbending executive.

Parekh, in a way, had to continue with Choksi's strategy due to force of circumstances. He avoided taking any major policy initiatives or reforms, instead trying to contain the influence of the militant Coordination Committee and supporting the Federation for the smooth working of the Bank post nationalisation.

Accordingly, CEO Parekh yielded to many new demands of the Federation. The 14-day strike by the Federation, leading to concessions for employees beyond the industry-level agreement, was a dramatic illustration of the growing power of the Federation. It showed as to how under changed environment, the management had to toe status-quoist policies despite their reluctance to do so.

Some people in the Bank interpreted this strategy as a convenient ploy by Parekh to buy peace from the union leaders in order to resolve the power politics at the top level of management and reduce the uncertainty of his tenure. However, it was a necessary part of strategy if he was to avoid the disruptive potential of militant unionism and achieve business results.

Concurrently, Parekh also continued with the process of building a specialised personnel–IR function at the Bank by recruiting specialists at the corporate level and by decentralising the function at the regional level. This strategy served the main objective of maintaining peace for the transition immediately after nationalisation and for undertaking the process of expansion and growth.

One of the consequences of the management strategy of buying peace was the increasing power of the Federation leader to influence the management in day-to-day administrative decisions such as transfers and postings, not only of workmen but of officers too. With enhanced power, the Federation leader could browbeat many operating managers into doing things that helped Federation members. The balance of power in BoB had thus begun to tilt in favour of the unions, and as Flanders (1970: 155) puts it, 'Peace at this price, apart from obstructing economic and social advance, merely stores up trouble for the future.' The events after 1971 amply confirm this, as we shall see in the next chapter.

Chapter 4

FIGHT TO THE FINISH (1971–74)

V.D. Thakkar took charge as CEO of the BoB in September 1971 when M.G. Parekh finally retired. Like his predecessor, Thakkar had grown with the Bank and understood its culture. Thakkar had made a name for himself with his path-breaking report on social banking post nationalisation, in which he had recommended financial and non-financial (consultancy) help for the self-employed, thereby creating employment. Little wonder then that immediately after taking over as CEO, he set up a Multi Service Agency (MSA) at the BoB, charged with the specific responsibility of implementing the social banking scheme.

In the changing banking scenario in the country, on the one hand, Thakkar had the challenge of putting BoB on a growth track, including overseas expansion, while, on the other hand, he faced the mammoth task of preparing the Bank to respond to the challenges of the change posed by its rural expansion. With increasing government control and monitoring, the Bank had to change fast and deliver results even more swiftly. All this required a new thought process to re-examine and re-evaluate its existing culture, systems, processes, and response mechanisms. In the new environment, personnel management required a new emphasis on training and development and preparing both existing staff and new inductees for their new roles.

A challenge of formidable proportions was, however, to reconstruct the IR system. The earlier informal culture and quid pro quo relationships had to be reviewed in the context of the many changes contemplated, if the Bank were to adopt the new paradigms.

Between 1956 and 1970, the Bank had pursued IR strategies with the clear objective of promoting its growth and image. Its IR climate had been characterised by informality and shaped by personal equations between the CEO and the key leaders of the Federation and the Association.

Thanks to this strategy, the Bank had experienced a long spell of industrial peace, with each side showing understanding and working together to achieve its goals. However, an unintended consequence of the management's accommodative strategy was the reinforcement of the power of the Federation and the Association. Both organisations expected management to consult them in the matters of transfers and promotions of the executives. They also interfered in many day-to-day administrative matters.

Attempt to Formalise IR

In the changed scenario, the management found it increasingly difficult and impractical to consult unions as quick action was needed to carry out government directions relating to expansion of branches in rural areas. It could no longer wait for the unions' nod on key issues. The management thus decided to formalise its relations with the Federation to minimise the existing ambiguities in the roles of the management and the unions regarding their respective rights.

As mentioned earlier, the Bank was obliged to undertake a major and quick expansion programme in the early 1970s under the Lead Bank Scheme. The new rural branches were to be set up mainly in the states of UP, Rajasthan, and Gujarat. The Bank had a limited number of branches in UP and Rajasthan. The AIBEA held a majority in union membership in most of the banks in UP and Rajasthan, except at the BoB. As a result, the new employees in UP and Rajasthan were mobilised by the AIBEA. The expansion in these states was so rapid that the Bank had to import officers from Gujarat to get work going in the newly opened branches. During 1972–73, the Coordination Committee started an agitation in UP and Rajasthan against the posting of officers from surplus areas of Maharashtra and Gujarat to the branches in their region. They wanted local staff to be promoted to man these branches. As a newly recruited officer in 1971 in Rajasthan, I experienced first-hand the impact of this agitation at the Johari Bazar branch in Jaipur (where I was posted) which was the hub of agitation. I cut my teeth in IR during this agitation in my own branch, which was one of the worst affected, leading to the suspension of nine clerical staff in this branch.

Although the Bank took a firm stand and forced the Coordination Committee to call off the long-drawn-out agitation unconditionally, the management realised that the Coordination Committee could no longer be ignored. The Bank also needed to review its relations with the Federation. One senior executive explained:

> We learnt a lesson that we could not run the Bank with only the co-operation of the Federation. If we wanted smooth development of our lead bank areas, we had to restructure our IR policy and review existing arrangements in dealing with unions.

Another significant development after the nationalisation of banks was the increasing control of the government over the functioning of PSBs. As an appointee of the government, Thakkar no longer enjoyed the freedom to grant benefits to employees beyond the industry-level bipartite agreements. Nor could he extend favours to union leaders as before. The IR policy was now guided by institutional arrangements rather than personal preferences.

An important consequence of nationalisation was the statutory provision for appointment of employee directors on the board of the nationalised banks. In terms of the scheme, the government appointed two directors, one each representing the workmen and the officers, on the board of the Bank at the beginning of 1973.

Thakkar's views about IR management in the Bank also appear to have played an important role in initiating changes in IR. Recounting his experience of heading the personnel function for a few months just before his appointment as CEO, Thakkar observed:

> Even though we had had no formal strikes or work stoppages in the Bank, the IR scenario was far from satisfactory. IR was conducted in an ad hoc manner with little guidance to operating managers.

This indicated that in the changed scenario, Thakkar intended to formalise the Bank's relationship with the Federation and the Association, clearly listing the areas of management control. The earlier strategy of pandering to the unions and some of their leaders had made these leaders very powerful and they were practically holding the Bank to ransom, so much so that managers and officers found their hands tied when it came to freely deploying staff where needed and taking disciplinary action. In an environment where the slightest exercise of supervisory authority was met with resistance from the unions, it was imperative for the management to lay down clearly the areas of its control and a system for the resolution of staff grievances. It can thus be seen that a combination of factors contributed to the Bank management initiating strategic changes in its IR strategies during this period.

As a first step, Thakkar reorganised the personnel function and took direct command of it, with a group of executives assisting him. CEO Thakkar's decision has to be understood in the context of management politics at the top. In order to understand these changes, it is necessary to first understand the top management structure and the positions of the top executives functioning in IR. Figure 4.1 shows the top management structure as it was before Thakkar became the CEO.

Thakkar, who was in charge of personnel and some other functions, and C.P. Shah, who was in charge of operations and other functions, were strong contenders for the CEO's position. When Parekh reached the age of superannuation and his tenure became uncertain, both executives lost no time in lobbying with the government for the top slot. The government's choice fell on Thakkar.

Immediately after his appointment as CEO, Thakkar totally sidelined Shah, assigning to him the planning and development portfolio rather than the more important portfolios of credit and operations. According to many senior executives, Shah was not involved in any important managerial decision-making at the time. He was not even invited to participate in the annual budget meetings in which regional managers finalised

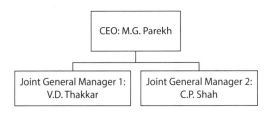

FIGURE 4.1 Structure of the Top Management at BoB until 1971

the Bank's business plan. A senior executive explained the reasons for sidelining Shah thus:

> It was essentially because of a sense of insecurity of Thakkar, who thought that if Shah was given any important portfolio, he could come into contact with government officials and create problems for him. Shah was, thus, made a non-entity.

Thakkar also sidelined Bhide, who had been head of personnel since 1958 and was the chief architect of the Bank's personnel policy. For the first time since 1956, an executive from operations, Kalyan Banerjee, was posted as head of the Personnel Department. Banerjee was much junior to Bhide and was recruited overseas. He did not understand the traditional IR culture of the Bank. He was a rising star and a confidant of Thakkar. Bhide was asked to report to him.

Over the years, Bhide had enjoyed the confidence of the top management and earned appreciation from both Choksi and Parekh, Thakkar's predecessors, for his contribution to the cordiality between the Bank management and the unions. Apparently in recognition of his contribution, in 1965, the Bank had sent him to London School of Economics at its own cost for a one-year programme in human relations, which in those days was considered a rare reward reserved for those enjoying the confidence of the top management. Bhide was also given additional increments in recognition of his services. He was respected throughout the industry for his knowledge. He also enjoyed great reputation with all the unions for his neutrality, although the new set of actors in the top management considered him close to the Federation leader and C.P. Shah, the superseded top executive.

Thakkar's decision to sideline him was ascribed to Bhide's close relationship with Shah. It was feared that Shah might influence the Personnel Department through Bhide and create problems for Thakkar. A note submitted by Bhide to Thakkar confirms this. In the note, Bhide explained his relationship with Shah and clarified the basis of certain decisions that were taken at Shah's behest. It can thus be seen that changes in the personnel functionaries were triggered by politics and the power struggle at the top.

The change in the roles of Shah and Bhide, who were considered close to the Federation, had important consequences for IR at the Bank. The

Federation strongly protested Thakkar's actions and considered them to be attempts to disrupt the cordial relations between the Federation and the management. This was also beginning of the strained relations between the CEO and the Federation leader.

In the new set-up, negotiations with the unions were conducted directly by Thakkar; and even circulars on critical personnel matters, which were earlier issued by the joint general manager, were now issued in Thakkar's name. A new group of advisors emerged within the management. These included a general manager, an ambitious and extrovert banker, R.C. Shah, known for his strong views against union power; Kalyan Banerjee, Chief Manager, Personnel, who was a bright young officer known for his typically British mannerisms; and a junior but aggressive personnel officer, V.J. Advani, who was known in union circles as the 'muscleman' of the management. The structure of the Personnel Department before and after these changes can be seen in Figure 4.2.

Thakkar and his new corporate advisors exercised close control over all aspects of the personnel function. In spite of all this, there were no early indicators of the changes to come in IR strategy. In fact, an internal note circulated by Thakkar acknowledged the cooperation of the Federation in maintaining good IR in the past and favoured continuance of support to the Federation. During 1971–72, the management followed the past policies of extending concessions to the Federation, and ideas and proposals for formalisation were discussed occasionally in an informal manner. The

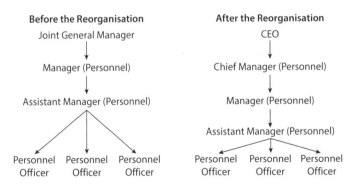

FIGURE 4.2 Structure of the Personnel Department at BoB (1972–74)

Association and Federation leaders were accorded all the attention they had received earlier.

For example, when the Bank introduced an innovative scheme called the MSA for granting loans to self-employed persons, the Association and Federation leaders were involved in the process of selecting 'cash collectors', who played an important role in the implementation of the new scheme.

The union leaders were also invited as principal speakers at various Bank functions. The Bank continued to consult the Federation and Association leaders in matters of executives' transfers, promotions, and postings. Such behaviour reinforced the power of the Federation leader who demanded more and more attention and concessions from the management. According to some senior executives, the Federation leader used to interfere in all aspects of administration, whether purchase of property or appointments of senior executives. Many senior executives resented the Federation leader's attempts to browbeat them through his circulars, some of which amounted to character assassination, if they acted independently.

However, the Federation leader's interference in administrative matters did not stop with the changes in the management structure because Thakkar's approach remained accommodative where the Federation was concerned.

During 1971–72, the Bank's expansion programme was at its peak. A number of rural branches were opened without enough infrastructure, staff were recruited and moved to these branches without the required training, and many staff members had to be moved from urban centres temporarily to fill rural vacancies till permanent arrangements could be made. The system received a sudden jolt and many staff problems appeared in the cracks. Many of the functionaries found it difficult to implement the various policies on business development because of the continuous interference of the unions. An executive who was in charge of the Priority Sector Department at the corporate office said:

> We had appointed agriculture clerks in branches with large agriculture accounts. In our circular to branches we had listed their duties. On this issue, the Federation leader created havoc by issuing nasty circulars against the executive concerned on the pretext that he (the leader) was not consulted about the duties of the agriculture clerks.

The duties were mentioned as per the existing awards and settlements, but the Federation leader made it an issue to demonstrate his power. Later, under pressure from the Federation leader, the top management instructed branch managers to keep the circular in abeyance.

A lot was happening on the management front in response to the process of change. The BoB recognised the need to reorganise its structure, review the delegation of powers, and improve operational efficiency. The Bank engaged two professors from IIM Ahmedabad to design a new organisational structure and a planning and information system. All these developments required a number of changes, and that too very quickly. The new organisational changes provided opportunities for the Federation to assert itself and seek consultations at every stage.

It was then that the management seriously considered redefining its relations with the Federation and the Association as, together, they made a formidable combination and could stymie the process of change. Thakkar's key advisors favoured a more business-like approach with the Federation and did not quite agree with his soft attitude. One of the advisors remarked:

> Although Thakkar wanted to formalise the relations with the Federation, he soft-pedalled [on] the issue because he did not want the Federation leader to make common cause with the sidelined C.P. Shah.

Apparently under pressure from his advisors, Thakkar did take some concrete steps towards formalisation of the relationship between the management and the unions. An IR consultant, S.R. Mohandas, was hired to draft proposals, which included a grievance redressal procedure, areas of sole discretion of management and union control, a check-off system, and providing facilities like office space and use of telephones and telex machines for union work, as well as allowing union work during the Bank's working hours. Meetings were organised in which Thakkar, his advisors, Mohandas, and the Federation leader participated. Proposals and counter-proposals were put forward. However, there were some issues on which differences persisted between the management and the Federation. The Federation insisted on arbitration as the last step in the grievance redressal procedure scheme, which was not acceptable to the management. It also did not agree to the Federation's proposal to permit its regional-level leaders to undertake union work during working hours.

One of the obstacles in the formalisation proposal was the lack of rapport between the Federation leader and Thakkar's key aides. As the Federation leader commented:

> Thakkar is sincere and understands the tradition of the Bank, but his advisors do not understand the Bank's fine tradition in IR. The advisors were obsessed with the idea of 'management prerogative'. They were basically anti-union and their strategy was to neutralise the influence of [the] unions.

A key aide of Thakkar said:

> The Federation leader dilly-dallied over the formalisation proposal for fear of losing his control over [the] employees. He did not want even a formal grievance procedure, lest his authority as 'sole grievance manager' [be] diluted.

While the formalisation proposals were under discussion, as a gesture of goodwill, the management recognised the Federation in May 1973 after verification of its membership by the government for the purpose of nominating a workman-director.

The recognition proved to be a shot in the arm for the Federation, which became more and more demanding in matters of executive transfers and promotions. Many senior executives, including Thakkar's advisors, put increasing pressure on him to check the Federation from interfering in day-to-day management.

Crossing Swords with the Federation

Under pressure from his advisors, Thakkar finally confronted the Federation on the issue of the promotion of a senior officer. This incident, as narrated by a close aide of Thakkar and confirmed by official record, triggered a major situation of conflict between the Bank and the Federation.

The management had promoted V.J. Advani, a personnel officer working in Thakkar's secretariat, and posted him as Officer in Charge of Central Office Administration. The Federation took exception to this on the grounds that it had not been consulted despite an understanding with Thakkar that it would be consulted on such issues. The Federation, in its letter of protest, quoted several instances of when it had been consulted in matters of executive promotions and transfers. In its reply, the management questioned the propriety of the Federation in raising an issue that did not relate to a member of the workman cadre. The Federation was informed that such matters were beyond the competence of the workmen's union and that informal consultations did not mean a veto or acquiescence. This was perhaps the first time that the management asserted itself clearly, advising the Federation to keep out of administrative functions. This episode marked the beginning of tension-ridden relations between the Bank management and the Federation. This shows as to how trade union's interference in day-to-day administration can force the management to redefine its traditional cordial relations.

Subsequent to the management's firm stand against the Federation's interference in matters relating to transfers and postings of officers, the Federation's attitude became non-cooperative and, at times, even hostile. This is evident from the many circulars issued by the Federation during that time, criticising the management's policy in various personnel matters. It objected to many routine decisions about transfers and promotions as well as other matters such as payment of allowances. The Federation also raised a dispute about the payment of bonus for the year 1973 and issued a number of circulars attacking Thakkar's attitude.

According to a representative of the top management, the Federation's strategy at that time was to find fault with the various administrative measures. The workman-director on the board, nominated by the Federation, also raised a number of issues about the functioning of the Bank with the intention of, as a top aide of Thakkar put it, 'embarrassing Thakkar before the board members'.

The increasing interference of the Federation and its obstructive approach to administrative matters confirmed the senior management's realisation that 'something needed to be done about the Federation'. At the same time, the management felt constrained in initiating any strong action against the Federation because the Federation wielded strong influence over the Association as well. The Bank could not have fought a united front of the workmen staff and the officers without major disruption of the Bank's operations. The main hurdle for the Bank in confronting the Federation was the close personal and institutional relations between the leaders of the Federation and the Association. Union and the Association solidarity, which was carefully nurtured and supported by the Bank (Chapter 2), now posed a serious threat to the Bank with the change of environment and consequential organisational changes.

Propping up the Association

After failure of formalisation efforts and continued challenges from the Federation, the Bank's strategy now focused on weakening the axis between the Federation and the Association. Members of the management described the two leaders as 'two sides of the same coin'. Of the two, the Federation leader was considered to be more of a force to reckon with because of his seniority in the trade union movement in the Bank, his organisational skills, and the certain aura around him on account of his clout with the top management in the past. The Federation leader's calibre and his negotiating and communication skills gave him an edge over the Association leader, who, as his deputy in the workmen's union, had been groomed by him to head the officers' association. Describing the difference in the two leaders, a senior union leader who had worked with both said that while the Federation leader enjoyed his role as king-maker, the Association leader aspired to become king.

The subservient position of the Association leader was exploited by the management to create a rift between the two leaders. A factor that helped in this process was the Association leader's nomination on the board as 'officer-director', which brought him into close touch with the top management. The Association leader was known to be ambitious and vulnerable, and this helped the management to entice him and break his nexus with the Federation. In pursuit of this strategy, the management began to 'give increasing attention to the Association leader and simultaneously ignore the Federation leader,' said a top executive of that time. Cases taken up by the Association leader were promptly resolved and special increments were given to officers recommended by him. According to a senior functionary of the Personnel Department:

> In those days, no formal meetings took place with the Association for discussing officers' grievances. The Association leader had free access to CEO, Thakkar and he personally took up the cases with Thakkar and got them resolved.

Apparently to boost the image of the Association leader, the management also extended personal favours to the Association leader and his colleagues. For example, the general secretary of the Association was promoted from a branch manager's position to the senior executive cadre. According to many senior executives, the management laboured hard to prepare a case for promoting the general secretary by diverting the business of other branches to the branch he headed and giving him credit for business development.

It was well known in the Bank that the Association leader spent most of his time on union work and neglected his responsibilities in branch development. His promotion as a senior executive, therefore, symbolised the growing affinity between the Bank and the Association. He was given a car and a flat in Mumbai, perquisites that were not extended to officers of his cadre at that time. The growing power of the Association leader cast him in a new image quite different from the earlier one of the Federation leader's protégé.

Bolstered by this new status in management ranks, board position, and being the general secretary, the leader was taken-in by this new persona and as strategised by the management, it had an impact on the Association–Federation relationship. The Association now began to act on its own and stopped consulting the Federation. The tilt in the Association's attitude clearly came into play at the time of promotion exercise from general manager's position to chief general manager in 1974. There was a keen tussle between two general managers, R.C. Shah, a close confidant of Thakkar, and C.P. Shah, who had been sidelined and who was considered close to the Federation. The Federation, through its nominee on the board, espoused the case of the sidelined Shah at the board level. The Association, however, supported the management's choice. For the first time, the Association and the Federation took different stands on a matter. This marked the beginning of their estrangement.

Escalation of Conflict

The growing tension between the Association and the Federation on the one hand, and between the management and the Federation on the other, culminated in a bitter conflict when the Bank sought to implement a scheme for reorganisation as proposed by its consultants.

In early 1974, a team of consultants submitted a proposal for the reorganisation of the Bank. The regional set-up was considerably expanded and dovetailed to a new system comprising zonal offices for specific geographical areas. A number of new positions were created to shoulder the increased burden of administration. Several new positions of area managers, assistant area managers, and development managers were created at the zonal level. Similarly, a number of new positions were created at the corporate level. The reorganisation programme provided major promotion opportunities to senior officers. The Association and the Federation also saw the reorganisation as an opportunity to push the claims of their supporters and maintain control over the officers. While the Association accepted the management's proposals, the Federation raised a number of issues and wanted more time for its own management consultants to study the proposals. The management rejected this demand. One top management executive observed: 'We did not want to make [the] reorganisation a subject matter of collective bargaining.'

From the point of view of the Association, the reorganisation provided an opportunity for development and growth of the officers and any disruption would have harmed the officers as well as the Bank. The Federation, however, claimed that the reorganisation 'was a ploy used by the management…to break the solidarity between officers and workmen.'

The various steps taken by the management during the reorganisation suggest that it wanted to neutralise the influence of the Federation on officers' matters by openly favouring the Association. The management offered promotions to office-bearers and activists of the Association. Of the 31 office-bearers of the Association, 24 were promoted to the executive[1] cadre. Many of these activists were posted in important places as regional managers and area managers. The general secretary of the Association was promoted as an executive in charge of a large office in Mumbai.

The reorganisation of administrative structure brought the general secretary of the Association into direct conflict with the Federation leader—once his mentor. In his administrative role, the Association leader took several measures to enhance productivity in the branches under his administrative control in Mumbai. Amongst the various steps to tone up administration, his attempt to control overtime invited the ire of the

---

[1] Executive positions are senior management positions.

employees, most of whom were Federation members. Many employees, including some activists of the Federation, had in the past claimed hefty overtime without actually doing extra work. The sudden monitoring and control of overtime was now resented by the employees. Many activists of the Federation challenged this action of the Association leader, who had been one of them not all that long ago.

The Federation leader challenged the Association leader on the issue of overtime. After this confrontation, the conflict between the Federation and the Association became much more pronounced and open. According to the Federation leader, the attitude of the Association leader in suddenly acting tough was the result of his desire to prove himself and impress upon the management that he could play his managerial role effectively. Managerial roles, by their very nature, bring exercise of authority and power by the role holders and if such authority has had strong past trade union affiliations, they are likely to face more challenges and even conflict with their one-time comrades.

The Birth of a New Officers' Association

As a consequence of the reorganisation, many officers complained of being neglected; they claimed that the Association had extracted the most number of promotions for its activists and office-bearers. An executive who was an officer at that time complained that he had not been promoted despite the fact that for three successive years, he had received awards for deposit mobilisation, and he claimed that this was because he had no contacts with the Association leader. Many other officers voiced similar complaints.

Some senior executives were apprehensive about the growing power of the Association leader and his growing arrogance. One of the senior executives who resigned in protest said:

> It was humiliating to take orders from the Association and suffer the dictates of its leader who behaved as the de facto Chairman. Top management did nothing to control him.

A majority of the officers in branches across the country felt alienated from the Association because their long-standing grievances, especially harassment at the hands of workmen unions in the branches, were not being resolved. Many also complained about the attitude of the general secretary of the Association in not meeting visiting officers without prior appointments. When he met them, he was curt and rude. A common refrain amongst the officers was that it was easier to meet the CEO of the Bank than the general secretary of the Association. Most members found it difficult to represent their grievances before the Association's office-bearers.

The alienation amongst the officers and the rising power and arrogance of his one-time protégé provided an opportunity for the Federation leader to launch a new officers' association, the NABOBO, which received a positive response from the officers. The NABOBO also received support from some senior executives. The members of NABOBO appointed the Federation leader as its chairman, while an ex-Federation activist was appointed general secretary.

The emergence of NABOBO symbolised the failure of the manage-ment strategy to undermine the control of the Federation leader over the officers—more so as most officers were promoted from workmen cadre on whom the Federation leader had huge influence.

The formation of NABOBO was seen by the Association as a direct challenge to its existence. It became a common adversary for both the management and the Association. Joined by common objectives, the management and the Association launched a combined attack to isolate the Federation leader. Over time, the conflict turned into a per-sonality clash between the key actors in the management: between the management and the Federation; and between the two organisations of the officers, each one denying the legitimacy of the other and attempt-ing to destroy each other's power base. The battle lines were drawn and each party competed with the others to sully the image of its adversaries and raise questions about the legitimacy of their leaders' actions.

Never before had the Bank experienced such an open display of conflict in which the management too was an active actor. When an exercise of reorganisation is used to distribute favours and to create schism in the trade unions, the management takes the risk of escalation of internecine conflict between unions, and also demoralisation of its officers and employees. The senior executive cadre, too, was divided into pro-Association and pro-NABOBO groups. Events in BoB demonstrated this in ample measure. There prevailed an atmosphere of allegations and counter-allegations.

For example, the Federation raised the question of the Association leader's legitimacy in simultaneously holding the positions of regional manager, member of the board, and general secretary of the Association. The Association also launched an attack decrying acts of omission and commission by the Federation leader. Amidst this warfare conducted via circulars issued by both the Federation and the Association, the atmosphere was further vitiated by Thakkar issuing a set of circulars titled, 'Union–Management Relations'. The tenor of these circulars, as illustrated next, demonstrates complete mistrust between the management and the Federation. One of the circulars of Thakkar read:

> I advised you in my circular of 26th September that the general secretary met me on 17th September and not on 18th September as stated by him.
>
> ...On 24th August, the general secretary of the Federation called on me and advised me of his securing a BA degree. The issue of method of payment of bonus was not raised by him. However, such an impression was given by him to the Manager (administration).

It was believed that Thakkar issued these circulars to the Bank branches under the influence of the Association in order to discredit the Federation. Whatever the motive, these circulars were seen as frivolous by many senior executives and symbolic of management strategy to actively discredit the Federation leader.

The management appeared to be fighting a war with the Federation on behalf of the Association. In continuation of the strategy to side with the Association and win their support, the management took a number of decision that signalled its desperation to keep the Association on its side. Some such decisions are mentioned here:

1. Permitted written communication with the Association at corporate and the regional level (the management had no policy to communicate in writing with any union).
2. Transferred executives considered close to the Federation leader at the behest of the Association leader.

3. Transferred L.B. Bhide, Personnel Manager, considered close to Federation from the corporate level to the zonal level.
4. Encouraged the Coordination Committee, the minority workmen union.
5. Supported the Association's efforts to entice some Federation members in Mumbai to join the Coordination Committee.

Encouraging the Coordination Committee was a complete departure from the management's hitherto consistent policy to discourage this union because of its militant postures. During this period, the Coordination Committee settled some of its long-standing issues with the management. For example, employees facing a departmental enquiry for acts of gross misconduct, including manhandling of managers, during the Coordination Committee-sponsored strike in UP and Rajasthan in 1972 were let off with just a warning.

Echoing the grievances of some executives, one senior executive who had handled the agitation as a regional manager observed:

> We had a very tough time at the hands of the Coordination Committee during the agitation. Many of us were physically assaulted by their members. We were assured by the management and the officers' association that strict disciplinary action would be taken against guilty employees and the honour of the officers would not be compromised. We are surprised that both the management and the Association subsequently backed out. Management let down us and the Association compromised the honour of its members.

The IR scenario turned chaotic with rival groups vying with each other to leverage their positions.

Suspension of the Federation Leader

Amidst all this, a development of far-reaching consequence in IR was the decision of the management to suspend the general secretary of the Federation on a small incident at a branch between him and a member of the Coordination Committee (who had recently left the Federation on the persuasion of the Association). The IR at the Bank had touched a new low. The Federation leader was suspended with support from the Association, which had nursed a grudge against him for launching NABOBO.

Several members of the management, including some of Thakkar's key advisors, did not approve of the decision to suspend the Federation leader and described it as an unwise act. Although there were only symbolic protests from the Federation members, which did not affect the functioning of the branches, the suspension had serious consequences, as revealed by subsequent events.

Unable to fight the war around IR issues, the Federation leader then fought the issue politically. The Federation leader was a socialist and had strong connection with politicians, several of whom were Members of Parliament (MPs). He took up the matter of a loan granted by Thakkar to a firm headed by one of his close relatives. The Federation leader accused Thakkar of corruption. The Federation alleged that its leader had been victimised for exposing Thakkar's corruption, though the records showed that the loan proposal had been approved by the board and that all procedural formalities had been observed by Thakkar. By mobilising the support of 40 MPs, the Federation managed to put pressure on the government to revoke the suspension of its leader. Subsequently, the government did not extend Thakkar's term as a CEO, even though he had two years to go before reaching retirement age. Thakkar, considered an imaginative banker, finally had to leave because of the bitter management–union conflict. It was a crisis for management, of management's making, and can be seen as the spur to a substantial change in IR and the social environment in the Bank.

One branch manager said about these divisive events:

> We now had to face problems from two associations, in addition to inter-union rivalry, at the branch level. The officers behaved like workmen staff, refusing to undertake additional jobs or shoulder responsibility. They questioned managerial authority on the basis of their affiliation to one or the other association.

A regional manager who supervised the Bank's operations in the lead bank areas observed:

> Our expansion programme during this period suffered. We could not open more branches, as there was intense inter-association rivalry, resulting in officers refusing to go to rural areas.

Another manager said:

> Apart from the trouble from the officers' association, [the] top management did nothing about the troublesome workmen staff. Even in matters

involving gross defiance of authority by workmen, the management soft-pedalled and often privately counselled officers at the operating level against raising any problem at that time.

This conflict-ridden period had an adverse impact on the Bank's development and growth. As against the target of opening 90 branches in 1974, the BoB could open only 39. Similarly, against a 15 per cent growth in deposits at the industry level, the Bank's growth rate of deposits was only 5 per cent. The poor performance could be attributed in part to the conflict, as Thakkar was preoccupied with it most of the time. The branch managers and officers could not concentrate on business development because they were involved in the Association's activities.

* * *

The nationalisation of banks brought in its wake newer responsibilities for the top managements of banks, requiring organisational changes and rapid expansion in rural areas for offering loans to the priority sectors. Massive recruitment of clerical and officer staff, their training, and consequent other changes posed several challenges for the personnel function. At another level, the Bank's management now had to respond to the new reality of the rising clout of its minority union, the Coordination Committee, affiliated to the militant AIBEA, especially in areas where the Bank was entrusted the leadership responsibility. Amidst all this, the earlier bonhomie among the Federation and the Association, as also these two bodies and the management, was put to severe test. It was no longer practical for the management to consult the Federation and the Association on the many new initiatives, given the pace of change.

The formidable combination of Federation and the Association, which had worked very well and helped the Bank attain uninterrupted development for about a decade, was now creating hurdles for the management in meeting the new environmental challenges, post nationalisation. The leaders' penchant for consultations on all the important decisions (personnel and non-personnel) together with the need for accelerated decisions in the new environment made the management see this combination with the potential to disrupt the Bank's ambitious expansion programme. What was hitherto considered as a great strength now appeared to be the greatest risk factor for the Bank.

In the changed scenario, the present CEO and his advisors seemed to believe that they should rid themselves of this burden of consultation, particularly involving the Federation leader, on officer and executive matters. With the Bank's officers' association gaining power on its own, perhaps without any more needing the crutches of Federation, the management decided to bell the cat. Tactically, the management decided to pamper and support the Association to keep officers on their side to run the operations, in case of any protest for work stoppage by the Federation. This led to a bitter conflict between the management and the Federation. It was difficult to believe that once the best of allies were now locked in a bitter war.

Fox (1974) noted that IR based on personal relations between dominant actors on both the sides can lead to bitter war with change of circumstances on either side, including replacement of key leaders. He mentions that this transition from adaptive cooperation (Chapter 2) is likely to be towards uninhibited antagonism (Fox, 1974: 307).

Organisational issues have a tendency to move from institutional conflict to personality clashes if either party targets key figures of the opposite side. The turn of events on account of changes in the context of IR from an informal relation to a more formalised pattern proved to be highly problematic for BoB. Consultation in administrative matters, which was extended as a courtesy to unions and the Association in earlier times, was now demanded as a matter of right. Hubris and arrogance of leaders is often a trigger for seeking change in the relationship, and BoB IR had all of it. The need to cope with environmental pressures required a free hand to take administrative decisions and restrict union's interference. This triggered a bitter conflict between the Bank and its major union. Purcell (1981: 81) observed that since it is the senior management which allows union access on grace and favour basis, it can withdraw the same as there are no constitutional safeguards in adaptive cooperation.

The 'Machiavellian mathematics' of the management in breaking the axis between the Bank's officers' association and the Federation fell through and led to many consequences, such as the creation of a rival officers' association and suspension of a key figure of the Federation (recognised union), which finally led to premature exit of the Bank's CEO. The question arises whether there was an alternative before the management other than meddling in union politics to achieve its objective? The search for an alternate conduct of IR is often time-consuming, and more so in an environment characterised by the need for fulfilling multiple expectation of various stakeholders. Notwithstanding the same, shortcuts in IR can be very damaging as evidenced by the turn of events.

The IR situation at the BoB during this period resembles what Fox (1974: 310–11) has characterised as the 'continuous challenge pattern':

> Here the union refuses to legitimize the management's claim to assert and pursue objectives. The union may be forced to submit, but it continues to withhold the legitimacy, fighting guerrilla skirmishes wherever possible, seeking ways to undermine the management's position and aspiring to mobilise enough power for an effective challenge.... No equilibrium relationship develops, only periods of uneasy truce as each side licks its wounds and watches the enemy for signs of a weak spot in its defence.

Chapter 5

DIVIDE AND RULE (1975–81)

The IR crisis during 1973–74 led to the premature departure of V.D. Thakkar and the appointment of one of his close aides, R.C. Shah, as his successor at the BoB in May 1975. Shah had been Chief General Manager under Thakkar. At the time of Thakkar's exit, the internal environment was chaotic and uneasy as a result of developments on the IR front. The executive morale was at the lowest ebb. The events had not only stumbled business growth but had also severely dented the reputation of the bank on account of premature departure of the CEO. Thakkar's departure was viewed as a victory by the leadership of the Federation. Unlike his predecessor, at 53, Shah was still young and had enough years left in him to pilot a new future for the Bank.

Shah was aware of the challenges that lay ahead of him and knew that his immediate task was to restore the image of the Bank and the general morale of its executive cadre. He was well equipped to face the challenges as he had climbed up from the ranks and had good experience of both Indian and overseas operations. As Thakkar's principal deputy, he was a key advocate of formalisation of the relationship between the management and the unions and, in some ways, the principal architect of the strategy to take on the Federation leader and break the combined power of the Federation and the Association by creating a schism between them.

With over 15 years' experience of working abroad, Shah was a professional to the core and believed in 'the management's right to manage'. He made no bones about his views about the unions and their role when he told me: 'As a senior executive in the Bank, I was never reconciled to the idea of pampering the unions and allowing their interference in management functions.' This clearly indicated that Shah was not willing to accord the unions as much importance as his predecessors had and was not afraid to challenge the existing culture of pampering the unions. In spite of the Federation's new-found confidence in instigating the premature removal of Thakkar, Shah appeared prepared to carve out his own strategy in dealing with the rising power of both the Federation and the Association. He seemed also to have learnt from Thakkar's mistakes. Shah told me: 'Thakkar's biggest mistake was to suspend the Federation leader.'

The IR scenario after the 1974 conflict posed a major challenge to the Bank in its effort to refurbish its image and regain lost ground in business. While, on the one hand, the Federation emerged even more powerful after its leader's unconditional reinstatement and the resultant premature exit of Thakkar, on the other hand, the Association had also become very powerful due to its clout in aligning with the previous management in its war with the Federation. The Association's penchant for interfering in promotions and transfers continued. Union power was at its zenith at that time and the credibility of the management had never been so low. In such a situation, Shah was naturally anxious about the management's ability to recover lost ground in terms of the Bank's performance. He described the prevailing scenario to me:

> There was general demoralisation among officers and executives. The officers hung around the union leaders for their promotions and transfers and the management's authority was severely undermined. The Bank's image had suffered very badly after the events of 1974 and...business was totally out of gear. There was so much to be done, but things looked grim and uninspiring. Under the circumstances, my main priority was to restore the credibility and confidence of [the] management.

Shah, as a key advisor to Thakkar, was seen by the Federation as having influenced the strategy to create a rift between it and the Association. Hence, there was already mistrust between Shah and the Federation. The Association, which had risen high during 1973–74, had become very powerful and its leader was now a force to reckon with. He was seen as a parallel power centre. Notwithstanding the above scenario and the state of nervousness in the top management, the events of 1975–81 showed that the management pursued with dogged determination a strategy to reduce the power of the Association and the Federation and to regain absolute control over the personnel and IR functions. Like a master strategist and tactician, Shah kept all the unions on tenterhooks and deployed multiple strategies to demolish them. Means were not important to him as long as they achieved his ends. Shah succeeded in his game plan and achieved extraordinary business results for the Bank. The BoB regained lost ground in business and achieved top position among nationalised banks in 1980.

In view of this success, it is important to understand the various environmental and organisational forces that shaped the managerial strategies of the time to neutralise the influence of the Federation and the Association and helped the Bank achieve top position.

Amidst the uneasy atmosphere that pervaded the Bank, the sudden declaration of national Emergency in June 1975 (barely a month after Shah took over) proved to be a god-sent opportunity for the Bank to consolidate and streamline its administration and operations. The general curb on trade union activities and the climate of discipline during the Emergency helped the Bank to redefine its relations with the unions.

The government's 20-point programme of socio-economic reforms after the Emergency placed heavy responsibilities on the Bank to undertake rural development through branch expansion and innovative financial schemes for the rural poor. Twelve out of the 20 points in the programme required the Bank's involvement. The BoB was expected to open about 125 branches a year and undertake intensive rural development, especially in the states of UP, Rajasthan, Karnataka, Maharashtra, and Gujarat. The Bank was also expected to deploy 60 per cent of its deposits through rural and semi-urban branches in these areas.

Apart from commitments under the 20-point programme, the Bank was asked to establish RRBs under its patronage in UP. This scheme aimed at creating low-cost autonomous banking institutions at district level to provide credit facilities to small and marginal farmers, agricultural labourers, artisans, and small entrepreneurs in rural areas.

The Bank's responsibility was to provide various kinds of managerial and financial assistance to these newly created institutions. The responsibility of the Bank in UP further increased with the allotment to it of two small sick banks by the RBI: the Bareilly Corporation Bank and the Nainital Bank. This meant providing managerial resources to these two banks.

The new business responsibilities and commitments under the various government schemes had a major impact on the Bank's personnel policies in terms of recruitment, promotions, and mobility of staff. In view of the major developmental responsibilities in UP and Rajasthan, two manpower-deficit areas, movement of officers from surplus manpower areas like Gujarat and Maharashtra was unavoidable. Heavy expansion in certain areas also involved transfers of senior officers to main branches and administrative offices.

The management traditionally discussed the transfer policy of officers from one zone to another with the Association. The Association ensured that its activists were not transferred without their approval. The Shah management, however, did not favour continuance of this practice. It regarded transfers as a 'pure management function' and transferred officers from surplus to deficit centres irrespective of affiliations with any union.

Using the Emergency, the management stopped formal/informal consultations with the Association on officers' issues, such as mobility. Shah took certain confidence-building steps to improve the morale of officers by improving direct communication with them. Simultaneously, he also undertook various measures that aimed at building the management's credibility with the officers. These measures included rehabilitation of some key executives and senior officers who had been sidelined earlier and seeking employees' cooperation in the task of creating business growth. Shah visited many important centres in the country and met the staff there. According to those who attended the meetings, Shah listened patiently to the problems of the officers and other employees and shared with them the Bank's plans to revive its past glory. A manager who attended one such meeting said:

> For the first time in my career of 20 years, a chief executive visited our branch and was talking like a colleague. His approach was one of seeking help from the rest of the family for the common good. The entire staff of the branch was very happy talking to the CEO.

These meetings helped Shah, as he put it, to gauge the pulse of the organisation. He was amazed at the overwhelming response and the concern demonstrated by the staff for the Bank's growth and development. An important discovery, according to Shah (as revealed to me in an interview), during these visits was the general frustration of the grass-roots employees with their union/association leaders, mainly on account of their attention to look after the interests of their activists and office-bearers who always managed to get preference in transfers, promotions, and postings, including foreign postings. In short, these meetings helped the management to bridge the communication gap between them and the rest of the organisation.

After establishing an initial rapport with the officers, Shah took several steps that demonstrated his resolve to be business-like with the Association and not permit the interference of any extra-constitutional authority (as he called them) in personnel administration. He wanted to restore management credibility, as he often remarked. The management initiated a number of changes that clearly indicated that it meant business with the Association and that it would not allow it to interfere in the administration of the Bank.

These changes included transfer of many officers (who had managed to stay at the same centre), including the office-bearers of the Association. The management also withdrew many privileges that were earlier accorded to the Association. For example, the management refused to pay the salary of office-bearers who did not work and stopped paying the telephone bills of union office-bearers.

During the 21 months of the Emergency, the Bank consolidated its grip on the personnel function and kept its distance from both the Association and the two workmen's unions (the Federation and the Coordination Committee). While the Bank was aggressive in dealing with the Association, it handled the workmen's unions with kid gloves.

After the lifting of the Emergency in March 1977, there was a general upsurge in the trade union movement across the country. Strikes, go-slows, and many other militant modes of trade unionism against the so-called 'Emergency excesses' of the employers were the manifestations of this upsurge. In the banking industry, the militant AIBEA spearheaded a number of agitations in many banks against what it called the suppression of trade union rights during the Emergency. The Bank, however, did not face any problem from the AIBEA's affiliate, the Coordination Committee, apparently because of its kid-glove treatment during the Emergency. Its leaders acknowledged that unlike other banks, the BoB had not created any problems for the Coordination Committee.

As expected, the Association made a lot of noise about the high-handed treatment of officers by the management. The Association, through a number of circulars, raised several issues against the management, such as victimisation of its members, the partisan attitude of the management, and transfers of officers in mid-academic year. The Association also raised the issue of the poor performance of BoB as compared to other banks and attributed it to the coercive tactics of the management in dealing with officers.

The management's decision to transfer officers, in fact, became a chief grievance of the Association. The focus of the attacks was CEO Shah and his policies in 'harassing Association activists through transfers'. One particular transfer triggered a conflict between the Association and the management. The Bank had transferred a chief manager (who was also a central committee member of the Association) from Chennai to Delhi. He suffered a heart attack while in Delhi and requested a transfer back to Chennai. The management granted him leave, but refused the request for transfer. In the context of the already existing tension between the Association and the Bank on the question of transfers, this marked the beginning of what was to be a long-drawn-out conflict between the management and the Association.

The Association set a long list of grievances before the Justice Shah Commission, which was appointed by the Janata Party government to look into the excesses committed during the Emergency. CEO Shah told me that the Association submitted a list of 140 points against him, which included items such as whether, during his visit to London, he paid from his pocket for his wife's share of their hotel room! Shah had, in fact, paid the amount himself and produced the receipt before the Shah Commission. Thereafter, the Commission did not pursue the long list of complaints posed by the Association. R.C. Shah told me that since he was aware of the blackmailing tactics of the trade unions, he had been extra vigilant in everything he did, paying even his personal tea bills himself while he was CEO.

It is amazing to note the quick turn of events in such a short time. The Association, which had been earlier pampered to the hilt, now faced an identity crisis due to the policies of a CEO who had been a key advisor to his predecessor in planning all the IR strategies that had indulged the Association leader. In Shah's scheme of things, there could not be two power centres, and he had no hesitation in articulating his view that it is the management's right to manage. He told me: 'As I have no right to choose the office-bearers of trade unions, they have no right to choose my senior executives or meddle in such matters.'

The Association's Call for Agitation

With Shah's determined efforts to regain control on career decision of the officers and a policy to keep the Association at a distance, the relations between the management and the Association hit an all-time low. The daily skirmishes between them on a variety of issues, including the trans-fer policy, finally culminated in a call for an agitation by the Association that included advice to the officers in the branches to desist from doing clerical work and stop sending various performance statements to the higher authorities, among others. As a part of the agitation programme, the Association also called a one-day strike. The agitation and strike marked the climax of the tension between the Association and the management.

While Shah knew the strike was in the offing and clearly saw it as an opportunity to rid the Bank of an arrogant leader and discipline the Association, he had learnt valuable lessons from his predecessor's failure and did not want to lose the battle. He knew that in the public sector con-text, things can blow out of proportion and therefore, he carefully planned his moves to neutralise the influence of the Association on the managerial staff who were the prime movers in the Bank's growth and development. Unlike his predecessor, Thakkar, who had relied chiefly on his advisors, Shah planned his own strategies and made sure that the government was on his side. He was sensitive to the fact that any disruption in the Bank could become national news and provide an opportunity for politicians to interfere. He did his homework and left nothing to chance. He told me that he met the Prime Minister, Morarji Desai, who gave him the go-ahead to deal with the strike if he was confident about dealing with it.

Shah also met the Finance Minister, H.M. Patel, and the Governor of RBI, I.G. Patel, and sought their support. According to Shah, he had the advantage as all the three top functionaries were from his own Gujarati community and he could build a rapport with them. He took complete command of the job of frustrating the strike call by the Association, planning each move tactically. Only a chosen few executives who enjoyed his confidence were given specific instructions for the implementation of his plans, and even they were not told the rationale or logic of his strategy. Certain changes were made in the Personnel Department to ensure complete confidentiality of his strategy. A senior executive from the Credit Department (known to be close to Shah) was made the head of the Personnel Department to guard against any leakage of information. Shah told me, 'He would not have allowed any Association man to know what was happening.' The Personnel Department reported directly to Shah throughout the strike period.

Shah did not hesitate to adopt any strategy that would achieve his purpose, notwithstanding the merit of such a strategy and its long-term implications for the IR climate of the Bank. He issued threats over the telephone to senior executives and officers who were activists of the Association and warned them against joining the strike. He removed pro-Association executives from strategic positions and replaced them with anti-Association executives. The management also sought the support of the rival officers' association, the NABOBO, which had 25 per cent membership of the officers, and asked it to be ready to run operations should the strike materialise. The NABOBO was also extended facilities such as office space and telephones to ensure speedier communication between its leaders and the units. During this period, NABOBO issued a number of circulars to the officers denouncing the strike call by the Association. It was no secret that many of these circulars were issued at the behest of Shah.

Shah's strategy ultimately divided the ranks of the officers and mobilised public opinion against the Association, which became so rattled that it withdrew its strike call at the last moment, signalling its clear defeat. This was symbolised by the resignation of many of the central executive members of the Association. The failure of the strike can be attributed to lack of support for it from the officers, most of whom saw it as a power struggle motivated by the personal ambition of the general secretary of the Association.

Echoing the popular sentiment, one officer said:

> Our leaders were all along busy in power-broking. They were more interested in executive promotions than in the plight of the officers in remote

branches or the harassment by the workmen staff. The Association leaders never thought of asking for a transfer policy until the office-bearers were transferred.

Another officer said:

> The Association had become a shadow of the management. When we approached them with our problems, we were berated by the leaders, most of whom were senior officers and executives with whom we could not communicate freely. They had become 'king makers' and many of them wanted to become kings themselves.

In a situation of poor union–member connect, there is hardly any chance to mobilise members against the management and their frustration with their own leaders becomes the biggest advantage for the management. During adverse times, members punish their leaders by being apathetic to the union's call for protest. Member's apathy manifests as psychological revenge (apathy) against their leaders.

Regaining Management Control

Although the strike failed, there was no guarantee that the Association or its leaders would not create problems in the future. The management did not appear too thrilled with its success because, already, it was worried about the future should the Association regain its power and influence.

In the management's view, the real problem was the nomination of the general secretary of the Association on the board as officer-director, which gave the Association legitimacy in interfering in executive matters, as senior management promotions were decided by the board. Shah told me:

> The real IR problem started in the Bank from the time the scheme of worker and officer/director was introduced as a part of nationalisation of banks and union leaders representing workmen as well as officers were nominated on the board of nationalised banks.

Having regained control in most areas of management, Shah now appeared concerned about the problems that he could still encounter with the Association representative on the board. Shah wanted his own nominee on the board of the Bank. In a strategic move, he pleaded before the government that the scheme of the officer-director on the board only provided for nomination of an officer on the board and did not suggest that the officer must be nominated by the officers' association, as was the procedure in nominating the workmen's director. Shah's contention was that the nomination of an Association activist on the board could vitiate the IR climate in the Bank. Shah successfully manoeuvred the nomination of a non-controversial and mild officer from Surat (Gujarat) to the board of the Bank. Shah's rapport with the government facilitated this move. This demonstrates as to how owner (government) and management conspired to weaken the hold of the Association in the Bank. This was in sharp contrast to government action at the behest of the trade union to order premature departure of Thakkar, the previous CEO (Chapter 4). In public sector, this unpredictability of owner's response is something the CEOs have to be aware of and work on before embarking on any big strategic move that is likely to disturb industrial peace.

Shah appeared determined to radically dilute the influence of the Association in the Bank and, in a calculated move, transferred the key office-bearers of the Association who were in the executive cadre to somewhat remote and relatively unimportant overseas centres. For example, he transferred the powerful general secretary of the Association to Fiji and another important activist to Guyana. These transfers came to be known in the Bank as 'exile postings'.

Many of the actions taken by the Bank and its continued tough stance demoralised the Association and there was clearly a mood of remorse and reflection within it. This culminated in the resignation of its general secretary and the restriction of its membership to non-executive cadres. With its determined strategy, the management was able to give a clear signal that it would not allow executives to be members/office-bearers of the Association.

Thus came to an end an era of the Association's rampant interference in executive transfers and postings. The subsequent behaviour of the Association, according to some top executives, was subdued and shorn of the arrogance that was typical of its previous leaders. The new general secretary attempted to build a relationship with the CEO, instead of constantly confronting and fighting with him. Perhaps he had learnt a lesson from the earlier experience.

Rising Power of the Federation Poses Worries

Although the management had successfully tamed the all-powerful Association, it was worried about the growing influence of the Federation leader on the officers and junior executives. It may be noted that during 1977, when the management faced problems in its dealings with the Association, it had sought cooperation from the new association, NABOBO, which, during this time, had consolidated its position. The Federation leader, who was also chairman of NABOBO, through extensive travel in the lead districts of UP and Rajasthan, had canvassed substantial membership, especially from among those officers who had been Federation members before their promotion to the officers' cadre.

In the prevailing tension between the top management and the Association during 1977–78 and the cooperative overtures of the management towards NABOBO, a number of officers had joined the latter. At one stage, it had staked its claim for recognition as a majority association of officers. In the atmosphere of claims and counter-claims, the management maintained the status quo and did not recognise NABOBO, but it was able to make its presence felt and the management had to discuss with it matters relating to its members at the regional/zonal and central levels.

The Federation leader, as chairman of NABOBO, frequently raised issues relating to officers' transfers and promotions. Shah strongly expressed his views against allowing the Federation (representing workmen) leader to take such a deep interest in officers' matters, but found it difficult to prevent it as the Federation leader also represented the officers in his capacity as chairman of NABOBO. Thus, the interference of the Federation leader in officers' matters became a major irritant for the management, and Shah frequently reiterated that this nexus between the workmen and the officers was not acceptable to him.

Shah's antipathy to trade union interference in management issues was at the core of his strategies. He now began focusing on weakening the influence of the Federation leader among the officers. The Federation leader, a veteran trade unionist in the Bank—who had enjoyed the confidence of earlier CEOs such as N.M. Choksi and M.G. Parekh and who was well respected by the former LWO, L.B. Bhide, for his knowledge—became an eyesore for Shah because of his enhanced power as general secretary of the recognised workmen's union and chairman of the minority officers' association. The following episode illustrates how Shah now began targeting the Federation leader.

In 1978, the management announced a promotion exercise for senior officers. The Federation leader, in his capacity as chairman of NABOBO, in one of its communications to Shah suggested that there was frustration amongst the senior officers because the norms for selection had not been shared with them. The Bank was asked to declare the number of vacancies in advance, lay down the eligibility criteria, and declare the policy for promotion of officers to the executive cadre. The Federation leader also approached the board to intervene in the matter. The board, thereafter, laid down the norms for promotions and selection of officers. This was claimed by the Federation leader as one of his major achievements.

In the context of the management's strategy to exercise full rights in the matter of promotion of executives, this successful intervention by the Federation leader using the board was considered by Shah as 'interference in [the] management function'.

It is thus evident that what the Federation leader considered to be his legitimate role was interpreted by the management as an act of interference. Apart from the Federation leader raising issues relating to officers and executives, another matter that apparently bothered the management was the Federation leader's attempts to unite the two officers' associations. The management termed this initiative as 'a tactical move' by the Federation leader to control the officers and eventually enter the board as officer-director. Needless to say, the management was opposed to this unification move.

A Strategy to Weaken the Federation

Against the backdrop of the management's strong opposition to solidarity between the officers and the workmen, the management strategy now focused on neutralising the influence of the Federation leader in NABOBO. This was attempted to be achieved by creating a rift between the general secretary of the NABOBO and the chairman (the Federation leader), the two key leaders of this association, by offering favours and concessions to the general secretary. For example, a liberal view was taken of his spending time on association work during working hours. Cases sponsored by him were promptly resolved. It was common knowledge at that time that the general secretary had direct access to Shah and could resolve speedily pending issues relating to the members of his association.

The special attention given by the management to the general secretary helped him to establish an identity of his own. According to a senior personnel executive:

> The general secretary suddenly became active in association work. He would often visit the Personnel Department and discuss various issues. The chairman of the [new] association (Federation leader) often cross-checked with the Personnel Department about the general secretary's visits and the matters discussed by him.

Shah's strategy created a bitter power struggle within NABOBO. According to an office-bearer of NABOBO, 'The general secretary and the chairman often rebuked or attacked each other during meetings; they also conspired against each other.' Later, in a hard-hitting circular, the chairman of NABOBO (who was also the Federation leader) openly talked of the general secretary's collusion with Shah and his tendency to sidetrack, humiliate, and ignore the chairman.

Senior officers and executives believed that the special attention paid to the general secretary by the management was on the understanding that he would dislodge the Federation leader from the chairmanship of NABOBO. During the next election, the chairman's re-election was opposed by the general secretary, but the chairman was re-elected ultimately.

After the failure of the general secretary of NABOBO to dislodge chairman, the management started ignoring the general secretary. This fact was acknowledged by then executive director, a close aide of Shah, who told me: 'We initially encouraged the general secretary. When he failed to overthrow the chairman of the association, we started ignoring him.'

Although the management failed to dislodge the Federation leader from the chairmanship of NABOBO, it succeeded in creating a power struggle within the association, which resulted in many members leaving it and joining the old Association. This led to increasing intra-association and inter-association rivalries at the operating level. It was evident that the management strategies to create a schism in the union organisations had further complicated the IR environment. This soured environment was a major reason for the deteriorating IR climate in BoB at that time.

New Overtures

While all these IR problems were going on, Shah simultaneously gave a new orientation to the personnel function by formally creating an HRD Department in Vadodara in 1978, which reported to the Deputy General Manager, Personnel, in Vadodara. Shah intended to introduce manpower planning, refigure the existing training system, and introduce a new appraisal system. Trade unions in general were quite cynical about the new HRD Department, which they thought was a clever ploy by Shah to undermine IR and divert attention from the more pressing issues in IR. The IR functionaries too were cynical about the role of the HRD Department in the Bank. Evidently, the introduction of the HRD Department in such a mistrustful environment invited cynicism. Human resource development is not a technique but a philosophy and needs conviction and credibility, and the management at that time seemed to lack both.

Events in IR had impacted the Bank's growth and this obviously worried Shah; his ambition to take the Bank to number one position appeared difficult to achieve in the prevailing environment. In a change of strategy, Shah softened his stance and sought the unions' cooperation in business development. Towards the end of 1979, the management organised meetings with trade unions to seek their commitment to business development. The leaders of the trade unions saw this initiative as being out of line with the management strategy of 'divide and rule'. However, their response was generally positive.

The management organised separate meetings with the two workmen's unions and the two officers' associations to discuss issues relating to the Bank's deposit growth, housekeeping, profitability, and image. According to the top management, these meetings with the trade unions were aimed at 'comprehending the problems of each other with a view to finding solutions to various problems and attaining corporate growth'. Shah, in particular, shared his concern regarding the slow deposit growth of the Bank in

1979, as compared to the 25 per cent deposit growth rate witnessed by the banking industry in general. Shah sought the cooperation of the trade unions in taking BoB to the top position in 1980–81.

All the trade unions submitted detailed proposals for improving the Bank's deposit growth, profitability, housekeeping, and image. According to those who attended these meetings, the response of all the trade unions was generally positive. The trade unions suggested that such dialogues with them should be a regular feature and should also percolate down to the zonal/regional level. During the meeting, the Federation contended that a good IR climate was a prerequisite for the participation of trade unions in such meetings. It also made a number of suggestions to improve the IR climate, which included training of branch managers and regional managers in IR management, expeditious disposal of employee grievances, and regular participation of trade unions in planning and business development matters.

Although the trade unions generally demonstrated a positive attitude towards the Bank's growth and development, this experiment in participation was soon given up. The management developed cold feet about the exercise because of the Federation's objections to inviting the Coordination Committee (minority union) to the meetings and its insistence on raising IR issues in such forums. The prevailing mistrust between the management and the Federation appeared to be the main reason for the failure of the experiment. This is suggested by a circular of the Federation, which pointed out:

> The kind of experiment contemplated can succeed only in a situation where…IR problems are attended to satisfactorily and the exercise would be hypothetical if…basic IR issues were not settled. In an environment of mistrust between the unions and the management, no overture in seeking the participation of the unions in business development can flourish.

It is thus evident that in an environment of mistrust, seeking any co-operation from the trade unions in the business growth could be far-fetched. In the absence of management efforts in resolving IR issues, trade unions may not respond to management's overtures to seek their involvement in business.

Targeting the Federation Leader

Soon after the failure of the business meetings, the management hardened its attitude towards the Federation, and more particularly towards its leader. In a series of actions, Shah attempted to weaken the latter's control over personnel matters, chief among them being denying the Federation leader access to reach out to personnel functionaries, with whom he enjoyed good rapport.

In a sudden strategic move, a large part of the personnel function, including recruitment, promotions, disciplinary action, officers' service conditions, and IR, was shifted from Mumbai to Vadodara, retaining only a small IR policy cell in Mumbai.

Commenting upon the shifting of the Personnel Department, an office-bearer of the Federation said: 'It was like Akbar suddenly deciding to shift his capital from Delhi to Fatehpur Sikri.'

Prior to this reorganisation, only the HRD and staff administration (wage and salary administration and staff loans) functions had been administered from Vadodara. The structure of the Personnel Department before and after the reorganisation is given in Figure 5.1.

Although the management officially ascribed the relocation to acute shortage of space in Mumbai and the ready availability of such infrastructure at Vadodara, the dramatic manner in which the move was carried out created surprise and resentment among the unions and employees. It was widely believed that the relocation of the personnel and IR functions was aimed at reducing the power of the unions and at blocking the access of the Federation leaders to the central management in Mumbai.

It is important to analyse the strategy of the Bank in relocating the Personnel Department and the reasons for the resistance of the Federation. When the Personnel Department was in Mumbai, the Federation leader had free access to it to raise employees' grievances and discuss and influence decision-making on various matters. It was widely known in the Bank that the relations between the Federation leader and the personnel specialists were cordial. The Federation leader and senior personnel specialist, L.B. Bhide, had dealt with each other since 1958 and architected many policies which worked well over a period of time. Management politics at the top (Chapter 4) and subsequent actions on both the sides had ruptured the relationship between the Bank and the Federation.

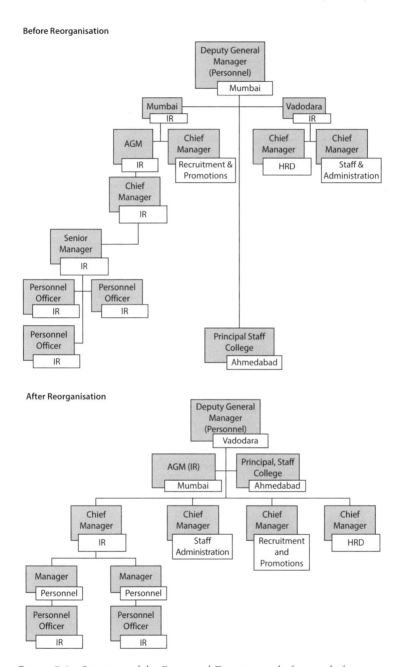

FIGURE 5.1 Structure of the Personnel Department before and after Reorganisation

In the top management's view, this closeness was detrimental to its strategy of clipping the Federation leader's wings. One top management representative observed:

> The Federation leader, through his influence with the personnel specialists, was often able to delay or stall the implementation of various decisions in personnel matters on the plea that he would discuss the matter with [the] top management. This delayed the implementation of decisions.

From the point of view of the Federation, shifting the Personnel Department to Vadodara meant loss of power in influencing the personnel decision-making process. The Federation leader observed:

> Whenever a problem was referred by our outstation unit, we could contact the Personnel Department, brief them about the facts of the case promptly and help sort out the issues fast. Similarly, whenever the Personnel Department had any problem with any of our units, they contacted us and we helped them to sort out issues. This reciprocity helped to maintain equilibrium in IR even during times of tension.

The shifting of the Personnel Department to Vadodara reduced the influence of the Federation leader over personnel matters and, by implication, also over the members. There were other structural changes which appeared to be aimed at marginalising the Federation further and reducing its influence over personnel decision-making. Among them, individual functionaries in the Personnel Department were divested of their power and decision-making was centralised in a newly created committee called the Personnel Committee (PC). The PC was based in Vadodara. Its members included General Manager (Personnel), the Deputy General Manager (Operations), Deputy General Manager (Personnel), and Assistant General Manager (IR). The Deputy General Manager (Personnel), an operational executive, was appointed its convener.

According to a circular from the CEO, the PC was expected to facilitate the process of personnel decision-making in the Bank and to decide matters requiring interpretation of awards and settlements where differences of opinion existed. It was also expected to scan the IR environment for signs of unrest from time to time.

Although the management claimed that the PC had been set up to facilitate decision-making, senior executives believed that the real intention was to reduce the authority of the personnel specialists and the power of the union leaders who enjoyed a good rapport with them. The creation of the PC neutralised the potential influence of the Federation leader over the personnel executives in Mumbai.

The power of the personnel specialists at the zonal level was also reduced by reorganising the personnel function, which was divided into two departments: a Staff Department to be headed by an operational functionary to look after all officers' matters; and a Personnel Department headed by the personnel manager to look after workmen-related issues, IR, and industrial law matters. A new post titled, 'Senior Manager (Staff Administration)', was created in four major zones alongside the existing post of personnel manager, which was held by a personnel specialist.

Ex-activists of the Association, who had been sidelined after the failed strike call in 1977, were appointed as Senior Managers (Staff Administration). These activists were known to be anti-Federation and the intention of the management, as one senior executive revealed, was 'to give the Federation a tough time at the operating level'.

The Senior Managers (Staff Administration) were assigned the function relating to officers and executives, including promotions and transfers. These functions had been handled earlier by the personnel manager, whose job was made merely advisory with responsibilities to attend to union negotiations and give an opinion on the interpretation of awards and settlements. The management officially announced that these changes were aimed at strengthening personnel management at the operating level. However, the real intention of the management, according to a close aide of Shah, was to prepare itself for any eventuality, like an agitation by the Federation, and to neutralise the power and influence of personnel managers in IR matters.

These measures led to a significant change in the management's approach to IR, especially in relation to the Federation. Shah and the Federation leader clashed on virtually every issue. As one top personnel functionary put it:

> It was common in those days for the Federation leader to issue threats of agitation and disrupt the working of the Bank. Shah retaliated by creating one or the other problem for the Federation leader.

Shah perhaps understood the weak connect between the Federation and its members and was confident of the Federation giving any call for work stoppages being disregarded and therefore, did not take any such threats seriously.

The power politics and the Federation leader's obsession to interfere in officers' matters, as also perceived loss of influence with the management, had diluted his influence over his members. Members find it difficult to relate with their leaders when they become inaccessible to their members and busy themselves with corporate politics.

New Demands by the Federation

In 1980, Shah made an attempt to formalise the management's relations with the Federation by clearly laying down the areas of negotiations and consultations, and demanded an agreement on this. In response, the Federation submitted the following charter of demands in return for arriving at any such understanding:

Facilities to the Federation:

1. 100 office-bearers (whether officers or workmen) of the Federation to be relieved from their duties for trade union work;
2. office space with telephone and other equipment like typewriters, cabinets, and so on, to be made available in the various zonal headquarters;
3. written correspondence by the zonal/regional authorities with the Federation and its affiliate units;
4. check-off facility;
5. subsidised canteens and appointment of canteen boys in branches in metropolitan cities;
6. assistant head cashier allowance to cashiers;
7. shifting of Personnel Department from Vadodara to Mumbai; and
8. formation of an IR council at the corporate level.

The management, for the first time, prepared its own agenda for discussions, which included:

1. norms of behaviour for the Federation leaders;
2. the Federation to vacate premises usurped by their leaders in various zones;

3. the Federation to cooperate in the implementation of the Bank's policy in respect of regulating payment of overtime;
4. the Federation leaders at all levels to desist from indulging in activities like gherao[1] and so on;
5. norms of job rotation with emphasis on mobility of staff;
6. redeployment of staff from surplus branches to deficit branches;
7. transfer of office-bearers of the Federation on their promotion; and
8. time-bound implementation of agreements/understandings reached between the Federation and the Bank.

The long list of counter-demands by the Federation leader only symbolised the remote possibility of any understanding on the issue of formalisation of union–management relations.

The management refused to discuss and settle the demands of the Federation until the Federation agreed to discuss the 'management agenda' as well. The management insisted on a 'package deal' which would include 'give and take' on both sides. Due to the uncompromising stand taken by both sides, none of the issues raised by the Federation, both policy matters affecting a group of employees as well as individual grievances, could be resolved. Thus, one more attempt by the management to formalise IR failed. Failed efforts in formalisation heightened the tension between the CEO and the Federation leader. In a mistrustful environment, any initiative on either side, howsoever well intentioned, has a huge chance of failure.

The personal mistrust between the two key actors, CEO Shah and the leader of the Federation, had reached a high pitch with little hope of reconciliation. Each side appeared determined to destabilise the other. The mistrust stemmed from Shah's 'conspiratorial style' of functioning, as told to me by the Federation leader. He cited many cases of Shah meddling with the internal dynamics of the unions by distributing favours to the leaders. The Federation leader was peeved at the way in which Shah, through his government contacts, got the Federation's choice for workman-director rejected and got his 'clan man' from his home state appointed. Shah admitted that he did it to weaken the influence of

---

[1] A protest in which workers prevent employees from leaving the place of work until certain demands are met.

the Federation leader by prevailing upon the government to nominate another candidate. He told me:

> The Federation leader often interfered in the matters raised in the board by briefing the workmen's director. Sometimes he used the information collected informally from the workmen's director on the board against the Bank. This often created controversies and it was not in the Bank's interest. In 1978, after the expiry of term of the workmen's director, the Federation had sent three names in order of preference to the government for nomination to the board. The person at number one was considered close to the Federation leader and his nomination would have strengthened the Federation leader and given him access to board matters. The Bank prevailed upon the government to nominate the person at number two. The Bank had no interest in this person, but it was known that he was not close to the Federation leader and hence could not be influenced by him.

Shah, with his repertoire of tactical manoeuvres, was able to successfully weaken both the Federation and the Association. And though these tactical moves kept the unions on tenterhooks, they created more problems at the operating level and created a new bureaucratic environment in personnel decision-making.

The episode also brings out the role of the government in IR. It illustrates how the Government of India used the scheme of participative management to tilt the power balance in favour of the Bank's management. It also brings out the need for political skills for PSB CEOs to network with the government in difficult situations.

After taking on two powerful unions which were once the conscience keepers of the management, Shah was able to regain power in the personnel function without resistance at any level. In a dynamic competitive scenario, this helped the management to redeploy officers and executives as per the needs of the Bank without any interference.

· By managing IR in this cavalier manner, Shah was able to assume unfettered control over the management functions of promotion and deployment of executives as per need, business requirements, and demonstrate excellent business growth. The Bank made rapid strides in business. It almost doubled its number of branches. Deposits multiplied about four-fold, advances nearly three-fold, and priority sector credit more than four-fold. The Bank expanded its overseas business and opened branches in the advanced countries. A summary of the developments is given in Table 5.1.

TABLE 5.1   How BoB Grew under Shah (1975–81)

Activity	1975	1981
Deposits	Rs 7,450 million	Rs 25,770 million
Advances	Rs 5,240 million	Rs 14,820 million
Priority sector advances	Rs 1,310 million	Rs 5,550 million
Number of branches	798	1,502
Number of foreign branches	37	51
Profit	Rs 26 million	Rs 56 million
Number of staff members	17,100	28,419

Turbulence at the Operational Level

Although the management had wrested total control at the top by reducing the power of the unions to interfere in the day-to-day running of the Bank, and also restricted their access to the Personnel Department for resolution of their member's grievances, the branches faced the real problems.

At the branch level, managers often had to cope with rising militancy of the workmen staff. The support of the top management in handling IR problems at the branch level, as one manager put it, was minimal. Managers were left on their own to deal with issues of inter-union rivalry, restrictive practices, and the increasing indifference of the staff towards customer service. The branch managers and their immediate bosses, the regional/zonal managers, bought peace and ensured completion of day-to-day work using the carrot of overtime.

A team of management consultants from IIM Ahmedabad confirmed the chaotic state of IR environment at the branches (Govindarajan et al., 1979). Their report observed:

1. The managers did not have time for developmental work.
2. Staff indiscipline was a severe problem. The managers were helpless in managing their staff due to union problems.
3. The managers did not have the administrative powers to deal with the staff.
4. The top management needed to be firm before the unions and not give away their powers and sacrifice their authority and credibility to the unions.

5. Communication between the regional managers and branch managers was poor.

6. Decisions on personnel matters were being delayed unconscionably.

7. There was no system of reward and punishment in the branches.

8. Inter-union rivalry was a big problem and it was affecting work at the branches.

9. Absenteeism was a problem. Staff members were coming late to office.

10. The regional managers were not helpful in sorting out the problem of branches.

11. Everyone at the senior and the top level was afraid of facing union and staff problems and was leaving such problems to the branch managers to sort out.

12. The regional offices did not respond to the problems of:

    (a) replacement of staff;

    (b) provision of staff during leave; and

    (c) clarification sought regarding staff matters.

The following excerpt from the consultants' report[2] on branch-level organisation is pertinent here:

> The main problem at the branches is the staff problem. Most Managers state that a large portion of their time is spent on the staff problem and the Branch Manager has no control whatsoever over the workmen staff. The workplace has become a place of tension and work a source of dissatisfaction for the Branch Managers. The Branch Manager is not perceived as effective. In case of any problems, there is no support from the higher management. Unions are seen as having the capability of getting any decision they want from the regional levels.

The rising number of cases of fraud at the Bank and the overtime bill of the staff showed a lack of control at the branches and loss of managerial authority. Many managers attributed these problems to lack of concern among the lower-level staff about completing their day's work, as also to the inability of the managers to ensure completion of work in the face of mounting staff resistance. The overtime payment bill at the Bank reached

---

[2] 'Management Control in Bank of Baroda', a report by Professors V. Govindarajan, N.R. Sheth and T.V. Rao, Indian Institute of Management, Ahmedabad, 1979.

an all-time high in 1980 and recruitment of additional staff did not control it. According to many senior executives who were managers at that time, the overtime was claimed and paid irrespective of the work done by staff after their normal working hours. Records also reveal that in some zones like the Eastern Zone and at the Mumbai main branch, overtime was paid much beyond the ceiling of 175 hours per year. Union activists who did not attend to even normal work were also paid overtime.

It is important to analyse the reasons for the deterioration in the IR climate at the branch level, even though union power at the corporate level was considerably reduced. The answer to this lies in the managerial strategies in IR pursued during the period between 1975 and 1981. The management's strategy to weaken the Association and encourage the rival NABOBO had its impact on workplaces, with officers of rival groups showing increasing militancy and aggressive postures in raising officers' issues with the management, each trying to score a point over the other. The alliance between NABOBO and the Federation had its impact on workplace discipline when workmen activists of the Federation were favoured by managers belonging to NABOBO. All this raised a big question mark on the credibility of the managerial staff, who were divided into two warring groups. This led to deterioration in workplace discipline with each group playing off the other.

The top management's later efforts to weaken the Federation leader also had consequences at the workplace, with increasing cases of indiscipline and total breakdown of managerial authority. The weakening of the Federation had its main effect in the Mumbai main office, a place of perpetual union problems, where a small group of employees affiliated to the INTUC, the trade union wing of the Congress Party, added a new dimension to the problem. Encouraged by the management's antipathy towards the Federation, it started mobilisation of membership and claimed unauthorised facilities to run its organisation.

Another consequence of the weakening of the Federation on branch-level IR was the growing militancy of the Federation members at the operating level. The failure of the Federation leader to get things done and resolve the grievances of employees resulted in growing frustration amongst the Federation members at the operating level. This is evident from the increase in the number of cases filed by the Federation units in various states in conciliation and tribunals against non-resolution of grievances of employees, as shown in Table 5.2.

TABLE 5.2 Cases in Conciliation and Tribunals (1976–81)

Year	Cases in Conciliation	Cases before Tribunals
1976	9	2
1977	6	3
1978	9	4
1979	14	5
1980	22	11
1981	36	16

Apart from the sharp rise in litigation between the Bank and the Federation, many cases concerning the militant acts of Federation leaders were reported from various zones. For example, in 1980–81, six cases of gherao and five cases of strike undertaken by Federation units were reported by various zones. In one case, the secretary of a regional unit of the Federation usurped the office of an executive and declared it to be a 'Federation office'. Against the history of the Federation's docile profile, such actions symbolised the growing frustration in the ranks of the Federation.

It is thus evident that the management's ploy to weaken the Federation led to the emergence of a rival union as well as militant acts by Federation activists at the operating level, complicating their management at the operating level. Together, these developments considerably vitiated the IR climate at the operating level, with managers struggling to deal with the increasing IR problems and inter-union rivalries. In the prevailing environment in the Bank, the top management responded to the branches' problems in an 'ad hoc and often unpredictable' manner, as one manager described it.

* * *

This period in IR in the Bank's history is an example of complete mistrust between the trade unions and the CEO. In a scenario of fractured relationship between the management and trade unions inherited from the preceding management, the IR conflict was exacerbated by the management's belief and assertion in 'right to manage' and disallow union interference in areas of management domain.

The CEO, Shah, successfully used Machiavellian methods of taming the unions. He used every arsenal in his armoury to marginalise them. He blocked all the channels for them to have a semblance of influence in the personnel matters. His actions lent credence to the adage, 'Everything is fair in love and war'. To pursue his goals, he did not mind going to any lengths, including creating storms in the trade unions, causing schism among the union leaders, pampering and promoting divisions in the unions, and using and dumping them. At the organisation level, he tinkered with the structure of the personnel function, disempowered and sidelined the key personnel functionaries, and installed committees for personnel decision-making that created prolonged delays in decisions.

With extraordinary focus on reducing the influence of trade unions at the corporate level, the management busied itself in tackling the unions at the top, with little time to attend to the problems of the operating units. On top of it, emasculation of personnel function by weakening the personnel functionaries and creating bureaucratic structure of decision-making in personnel further added to the woes of both the line managers and employees, who found the problem-solving process archaic, with deleterious consequences at the operating level.

Left to fend for themselves, the operating managers managed by compromising on discipline and productivity issues. When top management does not listen to operating managers regarding their problems, they tend to react by inaction even on issues under their control and discretion. Thus, while the top management attained complete control at the corporate level in personnel and IR management, the operating management's control weakened considerably. During this period, the workplace unions posed what Fox (1974) calls a 'challenge from below'.

Some of his strategies included shifting of personnel department to Vadodara, setting up of multiple committees for personnel decision making, weakening the authority of personnel executives, meddling into internal dynamics of the unions and fiddling with the appointment of workmen and officers nominees on the board. While these strategies put Shah in the driver's seat in calling the shots in IR, they also led to bureaucratic delays in personnel decision making, fostering an environment of mistrust in union management relations and a perpetual guerrilla warfare like situation in the branches.

Why did Shah succeed, whereas Thakkar failed, in disciplining unions? Unlike Thakkar who rushed into serious action against a powerful leader too fast without much preparation to handle its consequences, Shah led his assault on trade unions with clinical planning and government support, deploying himself completely. Dealing with complex IR situations requires multiple strategies which do not follow any sequence. Depending on the muck, a lot of cleansing may be called for that may defy any neat approach; and if both management and unions do not change their stand, the management may resort to manoeuvring, manipulating, and even crafty steps to deal with the disruptive potential of the actors, as we see in this case.

In this sense, IR can never be just a value-based relationship or ethical transaction, but always a relationship held in balance by the application of pressure and counter-pressure to gain advantage in the bargaining position. Good IR are about defining the larger purpose and creating a balance between what is asked and what can be given, to achieve a win-win situation. Getting entrenched in a particular style is problematic. As IR situations are unpredictable, it is difficult to speculate on any particular managerial style to deal with all the problems all the time. Trust is key to develop good IR and a cycle of mistrust is extremely risky in crafting good IR.

As seen in this chapter, the IR pattern during this period was mostly entrenched in personal animosity between the CEO and the key leader of the Federation, reaching a new low which precluded any alternative form of conduct of IR. In this pattern, there is essentially a denial of legitimacy of ends and means of the other party. This mutual dislike assumes irrational proportions (Walton and McKersie, 1965: 186). In such a scenario, it was a major challenge for succeeding CEOs to build back a cooperative relationship. The quality of IR at the Bank during 1975–81 fits the 'uninhibited antagonism' pattern, as described by Purcell (1981: 63):

> Under this pattern, the IR are conducted in an ad hoc, conflict based manner with bargaining advantage frequently exploited by either side when circumstances permit. The relationship is marked by mutual suspicion and distrust. The behaviour of one party is often seen by the other as irrational and unpredictable. Management in IR tends to be reactive and concerned with coping with short-term crises. The role of personnel management is limited.

Chapter 6

SOFT PEDALLING (1982–84)

After serving more than six years at the BoB, the longest by any bank CEO in recent times, R.C. Shah was asked by the government to take over as CEO of the newly established Export-Import Bank of India (EXIM Bank) in December 1981. He was succeeded by his deputy, Y.V. Sivaramakrishnayya (better known in the Bank as YVS).

YVS was essentially an industrial finance banker who had come to BoB from the RBI in the late 1960s. The Bank was in good shape, but its IR environment was abysmal. Shah's strategies had created a complicated IR situation marked by intense rivalry between the two officers' associations, the AIBOBOA (the Association) and the NABOBO; the rising power of the leader of the Federation; a chaotic work environment; demoralised personnel functionaries; and bitter enmity between the Federation and its rival workmen's union, the Coordination Committee. The unions were very angry with the management meddling in the internal dynamics of their organisations. They wanted quick restoration of a positive climate along with resolution of their long-pending issues. They expected the management to undertake confidence-building measures to restore its credibility.

On the business front, YVS had to carry forward the tempo of business and deliver consistent results to enable the Bank to maintain its prime position when it celebrated its platinum jubilee in 1983.

During Shah's time, the Board of Directors had already approved a long-range plan for the years 1982–85 outlining the business priorities of the Bank. Its entire thrust was to maintain its lead in the areas in which it was already ahead of the rest and reduce the gap between its own performance and that of its competitors in the areas in which it lagged behind. The plan included the following targets:

1. to achieve annual deposit accretion to the extent of 20 per cent;
2. to open 100 new branches per year;
3. to increase the share of priority sector advances to 43 per cent of total credit;
4. to increase the paid-up capital and reserves from Rs 350 million to Rs 450 million; and
5. to maintain the existing levels of productivity and profitability.

However, implementing the plan was not easy, more so because BoB faced cut-throat competition from other banks whose performance was not far behind it. The BoB was, however, determined not to lose the top position that it had achieved.

YVS appeared to be concerned about the IR environment, which could pose a considerable challenge to the management's efforts to maintain the Bank's top position. A diehard industrial finance expert, YVS had no experience in handling the complex challenge posed by the prevailing IR environment. A development which threw yet another spanner in the works, especially in West Bengal, was the split in the AIBEA, the majority union at the banking industry level, in 1980 and the formation of the BEFI, with its affiliation to the Communist Party of India (Marxist). The branches in the Eastern Zone in particular (comprising West Bengal and the north-eastern states) were torn by inter-union rivalry between the BoB's Coordination Committee (which was affiliated to the AIBEA) and BEFI, with each trying to gain a hold over the workmen.

In the context of the general militancy of the trade union movement in West Bengal, the inter-union rivalry at BoB posed special problems in this zone. The managers increasingly complained about the violation of the provisions of the Bank's settlement with the recognised Federation by the BEFI-affiliated union. All along, the Bank had avoided any confrontation with the unions in this zone; now the situation had deteriorated and posed a serious threat to operations.

Similarly, the emergence of the BOBETUC, affiliated to the INTUC in Mumbai during Shah's tenure (where the Federation had always held sway in the past) created tensions in IR right under the nose of the top management. As INTUC enjoyed government support, BOBETUC adopted a highly militant stance in the branches here. For the first time, the Bank's branches in Mumbai experienced problems on account of inter-union rivalry.

There were similar problems among the officers' associations, with inter-association rivalry running rife, especially in UP and Rajasthan, where maximum expansion had taken place under the Lead Bank Scheme.

The unions and associations complained about the non-resolution of their grievances, lack of information sharing, frustration among employees, and bureaucratic personnel decision-making. They called upon the YVS-led management to reintegrate the personnel function once again in Mumbai because they felt the bifurcation was the main cause for the delayed decision-making in employee matters.

Most of the operating managers cited increasing instances of indiscipline, restrictive practices, inter-association rivalries, and virtual loss of managerial authority to enforce discipline, leading to deterioration in productivity and customer service. Many of them were sceptical about achieving business targets unless the overall IR situation improved. They complained about the lack of support from higher authorities in their efforts to maintain discipline at the branch level. Many zonal and regional managers complained about the ineffectiveness of personnel decision-making at the corporate level, which led to confusion and the increasing militancy of the unions.

There were also problems within the top management. A.C. Sheth, the Executive Director, was reputed to be close to the earlier CEO, R.C. Shah, and was known to be quite parochial and prone to favouring senior executives like regional and zonal managers in placements and promotions. He also had his own agenda with the union leaders. For example, he did not like the Federation leader as, in the past, the Federation had complained to the board about Sheth's corrupt practices. Sheth was due to retire in 18 months and many senior general managers vied to replace him and aligned with the Federation leader for his support. Sheth did not like L.B. Bhide, the head of personnel, possibly because Bhide was known to follow rules and unlikely to violate them for expediency.

In addition to the murky internal climate, the government pressurised PSBs to improve customer service, reduce restrictive practices, improve workplace discipline, and initiate tough measures, such as reduction in overtime, job rotation of staff, and stopping the practice of allowing union leaders to do union work during working hours. On the other hand, the government in power encouraged its trade union wing, the INTUC. During the reorganisation of the boards of PSBs in 1983, the government had nominated activists of INTUC in most of the PSBs. In most of the large banks, there were no INTUC-affiliated unions, so these appointments did not have direct implications for IR. The BoB, however, had its recognised officers' association and a workmen's union, both of which were affiliated to the INTUC. The nomination of an INTUC activist on the board by the government enabled him to meddle frequently in union politics and openly canvass membership for the INTUC-affiliated unions in the Bank. The management thus had to cope with a variety of internal and external factors in IR.

A Softer Approach towards the Unions

The most difficult part of the Bank's IR problems during this period were the tensions and stresses at the branch level. In the management's assess-ment, much of the turbulence at the branch level stemmed from unresolved grievances—of both workmen and officers. One of the key priorities of the Bank then was to re-establish union–management interactions at all levels, so that long-pending employee issues could be taken up and resolved.

YVS took a major initiative to facilitate this: he introduced a system of structured meetings, with specific periodicity, with the unions at the cor-porate, zonal, and regional levels. This forum was created to deal with the grievances of employees emanating at different levels. Although union–management meetings were held in an ad-hoc manner at the regional level, now, a system of structured periodical meetings had to take place at the zonal, regional and branch levels as well. All the zones and regions were asked to draw up a calendar of meetings, which were monitored by the corporate management. The purpose of these meetings, as highlighted by YVS in a circular to the Bank branches, was to accord urgency to employee grievances and to ensure employee satisfaction. It was also laid down that the agenda of these meetings should be broad-based to include issues relat-ing to business development.

The management generally pursued a cautious policy in dealing with the unions and did not initiate any major changes, apparently to contain the unions' resistance. For example, it did not take any steps to improve the discipline at the branches by any policy pronouncement that could empower the branch managers to take initiatives in restoring discipline. Even the cases of indiscipline by the activists of minority unions were handled with kid gloves. When a branch manager in Mumbai complained about leaders of minority unions leaving office early and performing union work during working hours, he was advised against making an issue of it.

Similarly, official records and interviews with managers of Eastern Zone branches suggest that members of the BEFI indulged in browbeating tactics at the branch level whenever managers tried to promote punctuality or take steps to contain restrictive practices by the staff in the delivery of customer service. In many branches of the Eastern Zone, the housekeeping function (balancing of books) was in huge arrears as the staff did not attend to such work, which was part of their regular job. The corporate management soft-pedalled the IR problems despite pressure from the zonal management to lend support in tackling them. This led to a sense of helplessness among the local executives, and at one time, two top zonal executives threatened to resign if the top management did not act.

The management also softened its attitude towards the Federation and its leaders. Several matters raised by the Federation had remained unresolved because the previous management had insisted that unless the Federation agreed to discuss the management agenda, their agenda will not be discussed. These issues were now settled by the management without any insistence on discussing its agenda, which included issues such as norms for union work during working hours and acts of omission and commission by the Federation leaders.

The bipartite relationship between the Federation and the management, which had remained in limbo, was revived and they resolved some pending issues. For example, the management signed two important settlements with the Federation regarding: (a) sanction of a new allowance for the assistant head cashier in the branches allowing additional benefits to cashiers in the majority of branches; and (b) criteria for selecting special assistants and officers from the open market. YVS also accommodated the Federation leader's requests for transfers of employees, and even officers, and this created a thaw in IR in the immediate post-Shah period.

One of the principal reason for delays in personnel/IR decision-making was attributed to the split location of personnel/IR function. The Federation leader soon revived his demand to shift the Personnel Department back to Mumbai. But YVS placated him with small concessions. As one senior personnel functionary told me: 'Whenever the Federation leader came and raised issues of policy, he was favoured by the Bank with some small concession.' For example, the telephone bill for the Federation's office, amounting to Rs 22,000, was sent by the deputy general manager in charge of the Mumbai main branch (where the Federation office was housed) to central office for authorising payment. In view of the large amount of the bill, the Federation leader approached YVS and got his approval for payment of the bill. In another case, the Bank sanctioned a loan of Rs 50,000 to the Federation to celebrate its silver jubilee.

It is thus evident that the management, by extending these small concessions and favours to the Federation, avoided any problem that could disturb the prevailing equilibrium in the management–Federation relationship and eventually affect business at the Bank. It also shows how trade unions sought personal favours and compromised their trade union agenda.

The management also pursued a policy of accommodation towards the recognised officers' association. Many instances were cited by personnel functionaries as to how the top management accommodated the Association. For example, in a promotion exercise in 1983, six out of nine zonal secretaries of the Association were promoted and as per policy, they had to be transferred. The Association requested the Bank initially to defer the transfer of these officers until the election of new office-bearers. The Bank accepted the request and eventually the officers were not transferred for two years. According to a senior functionary of the Personnel Department, the Association was accommodated to keep them in good humour, although the Bank was not obliged to accede to such requests.

Similarly, in spite of persistent pressure from the government to abolish the practice of union work during working hours, the management did not initiate any concrete measure to discontinue such practice.

Failure to Resolve Fundamental Issues

Although by maintaining a soft and accommodative stance in IR, the Bank could retain its top position during its platinum jubilee year in 1983, it could not in any way improve the day-to-day IR climate at the operating level. The ad hoc 'Band-Aid approach' in IR could not guarantee a durable solution. In fact, the IR environment went from bad to worse. Almost all the unions complained about the moribund state of IR in the Bank.

An analysis of circulars issued by various trade unions during 1984 revealed their 'heightened concern' about the state of personnel management in the Bank. The intensity of their frustration was evident in the titles of the circulars they issued to their members at that time, such as 'Wanted: Management in the Bank' and 'Personnel Management in the Bank'. The Federation and the NABOBO passed resolutions against the deteriorating state of the personnel and IR functions in the Bank. Official documents show that during this period, the Federation addressed a number of communications to YVS about the deteriorating IR in the Bank and pointed out, in particular, the facilities enjoyed by the minority unions, lack of interest among line executives in resolving employee grievances, and failure of the system of structured meetings.

The Federation demanded shifting the Personnel Department back to the central office in Mumbai from the head office in Vadodara on the grounds that it led to pointless shuffling of papers between the two offices. The NABOBO also, through a number of circulars and communications, showed its frustration about the ad hoc decision-making in personnel matters.

An important development, symbolic of the growing frustration among the line executives during this period, was an unsuccessful attempt to form an executives' association by a small group of senior executives like the regional managers.

It is important to analyse the reasons for the deterioration of the IR climate in the Bank and the prevailing frustration amongst both the trade unions as well as the operating management with the quality of IR. While complaints from the trade unions related to delays in decision-making at the corporate level, the operating management complained both about delays in personnel decision-making as well as bias in transfers and promotions. In order to understand this situation, it is necessary to study the structure of personnel decision-making in the Bank, as well as the line of authority at the corporate level.

After the structural changes in the Personnel Department in 1980, the personnel function was divided between Vadodara and Mumbai. The entire Personnel Department, including IR, was shifted to Vadodara, leaving only a small IR policy cell in Mumbai. By the end of 1982, some more changes had taken place in the structure of the Personnel Department, which led to delays in personnel decision-making. The structure of the Personnel Department during 1980–81 and 1982–83 is given in Figure 6.1.

Documents show that the split locations of the Personnel Department led to considerable delays in transmitting decisions to the regions and zones, and in many cases, the delay escalated industrial conflict at the operating level. This also invited the ire of the operating managers against the corporate office. Though the top management acknowledged delays on account of the split location of the Personnel Department, it did not make any changes in the prevailing structure as demanded by the trade unions. The intention of the top management was apparently to avoid any step that could eventually increase the access of trade unions to the top management, even though the split location of Personnel Department delayed decision-making in personnel leading to a chaotic environment.

Management Politics Prove a Barrier to Reforms

As mentioned earlier, a factor that apparently contributed to obstruct any reforms in IR was the prevalent differences and mistrust among the key top executives. Among the three top executives, YVS (CEO), Sheth (Executive Director), and Bhide (General Manager, Personnel), Sheth was known for his anti-Federation attitude. Both YVS and Bhide acknowledged this and told me that the Bank's efforts to develop a working rapport with the Federation were usually scuttled by Sheth. For instance, YVS had agreed to give representation to the Federation leader in the House Allotment Committee headed by Sheth. Sheth protested against this decision and did not convene even a single meeting of the committee during his tenure of one-and-a-half years.

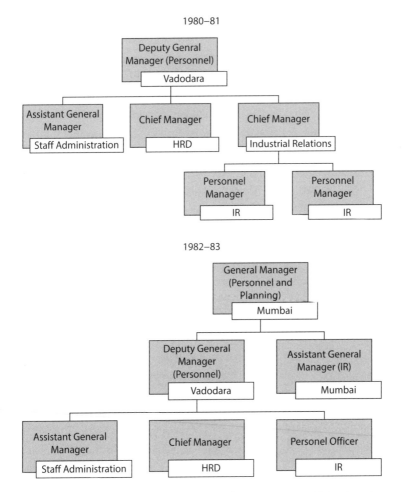

FIGURE 6.1 Structure of the BoB Personnel Department, 1980–81 and 1982–83

Similarly, the government had asked PSBs to constitute Customer Service Committees in their branches and give representation to recognised unions on them. According to a member of the top management, Sheth, who supervised this arrangement, did not allow representation of the Federation on the committee. The strained relations among the three top executives further delayed decision-making in personnel matters and demoralised the line executives. Bhide acknowledged that many proposals submitted by the unions and officers' associations and put up before Sheth or YVS for a final decision were delayed because each viewed the other with suspicion.

The lack of cohesion in the top management team and the uneasy relations among the top executives resulted in increasing frustration amongst executives at the regional and other levels, especially regarding transfers and postings. Records show that the executive postings in the Bank were decided by YVS and Sheth, and Bhide was not consulted. Many executives resented the absence of any policy in this regard. Several executives who were interviewed said that their grievances were not heard by the top management. As one executive put it:

> I have been away from my family for about eight years and I have two grown-up daughters of marriageable age. I have requested the management for [a] transfer back to my [home] place to fulfil this social obligation, but there has not been any response. In contrast, some executives have not moved at all from their original place of posting. You have to be close either to the CEO or the executive director to get a desired posting.

The executive cadre was divided along ethnic lines. The executives were frequently cited as belonging to the CEO's group or the executive director's group. It was, according to many senior executives, common for the executives to maintain direct relations with either the CEO or the executive director to seek personal favours in matters of promotions and postings, including overseas postings. An often-cited case in this regard was that of a regional manager known to be corrupt in his business dealings, who was rewarded with an overseas posting due to his contacts with the executive director.

It is thus evident that both the structure of the Personnel Department as well as the management politics at the top prevented the framing of any long-term IR strategy to improve the workplace climate. Instead, the management continued with the delay-producing, bifurcated structure in the Personnel Department, soft-pedalled the unions, and played on the vulnerable unions to buy peace by extending personal favours to some leaders.

Another important factor that enabled the Bank to take ad hoc measures in IR and avoid any long-term reforms was the absence of any sustained pressure from the Federation and the Association. Although both these unions often complained about the deterioration in IR and delays in personnel decision-making, their protests were feeble, apparently due to the favours they received from the management. The Federation leader frequently remained absent for long durations ranging from two to three months. He either went to his hometown or performed his union-related work from his residence in Mumbai. Although he occasionally issued circulars about the deterioration in the IR situation in the Bank and also shared his frustration about the delay in decision-making, he did not pursue it beyond a point.

The Association also privately shared its frustration about the state of personnel management in the Bank, but its strategy was to avoid confrontation. Although there was considerable pressure on the Association from the officers about the pressure of work, and improvement in service conditions, the Association failed to put up any serious pressure on the management and kept quiet in return for small concessions and personal favours.

It is thus evident that the lack of aggression and absence to put up any resistance was also a major factor in management pursuing status-quoist policy in dealing with employee issues. When both management and trade unions become apathetic to pursue reforms in IR, the workplaces face the brunt of alienated employees, and conflict-ridden state of IR in workplaces and general dissatisfaction of employees can be attributed to this.

Chaos at the Operating Level

The softening approach in IR helped the Bank to maintain its top position in the banking industry as it did not face any disruptions brought about by industrial action. Its domestic deposits in 1982–83 grew at an average rate of 19 per cent per annum, which was well over the 15.25 per cent achieved by the banking industry as a whole. Credit expansion also showed a similar trend. The BoB opened, on an average, 70 branches per year.

In spite of these achievements, the quality of IR, especially at the operating level, deteriorated. The impact of the soft-pedalling strategies of the management in IR and the ineffectiveness of the apex-level unions and associations in resolving their members' grievances was evident in the prevailing chaotic IR scene in the branches. Records show that during that time, there was an increasing number of complaints to the central office about inter-union and intra-union problems in the various zones.

The managers acknowledged that they had to yield under pressure from branch-level union representatives in matters of discipline. Describing the problems the branches faced during that time, a manager said:

> IR in the branches was chaotic. There was intense inter-union rivalry and the activists of the union undertook union work during working hours which the higher management failed to check. Unions interfered in matters of allotment of work, job rotation and discipline. For fear of lack of support from higher authorities and under constant pressure to achieve targets, we had to give in to union pressures. The management's authority at [the] branches was totally undermined, as there was little support from the higher authorities.

Many managers talked of the rise in restrictive practices, the violation of existing settlements, as well as unethical financial claims by staff members. Managers conceded that they had to spend a lot of time sorting out staff problems and they used overtime to get the day's work completed. During the period 1982–84, the Bank's expenditure on overtime to staff amounted to Rs 10.1 million, which was the highest amongst nationalised banks, and this invited an adverse reaction from the government.

Describing the situation in the branches at that time, branch managers made remarks, such as, 'the management did not exist in the Bank', 'the management had sold itself to [the] unions', 'the management was impotent', and the 'Unions were too powerful'.

The IR scenario at the zonal and regional levels was also quite muddled. The system of structured meetings introduced by the Bank to resolve employee grievances and ensure good IR was not implemented seriously by the regional managers, who complained about lack of time amidst their business pressures to attend meetings with the various unions. They also complained about the delay in decisions from the corporate level on matters arising from the structured meetings at the zonal offices. The overall IR situation was thus chaotic, although there were no incidents of strikes or go slow. Branches were, as one branch manager put it, 'in a permanent state of turbulence'.

Managerial strategies in IR pursued during this period were aimed at soft-pedalling IR issues and buying peace. Merely introducing the system of structured meetings, without initiating concomitant steps, such as unification of the Personnel Department, restoring the authority of the personnel functionaries, and providing support to the line functionaries to regain authority to deal with workplace problems, brought chaos and turbulence to IR. Thus, tinkering with small initiatives could not bring peace to the workplace. The management's reliance on short-term solution to combat union militancy by extending favours and concessions, and their apathy to reform the workplace IR through required steps, was the main angst of the operating managers and perhaps the biggest cause of prevailing IR situation in the Bank.

The continued neglect of reforming the workplace IR by successive management was not without grave consequences.

On the operating front, two major frauds were discovered in Kolkata, which pointed to the failure of the control systems. The government took a serious view of these developments and ordered YVS to proceed on compulsory leave. The services of the Executive Director of the time, Satish Master (Sheth's successor), were terminated. In 1984, Master was a rising star and very popular, and his sudden departure was a great shock to many in the Bank. The BoB also lost its top position in the banking industry. These developments were attributed to the failure of leadership at the top.

* * *

Y.V. Sivaramakrishnayya took over as CEO at a difficult time with a demoralised executive cadre, an alienated staff, and cowed down union leaders. The operating environment, marked as it was by intense inter-union and inter-association rivalries, posed a major threat to business growth. The mistrust between the management and the unions was at its zenith. The unions, which had suffered humiliation at the hands of the earlier CEO, R.C. Shah, wanted YVS to undo the various measures undertaken by Shah to reduce their power. They demanded structural reforms in the conduct of the personnel and IR functions and restoration of the credibility of the management through some confidence-building initiatives.

Against this backdrop, YVS chose to pursue a strategy of incremental changes, such as streamlining a system of structured meetings between trade unions at various levels with defined periodicity and ease the relations with the trade unions. It was perhaps in the belief that such a forum will by itself solve IR problems. Single-step reforms, as Parker et al. (1971: 77) have noted, are difficult to achieve and are prone to failure.

Except for such marginal changes, including occasional accommodative decisions on case-to-case basis, he failed to initiate any serious reform measures that signalled any major change. The strategy was largely status quoist on the IR front, avoiding any trouble that could pose a problem to the Bank's plans for growth and development. It sought to contain union influence in personnel matters by retaining the bifurcated structure of the personnel function in Vadodara and Mumbai, even though this caused more problems for the management than the unions in terms of delays in decision-making and the resultant loss of credibility. One of the key barriers to any reform, including implementing the instructions of the government to improve customer service, was the prevailing management politics at the top. The union–management relations failed to show any significant improvement despite the CEO's softened stance as the attitude of Executive Director A.C. Sheth was quite negative towards the Federation, and that stymied many initiatives to improve relations. It was widely believed and confirmed to me by a senior personnel functionary that the Federation leader had in the past complained to government against Sheth's dealing in some credit accounts, causing embarrassment to him.

Hampered by their own inner contradictions and lack of connect with their members, both the Federation and the Association lacked the will and the moral courage to question the management's apathy to changes, except for occasionally issuing circulars marking the growing frustration of the employees with the situation.

The management's status quo strategy served the main objective of avoiding any industrial strife that could derail its quest to achieve top position among the banks in the country for two successive years. However, its obsession with peace resulted in ad hoc decisions, compromises, and expedient solutions to IR problems at the operational level. Consequently, the unions at the operating level further strengthened their control over work and IR affairs. There was increasing incidence of disciplinary violations and perpetuation of restrictive practices, leading to accumulated problems in housekeeping and customer service. The workplace climate remained totally chaotic.

The management's inability to initiate long-term reforms in IR to improve the climate at the operating level and its 'expediency-oriented' approach to serious issues of indiscipline demoralised the managers and officers at the branch and regional levels. The discovery of two major frauds in 1984 and the subsequent fall in the Bank's ranking in the banking industry were symbolic of the increasing problems at the operating level. Failure to exercise leadership resulted in the unceremonious departure of YVS on the government's instructions. This period can at best be described as a period of indifference, leading to uninhibited antagonism at the operating level.

Chapter 7

MANAGEMENT APATHY TO REFORMS (1985–90)

A Feel from the Field*

The exit of CEO Y.V. Sivaramakrishnayya (YVS) and Executive Director S.S. Master in 1984, as a result of the discovery of two major frauds, shook the staff of the BoB, especially the senior executives. Executive morale was at an all-time low and there was a general mood of despondency among the top management. Many senior executives talked about the management's continuous neglect of affairs in the Eastern Zone, which was where the frauds had been discovered, and they all felt the need for drastic measures to ameliorate the situation there. The disturbed IR environment in the Bank was recognised as a crucial factor in the deterioration of its business growth and in the breakdown of systems in the various zones, especially in the Eastern Zone. The mood was one of introspection and self-criticism, and the consensus was for action.

In February 1985, the government brought in a new CEO, M.N. Goipuria, who came from another nationalised bank, but one that was much smaller than the BoB. For the first time in the post-nationalisation history of the Bank, an outsider was appointed CEO of BoB. Echoing the sentiments of the senior executives, a deputy general manager said: 'Our

---

* From January 1985 to December 1985, I undertook fieldwork in the corporate IR Department and the Maharashtra zonal office in Mumbai. These offices were the hub of IR activities in the Bank.

Bank has produced six CEOs for other banks after nationalisation. It is indeed a pity that today we have to have an outsider heading this Bank.'

After taking over as CEO, Goipuria, in an emotional speech to the members of top and senior management, assured that he was committed to the Bank's history and traditions. In private conversations also, senior executives experienced his warmth and gentle manner.

Soon the response from the executives changed. Senior executives praised Goipuria for his sensitivity regarding all that had happened and his positive approach towards the Bank's performance and potential for future growth. They praised him for his gentle manners, amiable nature, and commitment to rescuing BoB from its current crisis. Goipuria assured the executives of a collective and collaborative spirit in restoring the Bank's reputation, which had been hit hard by the unearthing of the fraud cases. He also met the top leaders of the various employees' organisations. During these meetings, the unions voiced their concern about the state of affairs in Kolkata, especially in IR, and complained about how the local union, the Eastern Region Council (ERC) affiliated to the BEFI, flouted the all-India settlements decided at the industry level. The unions complained bitterly about the neglect of Kolkata by successive CEOs and pointed out that the deviations in the implementation of the personnel policy in Kolkata and the total anarchy of the local unions had led to loss of managerial authority. They wanted the management to take firm action in Kolkata and promised Goipuria all their support in his endeavours.

Goipuria's First Challenge

It may be useful here to look at the background of the state of IR in Kolkata. Industrial relations in all PSBs in Kolkata were in a problematic state because of various environmental and socio-political factors. Traditionally, West Bengal has been a hub of trade union activities, which were supported by the Marxist government in power in the state. The ERC, an affiliate of the BEFI wedded to Marxist ideology, although in majority in BoB Eastern Zone, was however a minority union at the Bank level.

Its militant protest methodology hindered business growth and affected customer service adversely in the branches of the Eastern Zone. The management was equally culpable because it made no serious efforts to either resolve these problems or restore a healthier IR climate that would enable business to grow.

It was now realised by the management, as well as the Federation and the Association, that unless initiatives were taken to change the IR climate in the Eastern Zone, it would be difficult to improve business performance and customer service. After the discovery of the fraud cases, the government also demonstrated its concern about the deterioration in customer service and the vitiated IR climate and advised the Bank to take tough action against the erring union leaders and staff and restore discipline.

The management used the opportunity to take some measures that signalled its resolve to restore discipline in the Bank's branches. First, it replaced the senior management team. A senior executive with a reputation for being a 'tough guy', A.S. Krishnan, was posted as zonal manager and a bright young executive, N.R.C. Panicker, was posted as the regional manager to head the Kolkata region. A senior personnel manager, who had earlier worked for a long time in Kolkata and was known for his forthrightness, was posted there again.

Soon after these key personnel were put in place, the new management initiated several steps to improve the functioning of the Eastern Zone. These steps included insistence on attendance and punctuality of the staff and removal of restrictive practices. After some time, the local management initiated job rotation of the staff from one place to another. As per government guidelines, the staff in PSBs were to be rotated every three years as a safeguard against fraud. Although implemented everywhere else, the ERC had always resisted this in Kolkata, and thanks to its agitation-ready approach and the management's wary response, it invariably succeeded in ensuring that job rotation was not implemented.

As expected, the ERC resisted the management's efforts and began an agitation. The ERC contended that by initiating such action, the management was trying to divert the attention of the people from the frauds, which it attributed to the failure of the top management. Nevertheless, the local management, with the support of the top management, pushed on with its decision to implement job rotation.

The top management engaged itself fully to provide support to the local management by replenishing the management team so that the agitation could be dealt with firmly and discipline was restored. A positive development that encouraged the management was the assurance of the central government in Delhi that it would support BoB in its endeavour to improve the situation in Kolkata.

The top management's actions in handling the IR problems in Kolkata were widely appreciated by the operating management. Many senior executives complimented CEO Goipuria for this bold initiative.

A Surprise Move

However, in a surprise move, the Government of India shifted Goipuria as CEO of another large bank after just three months at BoB and replaced him with Premjit Singh, who took charge in April 1985.

Having served in the RBI and three commercial banks in responsible positions at different points of his career, Singh came with a huge battery of experience. His reputation as a tough executive preceded him. His deputy and Executive Director, A.C. Shah, was a home-grown executive fully aware of the culture of BoB. Singh continued with the policy of firmness in the Eastern Zone—a policy that was perhaps unavoidable because the agitation was on in full swing and the government supported the actions of the Bank. The agitation continued for about 54 days. This was perhaps the first time that BoB demonstrated its resolve to tackle the IR problems in Kolkata. On the intervention of the local Marxist government, an understanding was reached and normal work was restored in the branches. The Kolkata agitation was considered a moral victory for the zonal management and it helped to assert its right to maintain discipline. The subsequent business results were quite encouraging. Kolkata was the first centre to close its annual accounts that year, a rare achievement for the Eastern Zone.

The Kolkata case proved that given clarity of objective and corresponding action on the part of the top management, the operating managers could substantially improve IR. After the agitation in Kolkata was over, the management got down to business as usual. The atmosphere in the corporate office, and especially in the IR Department, was one of relief. Nevertheless, the change in IR in Kolkata was temporary because it was not followed through with a plan of action for a long-term strategy to deal with the union problems in the Bank as a whole.

Paradoxically, the Federation, which had always instigated the management to take action against the employees in Kolkata for their acts of indiscipline, did very little to instil any sense of discipline in its own cadres elsewhere, including Mumbai. Union leaders in Mumbai continued to do union work during working hours, workmen staff continued to leave office well before closing hours, and cases of indiscipline and restrictive practices were reported as usual. A consistent and long-term IR strategy continued to elude the management.

Singh came to the helm of BoB when the political–economic environment in India was improving very fast. The gloom the country had been plunged into following the assassination of Prime Minister Indira Gandhi had all but vanished, thanks to the optimism generated by her successor, Rajiv Gandhi. The country was flushed with hope, and the banking sector was no exception.

Singh's main challenge was to raise the morale of the executives and the rest of the staff, which had taken a hit after the Kolkata fraud case. He was keen to restore the management authority, which was severely compromised in the time of YVS. He made it amply clear with his initial actions that he was no pushover when it came to the unions. A single example will suffice to illustrate his attitude towards the union leaders. Soon after assuming charge, Singh took certain quick decisions on some promotions in the executive cadre. The Association protested against Singh's decisions, stating that there was a long-standing convention of consulting them first in such matters. Singh brushed aside the protest, saying he was not bound by any such traditions/understanding. After that, Singh rung in many changes. It was common knowledge that officers were randomly selected for foreign postings, with the Association's recommendations carrying huge weight in such decisions. Singh introduced a fair system for selecting officers for foreign postings by inviting applications and then conducting interviews to select the prospective candidates.

Singh did nothing to favour any union. Singh's deputy, Shah, however, liaised with the general secretary of the Association and opposed many of Singh's decisions. Singh seldom consulted Shah on important matters related to executive career decisions. Everyone in the Bank knew about the uneasy relations between the two top functionaries.

Reluctance to Initiate Reforms

During my fieldwork at the central office in Mumbai, I observed that the Federation and Association leaders frequently met Singh and made suggestions for improving and streamlining IR management. Both the Federation and the Association pleaded for the shifting of the Personnel Department from Vadodara back to Mumbai, the disbanding of the various committees that caused delays in personnel decision-making, and a greater decision-making role for the personnel specialists. Singh even appointed a committee headed by a general manager to conduct a comprehensive review of the personnel function in the Bank. The committee was, however, made ineffective soon after it was formed.

I also observed that during meetings and informal dialogues with the unions, the management gave assurances for undertaking reforms like the unification of the Personnel Department and for expediting the process of personnel decision-making. In reality, however, the management did not make any serious effort to deliver on its assurances. This was evident from the various notes on reform proposals put up by the Personnel Department, which Singh returned with remarks made on them such as 'noted' and 'seen'. The observation symbolised Singh's inclination to maintain the status quo in both the structure and policy in the personnel function. They also demonstrated the lack of enthusiasm in the management to take any significant measures to build trust and cooperation in union–management relations. The management appeared to be opposed to any idea that would even remotely restore the influence of individual leaders at the corporate level.

The management strategy was apparently to sanitise the corporate office of any such influence. It seemed to believe that if the Personnel Department was shifted back to Mumbai, the unions might increase their influence in the Bank by periodically bothering the top management to sort out key problems. Singh did not trust the senior personnel specialists at the corporate office who enjoyed a good rapport with the unions and feared that this could create pressure on the top management to sort out issues under pressure from the unions. In spite of multiple problems such as delays and confusion among the operating managers in getting decisions taken under the prevailing structure, the management seemed happy with the existing arrangements, to maintain peace at their level even at the expense of peace in the branches.

When the General Manager (Personnel), L.B. Bhide, retired in January 1986, Singh appointed a seasoned operational banker, B.K. Mukherjee, in his place. Mukherjee had the reputation of being straightforward, neutral, and business-like. He was not known to have any kind of relationship with the top union leaders, nor did he show any preference for any of them; as a result, the unions were apprehensive. There was complete rapport between CEO Singh and Mukherjee, and Singh trusted him completely. The unions were not very happy about the induction of Mukherjee because they could no longer get things done on the basis of understanding and rapport. Unlike his predecessor, Bhide, Mukherjee enjoyed the trust of the CEO and was happy to toe his line. Singh–Mukherjee combine created a communication gap between the top management and trade unions and from management perspective ensured greater freedom for them in managing personnel function.

As noted earlier, the administration of R.C. Shah (1975–81) saw the dilution of the unions' influence in decision-making at the corporate level, but the problems in the branches persisted in the absence of any initiatives to improve personnel decision-making, especially with regard to employee grievances. Now, under Singh as well, the management failed to initiate any reforms that could substantially improve the deteriorating IR climate at the branch level.

The hands-off policy of the top management in dealing with the unions at the corporate level complicated IR at the branches; inter-union skirmishes, work stoppages, misbehaviour by staff and union activists, and poor customer service became the norm. While top management may have ensured peace at the corporate level, it certainly contributed to tension and chaos at the operating level. The IR were conducted in an ad hoc manner and unless a crisis situation developed, the response of the management was tepid.

During my fieldwork in the Maharashtra zonal office in Mumbai, I observed that the second-rung leaders of the majority unions visited the Personnel Department on a daily basis without prior appointment and raised a number of issues, mainly to do with employee grievances in the branches in relation to work allotment, claims about special allowances, and other issues related to service conditions. Many branch managers telephoned the personnel officers about cases of restrictive practices or other acts of indiscipline by employees. In some cases, the managers personally visited the zonal office to report misbehaviour by union functionaries in the branches and to seek the support of the management. Barring some technical clarifications on issues of service conditions, the Personnel Department avoided giving any instructions for action, which they considered to be the job of their reporting operating managers. The branches were thus caught between the Personnel Department and the regional offices and no authority seemed able to render them any help in solving their problems. In fact, the branch authorities were scared to initiate any action against delinquent staff lest the issue got escalated to the corporate office. The policy at the corporate office was to keep away from branch issues. Local-level compromises were made even in matters of discipline. The message appeared to be, 'Handle all issues tactfully', and as one manager told me, 'Tact means compromise.'

The hub of union activity in Mumbai was the Mumbai main office (at a distance of a kilometre from the corporate office). It was the biggest branch of the Bank and performed multiple functions. It was overstaffed with some 250 employees on its rolls. It also housed the Federation office. Two minority unions occupied space in the main office without authorisa-tion. This office experienced IR problems frequently. The branch was, in fact, a hotbed of indiscipline, restrictive practices, and inter-union rivalry.

There was complete breakdown of managerial authority due to inter-union rivalry and the management of the branch was helpless before the staff's indiscipline. However, despite this chaos taking place in such close proximity to the corporate office, at no point in time did the latter try to enforce discipline here. Equally, the engagement of zonal management/ regional management in ensuring discipline in branches under their area of operation was marginal. Personnel managers/officers were expected to douse fire on a daily basis. In the many meetings between the unions and the management that I attended at the corporate, zonal and regional offices in Mumbai, I did not find the management raising the issues of indiscipline in the branches and deteriorating customer service with the unions. The meetings were one-sided, with the unions alone raising issues relating to their members' grievances. No wonder many branch managers whom I met complained about the lack of support from their bosses for any legitimate action taken against erring staff.

In all my conversations with branch managers and other senior operating managers, I was told about the delays in response from the corporate office, which were the main irritant in resolving employee grievances, and about militant intervention by the unions to force the resolution of issues to their advantage. With a view to understanding the issue, I investigated the process of personnel decision-making at the corporate and head office levels and how it impacted the IR climate at both the corporate and operating levels.

Personnel Decision-Making

Expeditious decision-making in personnel matters symbolises the management's intent to resolve employee grievances in relation to their work and its environment, thereby creating a better IR climate. Conversely, tardy decision-making signifies apathy in resolving such grievances, which can contribute to a negative IR climate.

At BoB, delay in personnel decision-making was considered one of the main reasons for its ineffective IR. While at the Bank of Baroda Staff College in Ahmedabad, in my role as senior core faculty member, I conducted sessions and programmes for senior branch managers and I consistently received feedback from them about how they felt handicapped in running branches for want of timely decisions in personnel matters. In my interactions with union leaders, they too complained about the delays in personnel decision-making, leading to frustration in the employees.

In my interviews with the senior executives as a part of this research, six out of eight executives in the general manager/deputy general manager category said that delay in decision-making was the main cause of the ineffective IR in the Bank. Similarly, 19 out of 22 zonal and regional managers and all the 18 union leaders interviewed expressed similar views. In the context of this near unanimity of views and the importance of timely decision-making in IR effectiveness, I decided to make a detailed study of this aspect of IR.

During the fieldwork, I identified three major variables affecting decision-making in personnel matters:

1. the structure of the Personnel Department;
2. infrastructure for decision-making, such as authority and power of personnel functionaries; and
3. the role of personnel specialists and executives.

The Personnel Department of the Bank operated from two locations, the head office in Vadodara and the central office in Mumbai. In order to understand the implications of the existing structure of personnel decision-making, we need to examine the following issues:

1. the division of functions and authority between the segments of the Personnel Department at Mumbai and Vadodara; and
2. the implications of the structural arrangements on IR effectiveness.

The structure of the Personnel Department in 1985 can be seen in Figure 7.1.

Matters relating to disciplinary action involving both vigilance (such as cases of misappropriation of funds, fraud, and graft) and non-vigilance (cases of staff indiscipline) relating to officers were handled by a separate cell called the Disciplinary Action Wing (DAW), which reported to the General Manager (Legal and Vigilance). Matters relating to industrial law/writ petitions in courts and other litigation on personnel matters were referred from time to time by the IR Department to the manager of DAW, who worked under General Manager (Vigilance). It is relevant to mention here that in 1983, disciplinary matters, which had been handled till then by the Personnel Department, were shifted to the Legal Department after numerous complaints about delays.

The Deputy General Manager (Personnel) at Vadodara was authorised to take decisions in the following routine personnel and IR matters:

1. leave for going abroad;
2. claims of compensation in case of injury or death while on duty;
3. voluntary retirement of workmen staff;
4. request for change of place of domicile;
5. reimbursement of medical expenses for treatment and investigations not covered under the officers' service regulations or BPS;
6. grant of special assistance to handicapped employees;
7. external training nominations for officers up to the non-executive cadre;
8. issues relating to wages and salary administration;
9. grant of housing and other staff loans;
10. matters relating to terminal benefits;

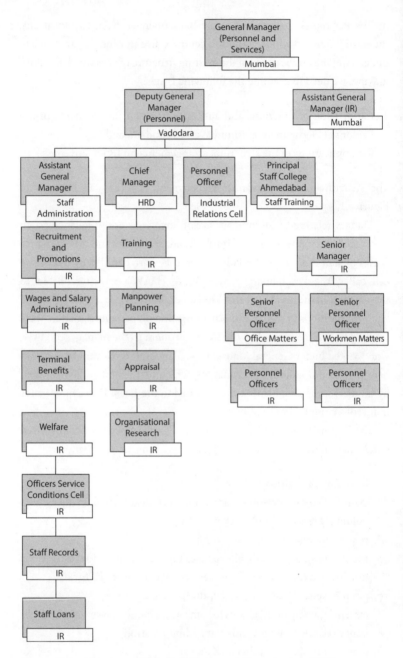

Figure 7.1 Structure of the BoB Personnel Department, 1985

11. acceptance of resignations of officers in the junior and middle management cadres;
12. suspending an officer in the junior and middle management cadres;
13. other routine matters relating to staff administration;
14. IR matters relating to interpretations of awards and settlements; and
15. financial grants to various employees' sports clubs.

Although a number of routine decisions on various aspects of personnel administration were taken at Vadodara by the Deputy General Manager (Personnel), the issues referred to by the zones/regions involving any conflict situation with the unions, matters relating to awards and settlements, and change in policy with regard to service conditions (such as recruitments and promotions) were invariably referred by Vadodara to Mumbai in order to avail of the expert opinion of J.N. Tandon, the Assistant General Manager for IR, who was a senior personnel specialist. In important matters, Tandon sought opinions/instructions of L.B. Bhide, General Manager (Personnel).

Every day, a large number of cases on the above-mentioned issues were referred by Vadodara to Mumbai. At Mumbai, the issues often remained pending, eliciting no response for a long time, while the zones kept reminding Vadodara of the pending cases. Sometimes, Vadodara asked the zones to contact Mumbai directly.

In this process, the decisions of the higher authorities were considerably delayed. In the given circumstances, under pressure from the local unions, the zones and regions made compromises even while the issues referred by them remained on the pending list in Mumbai. In one of the branches in a zone, the management refused to pay an allowance to a member of the subordinate staff on the plea that the existing settlement with the unions did not provide for it. The local union insisted on the allowance on the plea that it was the practice at other nationalised banks in the city. The issue involved interpretation of the BPS governing the service conditions of bank employees in the matter of payment of a special allowance to subordinate staff for maintaining office files/records, stitching vouchers, and filing papers. The branch-level union started an agitation and work at the branch was adversely affected. The branch reported the matter to the zonal office. The zonal office referred the matter to Vadodara, which, in turn, sent the matter for clarification to Mumbai. Given next is the sequence in which the matter moved between the zone, Vadodara, and Mumbai:

1. 14 September 1985: The deputy general manager of the zone referred the matter through an urgent telegram to the Deputy General Manager (Personnel) in Vadodara and sought clarification and guidance.
2. 29 September 1985: The Deputy General Manager (Personnel) sent a telegram to the zonal deputy general manager to refer the matter to the IR Department in Mumbai.
3. 13 October 1985: The Deputy General Manager (Personnel) also sent a telegram to the IR Department in Mumbai about the issue.
4. 29 October 1985: The zonal deputy general manager sent a letter to the IR Department in Mumbai.
5. 10 December 1985: The zonal deputy general manager sent a telegram to the IR Department in Mumbai requesting guidance.
6. 15 December 1985: The zonal deputy general manager received a letter from the IR Department in Mumbai seeking some clarifications on the issue.
7. 26 December 1985: The zonal deputy general manager sent a letter to the IR Department in Mumbai providing the clarifications.
8. 15 January 1986: The zonal deputy general manager sent a reminder telegram to the IR Department in Mumbai asking to expedite the matter.

Thus, a relatively small matter remained unresolved for about four months. Later, I learnt from the zonal manager that, eventually, under constant threat of agitation and disruption of work by the union, he was forced to authorise the allowance.

Commenting on the delay in the matter, the personnel manager of the zone said:

This may appear to be a small matter to higher authorities, but for us such matters have the potential to disturb industrial peace. Unfortunately, IR problems of the branches and the pressures created by inter-union rivalry are not appreciated at the higher levels. Such delays put us in a very embarrassing position and sometimes we have no alternative but to make unhealthy compromises with the local unions.

Apart from delays, the bifurcation of the personnel function between Mumbai and Vadodara also created a lot of confusion about the decision-making authority in personnel matters. For example, some zones referred matters to Vadodara, while some others referred the same kind of issues directly to Mumbai. Commenting upon the confusion, a zonal personnel manager said:

> The Vadodara/Mumbai affair caused a lot of confusion. As per standing instructions of the Bank in 1980, we refer all IR matters to Vadodara. In reply, we are informed by Vadodara that they have referred the matter to Mumbai. Sometimes when we talk to Mumbai, we are informed that they have referred the matter back to Vadodara.

A second zonal personnel manager said:

> We refer all the matters to Vadodara to the functional head, that is, the Deputy General Manager (Personnel) even though it involves delay. We do not want to bypass the authority of the Deputy General Manager (Personnel).

Yet a third personnel manager, however, differed from his colleagues in his observation:

> We refer matters to central office, Mumbai. We know that ultimately IR matters are referred by Vadodara to Mumbai. This being the situation, we do not waste time in going to Mumbai via Vadodara.

At this stage, it is necessary to understand how the IR Department in Mumbai operated in reality, and how lack of coordination there contributed to delays. The IR Department in Mumbai, apart from its main responsibilities of holding discussions/negotiations with the unions and the officers' associations on various policy matters, also attended to various references that were made by Vadodara or directly by the zones. In addition, it liaised with other banks, the IBA, and the government to collect information on various matters either at the request of Vadodara or on its own. The IR Department handled 'fire-fighting' operations with the unions, giving advice to various zones on a day-to-day basis during conflict situations. It also provided inputs on matters relating to industrial law, major conciliation cases bearing policy implications, preparing draft letters for the government and the IBA, and preparing background notes on various communications received from the unions for the perusal of the CEO. It had a small staff of about four–five personnel managers/offi-cers with very little experience of working in the field. The senior execu-tives, among them the Assistant General Manager (IR) and the General Manager (Personnel), worked like bureaucrats with little sense of urgency. They told me that CEOs do not see IR as a priority function and did not show willingness to engage in any long-term measures; they only want a disruption-free environment. Each CEO played politics with the unions, which is why the department did not enjoy confidence of the CEO. It, therefore, only offered advice and left it to the operational heads to act according to their circumstances.

It is thus evident that the IR Department in Mumbai, which was origi-nally designed to function as a policy-making cell in the reorganisation of 1980, played a variety of operational roles and mostly worked with limited authority and discretion. Lack of support from the CEO and the absence of a consistent policy towards the unions led to the personnel specialists steering clear of decision-making.

During my fieldwork in the corporate personnel/IR office in Mumbai, I observed that the bifurcation of the Personnel Department had created a messy situation, leading to delays and harassment of the operational func-tionaries. Most of the matters raised by the trade unions, the government, or the zones/regions relating to the various aspects of personnel admin-istration were referred to Vadodara for background information, as most of the basic information was stored there. The department concerned in Vadodara prepared elaborate notes and submitted them to Mumbai. While finalising the draft proposals, the IR Department examined these propos-als in the light of industry-level practices and government policy. If any changes were suggested in the draft, the notes were sent back to Vadodara for incorporating the necessary changes, and Vadodara would again send the revised draft to Mumbai.

After a final decision was taken in Mumbai on the matter, the entire bunch of papers was sent by the office of the Assistant General Manager (IR) to Vadodara so that circulars could be issued to the branches. If the circular needed to be issued under the signature of the General Manager, the draft circular would be prepared in Vadodara and then sent to the General Manager (Personnel) in Mumbai via the office of the Assistant General Manager (IR). If, for any reason, the General Manager made any corrections in the circular, the IR Department in Mumbai would send the draft circular again to Vadodara to carry out the corrections. The IR Department, Mumbai, thus used the Vadodara Personnel Department as its secretariat without any thought for the delays it caused. It was bureaucracy at its red-taped best!

This process invariably led to delays in the issue of circulars on policy matters and in final decisions on many important matters. On complaints from the unions and associations about delays in various personnel matters, Mumbai contacted Vadodara to expedite the matter at hand. It was common practice for both offices to exchange a number of telephone calls every day. Sometimes personnel officers at the Mumbai office conveyed the annoyance of higher authorities about the delays to their counterparts in Vadodara. Similarly, Vadodara executives often complained about the delays in receiving advice from the IR Department in Mumbai.

At times, the IR Department at Mumbai took decisions in urgent matters without referring the issue to Vadodara, although such matters were usually handled there. About matters on which immediate information was sought by the government or matters on which parliamentary questions were asked, the IR Department, Mumbai, sought information directly from the zones, compiled the notes, and submitted them to the government. For example, matters relating to job rotation and overtime were usually dealt with by the Staff Administration section in Vadodara, where they compiled the information on these issues for all the branches in India. But on two occasions, I observed the Mumbai office seeking information about the overtime paid to staff in a particular year directly from various zones. At this stage, it is important to analyse the causes of delay both in Vadodara and in Mumbai in various personnel matters.

Explaining the delay in decision-making at Vadodara, the Deputy General Manager (Personnel) observed:

Earlier in 1980–82, there were two personnel managers (specialists) and also a Chief Manager (IR), stationed at Vadodara to assist the Deputy General Manager (Personnel). Subsequently they were transferred from Vadodara and we do not have any specialist support as of now. We have to necessarily refer various matters involving interpretations of awards and settlements and industrial law matters to Mumbai. The real problem is the delay on account of inadequate attention given by the people at Mumbai to matters sent by us.

During my fieldwork in Mumbai, I observed that most matters referred by the zones either directly to the Mumbai office or via Vadodara were delayed. The IR Department attached priority to matters referred by the government, the board, or the CEO. Next in order of priority came matters raised and pressed by the unions. Then came fire-fighting issues in the zones. Last in the order of priority were matters raised by the zonal or regional offices or by Vadodara. It can thus be noted that problems of branches and at the other operating levels received least priority by the corporate office. As seen earlier, delays at the corporate office in such matters led to ad hoc understandings with the unions at the regional and zonal levels to prevent immediate disruption of work.

A number of factors contributed to delays in decision-making in the IR Department at Mumbai. First, as mentioned earlier, staff support was limited. Although the Assistant General Manager (IR), Tandon, often complained about the shortage of manpower in his department, no concrete steps were taken to augment the staff strength. The attitude of Assistant General Manager (IR) was one of unconcern, bureaucratic, and passive.

Second, the IR Department lacked staff resources with the requisite expertise and competence to deal with intricate matters relating to IR and law, which is why such matters had to be referred to the Legal Department, which took its own time to give its opinion.

The IR Department usually informed the zones that it had referred the matter to the Legal Department and official records show that some matters languished for more than a year before the Legal Department gave its opinion. Sometimes, the opinion given was considered vague by the operational functionaries and the matter was again referred to the IR Department and then back again to the Legal Department.

The last factor was the alienation and lack of involvement of the senior personnel specialists such as the Assistant General Manager (IR), who often referred even the most routine matters either to the PC or to the CoE, as explained later in this chapter.

Apart from delays, there were other serious consequences too of the prevailing structure in relation to application of rules and the conflict between operational executives and specialists in the Personnel Department, which, in turn, reduced the effectiveness of the IR function.

As mentioned earlier, zones referred personnel matters to both Vadodara and Mumbai. Each of these offices sometimes responded directly to the zones. There were instances when the clarification given by Vadodara on a particular matter to a zone and that given by Mumbai on the same matter to another zone differed. Once a zone asked Vadodara whether an employee who had submitted his resignation could be given privilege leave during his notice period. Vadodara advised: 'It will be in order to sanction leave even during notice period.' In a similar case referred to the Mumbai office, the verdict was to not grant privilege leave during the notice period.

Sometimes, different interpretations from the two offices also created union–management conflicts and vitiated the IR environment, especially when the management had to retract an earlier decision. An issue that generated considerable strain between a union and the management in one zone illustrates this point. As per the existing settlement with the recognised union in respect of 'special assistants',[1] it was provided that at the time of internal promotion from the clerical to the officers' cadre, some posts of 'special assistants' would be created by promoting clerks on a regional seniority basis. In a zone, one special assistant retired and the union demanded that the vacancy be filled up. When the zone referred the matter, Vadodara clarified that the vacancy be filled up as demanded by the union. Vadodara also endorsed a copy of this letter to Mumbai for information.

The Mumbai office immediately told Vadodara that its interpretation was incorrect and pointed out that the settlement with the union was silent on this issue and it was not advisable to fill the vacancy caused by the special assistant's retirement. Subsequently, Vadodara advised the concerned zone about this. The reversal of the earlier decision caused a lot of problems with the union, which threatened to go on strike.

Operational Executives versus Specialists

The dependence of Vadodara on Mumbai in IR matters sometimes brought the two offices in sharp conflict, each finding fault with the

---

[1] Special assistants are basically workmen with supervisory responsibilities. They are given the power to pass cheques and other instruments up to a limit.

other. The Vadodara office was headed by a Deputy General Manager (Personnel) to whom the Assistant General Manager (IR), Mumbai, reported. However, in practice, this reporting was at best theoretical as the Assistant General Manager (IR), who operated from Mumbai as a specialist executive, reported for all practical purposes to the General Manager (HR), Bhide, who was also a specialist. Most matters on IR referred by the Deputy General Manager (Personnel) were decided by the Assistant General Manager (IR). This divided the Vadodara and Mumbai offices into operational and specialist groups which did not see eye to eye, with the Vadodara group having the support of the top management and the Mumbai group bearing its antipathy. The two often exchanged mutually hostile correspondence. They accused each other of deliberate delays. The Deputy General Manager (Personnel), an operational functionary who was considered close to the top management, occasionally flouted the instructions of Bhide, to whom he reported. Some examples from official records prove this point. The General Manager (Personnel), Bhide, once instructed the Deputy General Manager (Personnel) in Vadodara to transfer a personnel officer from one zone to another. The Deputy General Manager (Personnel) did not follow this instruction under the plea that the Bank conventionally did not transfer non-specialist officers before five years of service, and therefore transferring a specialist officer before the completion of five years would set a bad precedent.

In another case, the office of the General Manager (Personnel) asked Vadodara to discontinue the officiating status of a junior officer as a senior officer had been posted to look after his officiating work. The Vadodara office did not discontinue the arrangement under the pretext that the motivation of the junior officer who was officiating in a higher position would suffer if the arrangement was discontinued.

At one stage, the management and the unions discussed the policy for promotion from the clerical to the officers' cadre in the UP Zone, where the Bank found it difficult to identify enough officers to keep up with its rapid expansion. A proposal under consideration was to hold a separate test for this purpose. The CEO and the executive director had agreed to the proposal. However, one of the senior executives at Vadodara prevailed upon the executive director to drop this proposal without consulting the General

Manager (Personnel), Bhide. It is thus evident that the rivalry between the operational and specialist personnel functionaries at the two locations created problems of coordination and coherence in decision-making.

The split locations of the Personnel Department and the delays arising out of this also led to strains in the union–management relationship. During union meetings, it was not uncommon for the management team to be embarrassed by the union leaders, who often brought up issues of non-implementation of decisions. An example from the official records illustrates this. In 1984, during a meeting between the management and the Association which I attended as an observer, the Association members pointed out that officers found it difficult to get their medical claims settled because of the questions raised by the insurance company. It was agreed that the management would streamline the procedure for early settlement of such claims. To this end, the management agreed to: (a) appoint a medical officer at Vadodara to examine doubtful claims before the claim was submitted to the insurance company; and (b) to appoint a joint committee comprising representatives of the Association, the Bank, the insurance company, and the Bank's medical officer to review such cases from time to time.

In a meeting with the management in December 1985, the Association pointed out that this decision was still to be implemented and it expressed its annoyance and frustration at the delay. Later, in a communication to the Deputy General Manager (Personnel) in Vadodara, the General Manager (Personnel) expressed his annoyance:

> In one of the recent meetings, the Association representatives pointed out the delay in implementing the decision of posting a doctor and appointing a joint committee for sorting out medical claim matters of the officers. The management was highly embarrassed on this issue of non-implementation of a decision already taken about a year back. Records show that the IR Department, Mumbai, had written three letters to your office pursuing the matter. I would like to know why no action has been taken so far.

The unions often showed their frustration with the 'shuttling of papers between Vadodara and Mumbai', as they called it, during meetings with the management. The situation became so hopeless that the Federation and the NABOBO (the new officers' association) passed resolutions in their annual conferences about unification of the Personnel Department and threatened to launch agitations if it were not done quickly.

Thus, it is evident that the split location of the Personnel Department created a number of problems like staff–line conflicts, inconsistencies in rule implementation, overlapping of jurisdictions, confusion of roles, mistrust between the unions and the management, employee dissatisfaction, and finally, as a consequence of all this, agitational culture and poor customer service.

So, why did not the management, despite the problems mentioned earlier, gather all the personnel functions under one roof? It may be recalled that in 1980, the management, as a part of its overall strategy (Chapter 5), had shifted a major part of the Personnel Department from Mumbai to Vadodara to contain the interference of the Federation in personnel matters, under the guise of easing the space problem in Mumbai and to use the unutilised infrastructure at Vadodara.

Although the functioning of the Personnel Department from two locations created a number of problems, it served an important purpose for the management of the time in reducing the influence of the unions on personnel decision-making in Mumbai and helping the Bank to maintain exclusive control over the personnel and IR functions, especially on sensitive functions like recruitments and promotions.

The Committees and Their Impact

The Bank had several committees that had been set up to facilitate decision-making in personnel matters. But it did not always work that way. From my research, I found that apart from the structural problems, the delays in decision-making in personnel and IR matters also arose because of the manner in which the Bank committees functioned. In order to understand the functioning of these committees and their impact on personnel decision-making, it is important to answer the following questions:

1. What were the various committees for personnel and IR decision-making? What was their jurisdiction and authority? What kinds of decisions were taken by these committees? What was the contribution of the operational functionaries in personnel decision-making?

2. What was the contribution of these committees in facilitating the decision-making process in personnel and IR and how did they influence the formulation of the management strategy in IR?

In order to answer these questions, it is important to first understand the background of the committees, their constitution, the kinds of issues referred to them, and their contribution to the conduct of IR.

At the time of my fieldwork, three committees of the top management were involved in personnel matters. These were:

1. the Personnel Committee (PC);
2. the Committee of Executives (COE); and
3. the Executive Management Committee (EMC).

Among these three committees, the PC was concerned exclusively with personnel matters. The other two committees discussed a variety of issues relating to the performance and growth of the Bank and, occasionally, items relating to personnel matters.

The PC

The PC was created as part of the restructuring of the personnel function in 1980, as an overall strategy of the then CEO, R.C. Shah, apparently to weaken the power of the personnel specialists in IR and, in turn, weaken the Federation. The General Manager (Personnel) chaired the PC and the Deputy General Manager (Personnel) was its convener. In addition to the General Manager and Deputy General Manager of Personnel, the Deputy General Manager of Operations and the Assistant General Manager of IR were also members of the PC. The committee meetings took place in Vadodara and all the relevant records relating to the PC were maintained there. There was no fixed periodicity for the PC meetings, and meetings were often convened to synchronise with the visit of the General Manager (Personnel) to Vadodara.

One of the principal objectives of creating the PC, according to a circular of the Bank, was to 'facilitate the process of decision-making'.

The specific roles assigned to the PC, according to a circular from the CEO, included:

1. dealing with matters which were beyond the purview of the delegated authority of individual executives;
2. dealing with matters involving differences of opinion in the interpretation of agreement, rules, and regulations; and
3. reviewing the IR environment in the Bank or in any particular region or zone and giving suitable instructions to deal with the situation as might emerge from time to time.

An internal note in the Personnel Department revealed that the PC would take decisions on:

1. major issues affecting a group of employees within the policy guidelines laid down;
2. important issues affecting individuals which, in the opinion of the convenor, should be brought before the PC for decisions;
3. all matters of policy/decisions requiring changes in the norms, which the PC would put up before the CoE with its recommendations;
4. issues requiring urgent attention;
5. cases of request for inter-zonal transfer on compassionate grounds;
6. individual cases not falling within the rules at the discretion of the Deputy General Manager (Personnel); and
7. interpretation of policies in cases of doubt and above the discretion of the Deputy General Manager (Personnel).

During my fieldwork at the corporate office in Mumbai, I observed that both the IR Department in Mumbai and the Personnel Department in Vadodara referred various matters to the PC. A number of issues relating to IR, such as interpretation of settlements, new demands made by the unions, and other assorted issues like the Bank's policy in giving facilities to unions, were referred by the Assistant General Manager (IR) to the PC. The personnel officers in Mumbai prepared detailed notes for the PC. Matters relating to inter-zonal transfers of officers and cancellation of transfer requests from one zone to another were put up to the PC by the Deputy General Manager (Personnel), Staff Administration Department in Vadodara. These items were sponsored either by the Deputy General Manager (Personnel) or the Assistant General Manager (Staff Administration).

Records show that during the five years of its working from 1980 to 1984, the PC held 42 meetings. Matters that were earlier decided by individual executives like the General Manager (Personnel) or the Deputy General Manager (Personnel) were now put up before the PC. About 82 per cent of the items discussed at these meetings related to requests for transfer from one zone to another or transfer on special grounds, such as marriage, medical reasons of family members, and academic requirement of wards.

Policy matters like the promotion policy, the IR climate in the Bank, general discipline, and the quality of IR in the different zones (as listed in the original mandate of PC) were not discussed by the PC. It also did not discuss IR strategy and policy in dealing with the unions. On an average, it took the PC about four–five months to decide on an issue referred by a zonal office to the central office or the head office.

A number of routine cases referred to the PC and the delays involved were cited by the representatives of the unions, both workmen and officers. They were critical of routine matters being referred to the PC relating to interpretations of service conditions, and so on, which they regarded as the job of specialists, legal experts, and the IBA. The Association, in particular, complained about the hardships caused to officers in matters of inter-zonal transfer due to the delays involved in referring such routine matters to the PC.

In a meeting of PC that I attended, there were 11 items on the agenda, of which nine pertained to transfer requests made by officers from one zone to another. The note submitted by the Staff Administration Department in Vadodara contained the background of each case. Most of these cases contained requests for cancellation of transfer from one zone to another zone on promotion. The issue was discussed in general for five minutes and it was decided that such requests should not be accepted in view of the basic policy of the Bank. A transfer request made by a lady officer on marriage grounds was acceded to in consonance with the existing policy on the subject.

An important item on the agenda was the case of suppression of educational qualifications by some subordinate staff at the Bank. The Personnel Department had collected information on the policy adopted by other banks in this regard. The PC was supposed to take a decision on the punishment to be awarded to such employees. During discussions, the Assistant

General Manager (IR) briefed the PC about the discussions that had been held with the Federation and the understanding arrived at with regard to punishment. The two operational executives who were present endorsed the views of the Assistant General Manager (IR).

The meeting lasted about 40 minutes. No mention was made of a long-drawn-out agitation going on at that time in the Eastern Zone. After the meeting, the Deputy General Manager (Operations) told me:

> These meetings are a waste of time for us. It is the personnel specialists who are in touch with the top management or the unions and are in the know of things.

It was interesting to observe that the PC generally avoided decisions on critical IR issues referred to it by the zones. If sometimes the PC took a decision on such issues, it was not uncommon for the top management to supersede the decision of the PC. Examples will prove each of these points.

In one zone, the Coordination Committee (AIBEA) wanted to include an outside leader in its team for holding structured meetings with the management. The zone sought clarification as to whether this could be permitted. This agenda was withdrawn from the list and no decision was taken, thereby avoiding giving any clear guidance to the operating unit. Later, the personnel manager of the zone told me: 'Clear decision by the management would have helped us to take a stand at our level. Our efforts to reform IR are discouraged by such ambiguous decisions.'

In another case, a zone sought the guidance of the central office about holding structured meetings with a minority union which had acquired majority status in a particular zone or region. The PC deliberated on this issue and advised the zonal management that on the basis of precedence in the Eastern Zone, the management could hold meetings with such unions. Later, CEO Singh reversed this decision on an intervention by the Federation, which did not want the management to deal with a union having minority status at the Bank level, notwithstanding its majority status at the regional level. Thus, crucial issues involving relationships with the unions remained outside the purview of the PC. In fact, decisions on strategic aspects such as the relationship with the unions and their office-bearers were handled by the CEO himself.

As a result, the articulated purpose of the PC that it would facilitate personnel decision-making, scan the IR environment, and discuss policy matters and matters requiring urgent attention proved to be a sham, given its actual working. In fact, if anything, it delayed the process of personnel decision-making and created dissatisfaction in the unions as well as among the well-meaning operating managers.

The marginal role played by the PC in IR management, as stated here, can be understood in the context of the management's IR strategy in weakening the trade unions influence in personnel decision making.

Even though Shah's successors softened their approach towards the unions, they did not initiate any steps to look at the issues that had contributed to the messy IR climate in the Bank. The continuance of the structure in spite of the change in strategy created a multitude of problems and consequences for IR, such as the centralisation of personnel/IR decisions, the loss of discretion of individual executives, the delay in personnel decision-making, and, eventually, a vitiated IR climate. As mentioned earlier, the structure of the personnel function and the committee-type decision-making effectively contributed to the prevailing mistrust in union–management relations.

The CoEs

There were two top-level committees at the central office in Mumbai to decide on various issues relating to the Bank's business and administration. These two committees were known as the Committee of Executives A (CoE A) and the Committee of Executives B (CoE B). While the CoE A discussed matters relating to credit, the CoE B discussed issues relating to inspection, general administration, housekeeping, premises, and personnel. Both the committees were chaired by the CEO, and all the general managers and deputy general managers at the central office were members of these committees.

Though, according to the functionaries of the Personnel Department, there was nothing on record about the terms of reference and powers of the CoE B in personnel matters, issues having financial implications were referred to it.

Records suggest that the Personnel Department maintained no specific distinctions in referring matters to the PC or the CoE B. For example, a number of routine issues relating to interpretations of awards and settlements as well as demands raised by the unions were referred to either the PC or to the CoE B. On enquiry, a functionary of the Personnel Department stated:

> No specific criteria are followed in referring the matters. Depending on the urgency of an issue, if a particular committee meeting was scheduled in the near future, the issue was referred to that committee.

An analysis of the items submitted to the CoE B revealed that apart from issues requiring interpretations, demands of the unions and a number of routine administrative matters, such as sanction of increments to officers who had reached 'Efficiency Bar' level and financial grants to the staff sports clubs operating in different centres, were referred to the CoE B.

Referring routine matters to the CoE B often invited the ire of the senior operational executives. For example, once the Personnel Department referred an issue requiring a decision on 'whether [the] clearing departments in the branches were a part of [the] Cash Department'. After the meeting, a senior executive remarked: 'Could it not be enquired from [the] DGM (Operations)? Why are such routine references made to [the] CoE?' Later in a meeting of the CoE, it was resolved that 'the Personnel Department should carefully examine the possibility of avoiding reference of routine issues to [the] CoE'.

It is important to mention here that while the CoE resented the referral of routine issues from the Personnel Department, it did not take decisions on critical issues that might have IR implications. Once, the Federation brought to the notice of the Bank the forcible occupation of office space by a minority union in various branches. The Personnel Department, in its elaborate note, also pointed out that the minority union had forcibly occupied the office space in various zonal offices and no action had been taken in the past. The CoE B did not take any decision in the matter and, in fact, advised the Personnel Department to withdraw the issue from its agenda.

A senior functionary in the Personnel Department later told me: 'Whenever important critical issues were referred to the committee, the issues were either postponed or withdrawn from the agenda.'

Thus, the CoE B, like the PC, also mainly dealt with routine administrative issues in personnel administration, and sensitive issues involving
policy towards unions and strategy formulation in IR were not discussed
and remained unresolved. Like the PC, the CoE too was ineffective in
resolving critical issues in IR and proved to be just one more appendage to
the personnel management bureaucracy in the Bank.

The EMC

The EMC was the highest decision-making management committee in
the Bank; it was chaired by the CEO and had all the general managers
as its members. It met once a fortnight and discussed important policy
issues in the areas of business, deposit mobilisation, credit policy, profitability, inspection, personnel, and IR. There was nothing on record as to
what kind of issues related to personnel function needed to be referred
to the EMC. However, from the records, it was clear that issues initiated
and raised by the government were generally discussed at this level. For
example, in 1985, the government advised the banks to improve the
quality of their personnel and IR administration by reducing payment of
overtime, implementing the job rotation scheme for employees, stopping
the Bank's discretion to give any new allowance to employees, and enforcing attendance and punctuality. All these matters were discussed by the
EMC, which discussed the steps to be taken within the Bank to comply
with the government instructions.

The focus of discussions in the EMC was on complying with government instructions, but creating minimum problems for the Bank. For
example, in compliance with the government's instructions to organise
surprise checks for attendance and punctuality, the EMC developed an
elaborate plan and assigned to each general manager the responsibility for
undertaking surprise checks in certain specified branches.

Apart from matters raised by the government, the EMC also discussed
various issues relating to personnel administration, such as categorisation
of posts in various administrative offices and the number of vacancies to be
declared in a particular cadre for promotion.

In sensitive matters like attendance and punctuality of staff or union
leaders doing union work during working hours, the top management did

not initiate any steps. Under pressure from the government, bare minimum action was taken by the management to issue circulars. Everyone understood that the circulars had been issued to create a record of compliance. The government too seemed to know the reality of the situation in the various PSBs, but did nothing to ensure actual implementation.

A close review of the functioning of these committees revealed that they spent most of their time on routine administrative issues. The committees were also used to put the official stamp of approval on many matters that had been decided already between the unions and the Personnel Department. Referral of various matters, especially those with IR implications, sometimes travelled from one committee to another, causing unnecessary delays.

The blurred jurisdiction and preoccupation with routine matters among the various committees led to the loosening of the control of the corporate office over the functioning of personnel policies at the operating levels, leading to inconsistencies, violations of rules, and a culture of compromise under union pressure. Such short-term measures and failure to engage with critical issues in IR were the bane of the chaotic and messy environment of IR in the Bank. Fire-fighting and 'Band-Aid' solutions to critical problems proved to be self-defeating for the Bank.

Structured Meetings

Union–management interaction at the corporate level was a subject that generated considerable heat among both the operating managers and the senior executives in the Bank. During my interviews with them, they expressed views that the bipartite meetings helped the unions to strengthen their hold over IR, but failed to provide the management any mileage.

During my fieldwork in the corporate IR Department, I had an opportunity to examine this issue in detail. In particular, I studied the union–management interaction at the corporate level in relation to: (a) its usefulness as a mutual problem-solving forum; and (b) its usefulness as a mechanism to create a better IR climate by developing a shared understanding on critical problems like customer service, discipline, and productivity.

In the given context, the following questions assumed relevance:

1. What arrangements existed at different levels for union–management interaction?
2. What was the content of the discussions and conclusions at the joint meetings? In what way did the management and unions resolve IR problems?

The BoB had laid down a system of regular meetings with the various trade unions. These meetings with the unions and associations were called 'structured meetings'. The details of such arrangements are given in Table 7.1.

The Bank held negotiations with its two major unions, the Federation (the recognised workmen's union) as well as the Coordination Committee (the minority workmen's union), on policy matters relating to promotions, transfers, staff loans, and criteria for sanction of various allowances, among other things. At the zonal and regional levels, discussions were held on matters such as individual grievances of the employees with both the Federation and the Coordination Committee. The Bank also held discussions with its two officers' associations, the AIBOBOA or the Association and the NABOBO, on various matters pertaining to officers.

In accordance with a settlement signed in 1973 with the Federation and the Coordination Committee, the Bank held discussions with both the unions on all important policy matters, but signed settlements only with the Federation, which had been given the status of sole bargaining agent. The Coordination Committee enjoyed only consultative status.

An analysis of the minutes of the meetings held between the Bank and the Federation revealed that apart from matters such as promotion and transfer policies, a number of other assorted issues such as the fixing of norms for assigning duties carrying special allowances, disciplinary action, policy for converting part-time employees into full-time employees, and new amenities and facilities to staff were often raised by the Federation in these meetings. Many similar issues were also discussed with the Coordination Committee. Records showed that in the past, many demands of both the unions about issues such as the promotion

TABLE 7.1 Structured Meetings between Management and Unions at BoB

Level	Frequency of Meeting	Who Could Convene the Meeting?	Number of Union Representatives Allowed	Payment of TA/DA	Were Minutes Exchanged?
Branch level	Once in a fortnight	Branch manager	Two	No TA/DA	No
Regional level	Once in 3 months	Regional manager	Five	TA/DA for three representatives	Yes
Zonal level	Once in 6 months	Zonal manager	Five	TA/DA for four representatives	Yes
Central office	Once in 4 months	General Manager (HR)/ Assistant General Manager (IR)	15	TA/DA for 10 representatives	Yes

Note: Travelling allowance (TA), Diem Allowance (DA).

policy, special allowances, and facilities to the unions had been settled in these meetings.

The meetings were invariably arranged at the request of the unions and the associations. The unions generally submitted their agenda in advance. Except for the period 1979–80, the management did not prepare any agenda in advance about its issues and problems.

As mentioned earlier, a common belief among the operating managers was that these meetings did not help in any way to improve the quality of IR in the Bank; they felt that, instead, they strengthened the unions' power. In order to understand these issues in the wider context of IR effectiveness,

I attended a few such meetings with the unions and the associations at the corporate level, as an observer.

At the meetings, the union was represented by the general secretary, other principal office-bearers, and central committee members from various states. The management was generally represented by the Assistant General Manager (IR) and personnel officers from the corporate IR Department. No management person from the line function attended the meetings. On rare occasions, General Manager (Personnel) or Deputy General Manager (Personnel) and officers of the Personnel Department in Vadodara put in an appearance. On every occasion, I observed that the discussion was initiated and carried on by the union representatives. Many state-level leaders raised issues specific to their zones. They also gave an account of the state of IR in their zones, pointed out inconsistencies in implementation of rules, and made observations about the managerial styles of the zonal managers/regional managers in IR. The participation by the management representatives was confined to issues raised by the unions or the associations. The management team generally listened to the union representatives in silence, and occasionally pleaded helplessness in dealing with the zonal and regional offices.

A case in point was a meeting with the Coordination Committee that I attended at the central office in September 1985. The union team was led by the general secretary of the Coordination Committee. The union had a negotiating committee of 10 members drawn from various states. The management side, for most of the negotiations, was headed by the Assistant General Manager (IR), Tandon, assisted by three personnel officers working in IR Department at corporate office. For a part of the meeting, General Manager (Personnel), Bhide, was also present. While opening the discussions, the secretary of the Coordination Committee pointed out a number of cases of ad hoc personnel policy. The Coordination Committee was agitated about a circular issued by the Assistant General Manager (Staff Administration), Vadodara, to the branches for the appointment of data entry operators for computers on the basis of an aptitude test. It strongly objected to this circular being sent out without the selection criteria having been discussed first with the unions. The Assistant General Manager (IR) told them that the circular could be ignored. Next, the union raised the problem of coordination between Vadodara and Mumbai, which, it said, was leading to delays in personnel matters, and thus complicating the IR environment.

After that, the Coordination Committee raised the issue of the functioning of the DAW under General Manager (Vigilance). The union questioned the need for non-vigilance cases to travel up to General Manager (Vigilance), especially when disciplinary authority was vested in the regional managers. It alleged that General Manager (Vigilance) interfered in disciplinary matters at the lower levels. It contended that in non-vigilance cases involving misconduct, such as disobedience of orders or non-performance of duties, the regional managers, as the disciplinary authority, should be fully empowered to take decisions. The Coordination Committee especially resented the delay in resolving disciplinary matters when they were referred to the corporate office. It wanted immediate redressal of the problem, failing which it threatened to launch an agitation. The General Manager (Personnel) responded by pleading ignorance on the subject. This was followed by a discussion on the proposals on the promotion policy, which had been under discussion for about a year.

The next item on the agenda was the conversion of part-time subordinate staff into full-time employees. The Coordination Committee wanted all daily wage workers who had completed 240 days to be absorbed into regular service, as per a recent ruling of the Supreme Court. The Coordination Committee stated that the management had agreed to such an arrangement in Kolkata. The union further questioned the legitimacy of having different policies in different places. The General Manager (Personnel) and the Assistant General Manager (IR) promised to look into the matter of the daily wage workers.

The union also demanded its representation on the Welfare Committee of the Bank on the basis of its consultative status. The General Manager (Personnel) replied that he would convey the workmen's feelings to the CEO.

The Coordination Committee also raised an issue regarding the installation of computers in the branches. The management's action in this regard was alleged to be against the spirit of the industry-level settlement. The Coordination Committee spokesmen provided a lot of data to prove that the machines installed were, in fact, computers and not ledger posting machines, which had been approved in the bipartite agreements. The management team pleaded ignorance about the difference between the electronic machine and a computer and called for two officials from the Computer Department to convince the union that the electronic machines were not computers.

Throughout the meeting, the personnel specialists maintained a low profile, listening to the union leaders with attention and responding gently with factual data. Although the meeting was held in an atmosphere of cordiality, the union demonstrated frustration with the delays, inconsistencies, and lack of coordination in personnel matters. At no stage did the management team raise any issues faced by the operating units.

A few days later, I attended another meeting between the corporate management and the Federation, which was the recognised workmen's union. At the very outset, the Federation leaders expressed their resentment about the fact that a meeting had been held first with the minority union, the Coordination Committee. The management explained that the meeting with the Federation had been scheduled first, but postponed on its own request; the matter was not pursued further.

At this meeting, the management wanted to sign a settlement on the procedure for the appointment of data entry operators for computers. The 15-member Federation team was led by its general secretary. The management side was headed by the Assistant General Manager (IR), who was assisted by three personnel officers. The Assistant General Manager (Computer Services) also participated and led the discussions on computer matters.

The Federation leader opened the discussion by expressing his frustration with the way things were happening in the Bank. In his lengthy opening remark, he said:

> There is a feeling among our units that things are not moving in our Bank. The feeling is that the top personnel specialists have no sense of involvement and lack initiative. Although they agree with us, they are not able to convince the management. The Personnel Department which at one time was very powerful is emasculated. For the sake of decency, we don't want to use harsh words. There are inconsistencies, delays, disowning of commitments made. The personnel function is totally fragmented. It has become a high-watermark of non-decision-making. This is destruction of the Bank's tradition in IR.

The Federation leader cited a number of cases awaiting decisions from the top management. He said he resented the absence of General Manager (Personnel) at the meeting, especially as the latter had attended the meeting with the Coordination Committee. Each regional-level leader spoke in turn about long-pending grievances and pointed out how their members were getting restive. They also complained about long-pending disciplinary cases against employees. Many of them spoke about not holding structured meetings at the regional level. The management team assured them of appropriate action in the matters raised by them.

Thereafter, the first item on the agenda, the computerisation at the branches, was taken up. The Federation questioned the fairness of the decision to leave Kolkata out of the implementation of the computerisation policy. The Federation also questioned why the management had taken no action to tackle the threat posed by the minority BEFI union in Kolkata. Thereafter, the main issue—the criteria for selection of data entry operators for computers at the branches—was discussed.

Some members of the Federation claimed that the electronic machines installed in the branches were, in fact, computers. The Assistant General Manager (Computer Services) explained that the machines were not computers. After a lot of discussion between him and some members of the Federation, the Federation leader said that he had requested General Manager (Personnel) to hold a computer-orientation programme for the union leaders; had he done so, problems of this sort would not have arisen.

After further discussion, the Federation agreed to the criteria for selecting staff as data entry operators. While negotiating this issue, the Federation demanded that some of their long-pending demands be settled; and later, the personnel specialists, after consulting with the CEO, agreed to two main demands. Special leave was granted to representatives of the Federation for attending conciliation proceedings under the Industrial Disputes Act, 1947. The second demand was for permission for representatives of the Federation to come for negotiations a day in advance and stay a day after the negotiations were over. Apparently, the pressure for computerisation of branches yielded concessions to the Federation from the management. It was thus evident that whenever the management had its own agenda to pursue, it readily extended an accommodative attitude to the Federation.

Although these corporate-level meetings mainly discussed policy matters with implications on an all-India level, it was common for the regional-level leaders, who were members of the negotiating committee, to raise issues relevant to or pertaining to their area. Such issues were sometimes discussed in smaller meetings. Sometimes, the personnel manager of the zone concerned was also called to the smaller meetings. In the meetings, pending matters, including individual cases and interpretations of settlements, were sorted out. In one such meeting relating to the Rajasthan zone, I observed that a number of pending matters such as ex-gratia medical aid to an employee, grants to local sports club, permission for deputing employees for workers' education programmes, and inter-zonal transfers of some employees were sorted out. These issues had been pending with the IR Department for a long time and were referred to the PC. It is thus evident that the meetings were used by the unions to sort out both policy matters and individual cases.

During both the meetings that I attended, the management did not raise any issues, whether of productivity, discipline, or customer service; nor were even concrete cases of violation of policy by state-level unions brought to the notice of the apex union, even though a number of such references were made to the central office by the personnel managers of the various zones.

Despite the fact that a Bank circular in 1983 stipulated discussions on business developments and deposit mobilisation in the structured meetings, none of these issues was discussed in any of the meetings that I attended. Nor did any of the minutes of the past meetings give indications that such discussions had ever taken place.

Thus, it is evident that the system of structured meetings discussed mainly the problems raised by the unions; the problems faced by the management at both the organisational and operating levels were not raised. To this extent, this mechanism worked to the distinct advantage of the unions and failed as an effective forum for mutual problem-solving. The reasons for this can be summed up as follows.

First, the management team in the structured meetings at the corporate level comprised mainly personnel specialists. The members of the top management, like the CEO/executive director or any general managers from the operations side, did not attend these meetings. The personnel specialists, by the nature of their job and the limitations of their role, did not have much information about operational problems such as business development, profitability, deposits, and housekeeping. They failed to collect basic information on business and confined mainly to personnel matters. This handicapped the management team in raising substantive issues of business, sharing problem areas, and seeking the involvement of the unions in the problem-solving process.

Second, the personnel specialists did not enjoy the confidence of the top management and played a low-profile advisory role. In a real sense, they did not represent the management in terms of authority and power to take decisions during negotiations. That is why they avoided making commitments during the negotiations. In their advisory capacity, they merely listened to the viewpoints of the unions for communication to the higher management. This reduced the value of these interactions as an effective problem-solving forum.

Third, the management did not use the negotiations with the unions as an opportunity to share information about business growth and customer service and to seek the cooperation of the unions and, through them, that of the employees in providing uninterrupted customer service. This is evident in the top management's policy of considering the negotiations to be the main show of the Personnel Department—a chore that had to be done by someone.

Fourth, the structured meetings were not based on relevant consultations with the operating managers, the people who had to implement the decisions and policies arrived at through the settlements with the unions. Even in critical matters like the promotion policy and special allowances, the operating managers were not asked for their opinion. The records showed that operating managers such as the zonal and regional managers were not invited to attend the meetings, although matters relating to their zones were often discussed.

To this extent, collective bargaining, which is a two-way mechanism for problem-solving, was reduced to an almost unilateral arrangement in favour of the unions. Bhide told me after one such meeting:

> The successive CEOs have their own agenda in dealing with union leaders. The union observations on delays are fully justified, but they [the CEOs] have little regard for [the] IR climate as long as it suits them to isolate [the] unions. Structure is supposed to facilitate

decision-making. Here in the Bank, it is created to delay decisions and weaken the trade unions. There is no long-term strategy, as each CEO wants to handle IR in his own way. They don't trust us [the specialists] because we act professionally and our decisions are based on rules and regulations and fairness to all, while often [the] CEOs base their decisions on individual likes and dislikes. The structured meetings have become a formality and it is embarrassing to face [the] unions on delays in personnel decision-making and ambiguity on many policy matters.

Personnel Specialists as Scapegoats

Most line managers and members of the senior management, such as zonal managers, considered the corporate-level personnel specialists to be the root cause of all the IR problems in the Bank. They held the personnel specialists responsible for the growing power of the unions and the deterioration of the IR climate. They ridiculed them by calling them academicians and theoreticians and observed that they (the personnel specialists) were not committed to the Bank and were pro-union in their leanings. Statements such as 'we are dying with the help of doctors' and 'all problems are due to personnel functionaries' revealed the extent of the dissatisfaction the operational functionaries felt about the personnel specialists in the Bank.

The issue of effectiveness of the personnel functionaries needs to be examined in the context of related issues, such as the nature of their authority and power, their orientation to operational problems, personal characteristics, and the managerial strategies in IR.

It is important to understand that at the corporate level, the Personnel Department was headed by a general manager who was a specialist. L.B. Bhide was recruited in 1958 as an LWO and reached the position of General Manager (Personnel) in 1982. He was allotted the Services Department, along with the personnel function, which looked after matters relating to premises and equipment. The other senior personnel specialist at the corporate level was J.N. Tandon, an Assistant General Manager, who headed the IR function. Records show that no formal authority or power was delegated to these specialists in the personnel/IR area.

During my fieldwork in the corporate IR Department, I observed that the Assistant General Manager (IR) mainly dealt with the matters raised by the various trade unions, coordinated the personnel function between the Vadodara and Mumbai offices, and attended to matters referred for technical opinion about the interpretation of awards and settlements from Vadodara as well as from the various zones or regions. The General Manager (Personnel) mainly attended to matters put up by the Assistant General Manager (IR) relating to issues to be referred to the board and the committees and matters raised by the government and the IBA.

A major role played by these specialists was to maintain active liaison with the various trade unions by meeting them and hearing their grievances and viewpoints. When demands were raised by the trade unions on policy matters, the specialists collected the necessary background information from the IBA and other banks, prepared notes, and submitted the matter for decision to either one of the committees or the CEO. They were usually cautious and conservative in their approach. Whenever there was a proposal to withdraw any facility from the unions and staff as per government instructions, or any change that could create a conflict situation, the specialists cautioned the higher management about the possibility of an IR problem. An example illustrates this point.

Once, the Federation pointed out through a written communication the tendency of its rival, the Coordination Committee, to usurp office space in various premises of the Bank. The Federation wanted strict action taken against the Coordination Committee. The Personnel Department submitted the information collected from the various zones about the Coordination Committee occupying office space and submitted it to the CoE, with the opinion that if any decision was taken to ask the Coordination Committee to vacate the occupied space, it could lead to IR problems.

When any union predicted an IR problem in any region or zone or complained about violation of any rules and regulations in any place or about the attitude of any executive in IR matters, the response of these specialists was generally non-committal. If a union insisted on taking any remedial steps in any zone, the typical response of these specialists was, as I heard in one of the meetings, 'We are like doctors, our job is to give advice and if the patient does not heed our advice, we cannot do anything.'

In their interaction with the zonal or regional managers on IR matters, the specialists gave their technical opinion on various matters, but whenever the zonal or regional managers telephoned them and sought an on-the-spot decision, especially in a crisis situation, they avoided taking a decision and invariably told the operating managers that they would consult the CEO and get back to them.

If a zonal manager reported a conflict situation like a call for a strike or agitation by a union, the specialist at the central office often contacted the senior leaders of the union and requested them to intervene. Occasionally, the regional leaders were called for discussions at the corporate level in such circumstances.

Thus, in the normal course of things, the specialists avoided getting involved in any problem unless there was a threatened or actual agitation. They stuck to playing an advisory role. This had several organisational consequences that affected the effectiveness of IR.

The third bipartite agreement at the industry level had provided for payment of an agriculture assistant allowance to clerks who performed duties relating to agriculture financing. A list of duties to be undertaken by them was given in the agreement. Accordingly, the Bank issued a circular advising its branches to pay the allowance to the clerks concerned. Some zones wrote to the IR Department, asking to know the exact criteria for sanctioning the allowance. The Personnel Department called for information from other banks, enquiring about the criteria they had followed in sanctioning this allowance. Meanwhile, it was informed by a union that in one zone, the zonal management had agreed to sanction this allowance in all branches where there were 300 or more agriculture accounts. The unions in some zones demanded this criterion to be applied uniformly. The Personnel Department did not question the zone, although the personnel specialists resented the unilateral decision of one zone that was creating a problem for the Bank. Later, the personnel manager of the zone stated:

> Our experience with the Central Office is that they do not respond to problems in time. This creates conflict at [the] local level. We have to promptly sort out the issues to avoid any agitations, etc., and to conduct business smoothly.

This was not the only example of a zonal management agreeing with the local union about an ad hoc criterion for an allowance. Other zones also entered into local understandings with the unions. A number of cases were cited in this regard where different zones favoured different practices. The Personnel Department acknowledged the variations, but claimed they were helpless in the matter because they were merely advisors and did not hold executive powers. The best they could do was to write to the zones and draw their attention to the anomaly and ask them to rectify the situation.

The advisory role played by the personnel specialists brought them into sharp conflict with their operational counterparts, who expected them to play an executive role like any other functionary of the corporate office, giving the line managers guidance, support, and encouragement in various day-to-day matters.

A number of such instances were observed. In critical IR matters, which threatened stoppage of work, or agitation, or involved the prestige of any executive, the personnel specialists avoided giving a decision. At best, they offered their guarded opinion subject to various 'ifs' and 'buts', and warned the operational functionaries of the consequences of the stand taken by them. An example supports this point.

Once, a zonal manager, who had the reputation of being straightforward and effective in his job, transferred a local union leader of the Coordination Committee from one branch to another, under the job rotation plan, within the guidelines of the corporate office. The local union resisted this transfer and made its reversal a prestige issue. On the other hand, the Federation threatened that if the transfer was withdrawn, their members would also not accept the job rotation plan. The zonal manager was therefore keen that the transfer of the local union leader should not be withdrawn. He referred the matter to the personnel specialists in Mumbai, who advised him that he could go ahead, but only after considering the consequences. The zonal manager later told me:

> I cannot go ahead on the basis of [such] guarded advice of the specialists. Unless I have the support of the corporate office, how can I go ahead? If anything goes wrong, they would say 'Look, I told you so'.

Eventually, the zonal manager did not implement the transfer order and the members of the Federation also flouted the job rotation plan. Thus, the job rotation plan could not be implemented in that zone.

The advisory nature of the role of the personnel specialists was itself the cause of their isolation; they were dysfunctional because they had no executive authority vested in them. Clearly, the lack of a clear definition of the specialists' role was at the root of the problem.

An important question that needs to be examined at this stage is: in spite of the widely expressed dissatisfaction with the personnel specialists across levels in the Bank, why did the management continue to recruit personnel specialists and post them at various levels? Another related question: why didn't the management accord the personnel specialists the necessary authority and power that would enable them to deal with the various personnel matters?

The answer to these questions should take into account the general style of the BoB management, its strategy and priorities, and the degree of importance it attached to IR.

In assigning the fire-fighting role in IR to personnel specialists without giving them any specific authority, the management had a definite strategy to rid itself of the irksome and difficult problems it would have otherwise faced on a day-to-day basis. The top management believed that routine IR functions should be left to IR specialists so that the rest of the management was free to deal with operational and strategic issues and problems. Under this system, the personnel specialists played the role of shock absorbers for the top management. In spite of the low profile maintained by the specialists, they remained at the centre of controversy and were blamed by a majority of operating managers for all the problems in IR.

By not vesting the specialists with any real authority in IR matters, the CEOs sought to keep control of strategic matters like relations with the unions, maintain their own powers to play one union against the other, and keep for themselves the authority to distribute favours. Bhide, the top personnel specialist, was well known in the industry for his knowledge and experience, and other bank CEOs and the IBA often consulted him. Bhide was very popular with the workmen's unions and he was trusted by all the workmen's unions for his knowledge and neutral stance. The officers' associations, however, were never comfortable with Bhide because they believed in cultivating the CEO to seek favours and concessions and leveraged this to become a parallel power centre. They also played one executive against the other to gain favours. Bhide's professional value system was in conflict with that of many CEOs, especially in the post-nationalisation period.

As we have seen earlier, most CEOs in the post-nationalisation period pursued ad hoc strategies in IR and found it difficult to execute their short-term objectives through Bhide, which is why he was sidelined, demoted, and made to work under operational heads. Even when he became General Manager (Personnel), his influence was effectively neutralised by creating a committee system of decision-making. Management politics was at the core of the IR function and personnel specialists like Bhide were reconciled to their perfunctory roles. Lack of trust between the CEO and the personnel specialists on one hand, and between the CEO and the unions on the other, buttressed by management politics at the top, was the cause of many problems in IR at the Bank.

For effective management of IR, there has to be congruence in the value systems of the CEO and the personnel specialists. Conflict in value system can stymie the trust between the organisation and the trade unions, as it is the personnel specialists who represent the management in dealings with the unions. Despite the widely prevalent management dissatisfaction with the personnel specialists, they continued in the Bank. The specialists were reconciled to their advisory role and knew they had no real authority to influence the conduct of IR. They were also torn between the expectations of the top management, which wanted to restrict them to an advisory role, and the expectations of the operating managers, who wanted them to play an executive role.

In sum, the policy of the management towards the specialised personnel function, and consequently the role of the personnel specialists, resulted in issues such as bureaucratisation of personnel decision-making, feelings of alienation among the specialists, loss of corporate control over the personnel function, and inconsistencies in rule implementation. These factors contributed to the ineffectiveness of the IR function.

Credibility of the Top Management

The top management continued to retain the old structure and system in the Personnel Department and avoided any initiative that signalled a desire to improve IR, but in the process, it lost credibility in the eyes of the operating managers. The operating managers spoke about the insurgency of the unions, the increasing cases of indiscipline, the restrictive practices, the attitude and behaviour of the union leaders, and they held the top management responsible for their problems, declaring openly that the management's policy of pampering the unions was responsible for the ineffectiveness of IR at the operating level and the consequent negative impact on business.

The branch and regional managers cited a number of instances of when disciplinary action initiated by them had had to be dropped halfway because of lack of support from the top management. Statements such as 'the management does not mean business in IR', 'the management is impotent', 'the management buckles under union pressure', and 'the management has abdicated its right to manage', made by managers, manifested their extreme dissatisfaction with the top management in IR matters. A manager described the prevailing scenario of IR and its implications for branch management wryly, using cricket metaphors:

> The branch manager is stripped of even a semblance of authority and his position resembles that of a last unrecognised batsman who is expected to hold onto a shattered innings and achieve success in [the] face of hostile bowling [union leaders] and a biased [or an equally helpless] umpire [regional manager] with his index finger ever raised towards the heavens. To top it all, he is unpadded [no support] and holds in his hands only the handle of a broken bat (his staff, which is left free to determine its own level of output)—an impossible task. But he carries on somehow, often getting flogged on the way.

Another branch manager said that the average manager was 'disliked by the staff [if he insists on discipline, punctuality, and output] and disowned by the management [if he ever carries a problem to them]'.

The senior management personnel, such as the regional managers and zonal managers, were also significantly negative about the top management's IR policy. Of the 22 zonal and regional managers I interviewed, as many as 17 expressed their dissatisfaction with how the top management dealt with the issues of IR, unions, and discipline. They pointed to the low priority accorded by the top management to critical issues such as indiscipline and union misbehaviour as the cause of the IR problems at the operating level.

Such perceptions among the senior management staff were symptomatic of the general mood of helplessness with regard to IR management in the Bank.

During my fieldwork, I investigated the reality by examining the following questions:

1. How did the top management deal with issues of IR and indiscipline in reality? How did they ensure effectiveness of IR at the operating level?
2. How did the top management deal with conflict situations and with pressures from the unions?
3. What impact did the top management policy have on discipline and IR at the operating level?

The Bank's central office and other administrative offices headed by senior executives symbolised the top management, and the manner in which the top management dealt with problems of indiscipline and tackled unions sent signals about its policy as a whole. Since the major part of my fieldwork was done in Mumbai, the observations in this section are based on the events I observed in the Bank's offices and branches in Mumbai.

I observed that a number of union leaders from both the majority and minority unions based in Mumbai visited the central office regularly. They called on various executives such as General Manager (Personnel) and Assistant General Manager (IR) and discussed their members' grievances and other policy matters. The personnel specialists enjoyed excellent rapport with these leaders, perhaps because the unions trusted them for their professional knowledge and for being apolitical in their approach.

A number of second-line leaders also visited, every day, the Mumbai zonal and regional offices without prior appointment with the executives concerned and held discussions with the personnel officers about the problems of members in the branches. During these meetings, they also pointed out the state of affairs in the various branches. They normally registered their protests against the actions of the branch managers and officers in enforcing punctuality and attendance and allocating work to their members. On an average, every day, about two to three hours of the personnel officers' time was spent talking to the union leaders.

The leaders also visited the various branches during the day and undertook union activities during working hours. They harassed the branch managers during working hours, even disrupting customer service. One day, while I was talking to a branch manager about IR issues, four local union leaders belonging to a recognised union from other offices barged into the manager's cabin and questioned the behaviour of the branch accountant (next in hierarchy to the manager) in asking their members to complete the day's work. There was considerable shouting and commotion in the banking hall.

Response of the Top Management

The top management was generally indifferent to the operating managers' grievances in such instances, as well as to pressure from the government to discipline the unions and the employees. Even the Association, which represented the officers, did very little to help the branch officials exert their authority to manage. An example explains this point.

In 1985, the government sent out a communication to all the banks to put a stop to the restrictive practices of the unions, including conducting union work during working hours. Accordingly, PSBs were advised to enforce discipline through a time-bound programme. In response to the government instructions, the IR Department sought information from all the zones about the number of employees who did union work during working hours. Many zones submitted the information, as did the office manager of the corporate office and the personnel manager of the main branch in Mumbai. In all, it was found that about 30 employees of both the offices undertook union work on a full-time or part-time basis. According to a rough estimate, the Bank spent about Rs 0.1 million a month on each of their salaries, allowances, and other perquisites.

It was revealed that a senior officer of the Bank attached to the central office had not attended office for many years and was, in fact, attending to the work of the All India Bank Officers' Association (AIBOA), an officers' organisation floated by the AIBEA at the industry level (a minority association of officers at the industry level having no membership in the Bank). In effect, this officer, who held no office in any of the unions or associations in the Bank, was being paid a salary for undertaking union work for the officers of other banks.

The EMC was informed about this case, but it decided informally to not take any drastic action against the officer as it was felt that such instances were not uncommon in other banks also. Formally, it issued a circular to the branches reiterating the government's concern and instructions. The circular was clearly a formality in compliance with the government instructions, as the management was not serious about initiating any concrete action with regard to stopping the indisciplined behaviour of the union leaders.

A regional manager of the Mumbai local branches ridiculed the gesture the circular represented and said:

> I know these kinds of circulars are issued under government pressure. Let the central office set their own house in order. I do not want to set my own house on fire on the basis of this circular.

Another branch manager commented:

> Everything is known to the management. Why do they keep issuing such circulars? This practice has been going on for quite some time. Why don't they [the top executives] refuse to meet union leaders during working hours? It may solve our problems.

From these comments, it appears that the line functionaries expected the corporate office to initiate action in the administrative offices first, and they did not seem to attach much importance to the circular issued by the top management. Obviously, the credibility of the top management was the main issue that encouraged the lower functionaries to live with the situation, such as it was.

Similarly, many branch managers in Mumbai reported acts of misbehaviour by the union leaders and their interference in the day-to-day administration. However, no action was initiated at any level on such complaints. The management's policy of undue caution and indifference was symptomatic of the malaise and inertia in reclaiming the basic management function to manage.

Impact on Workplace Discipline

The top management's cautious policy in IR and lack of focus on workplace discipline provided the operating managers with the perfect excuse to justify their own inaction in maintaining discipline and managing IR. When they were questioned, the operating managers quoted the examples of the higher authorities and expressed their fears about taking action at their level. For example, during fieldwork when I visited a branch in Mumbai, the joint manager of the branch reported to the manager that an employee belonging to a minority union had been leaving office two hours early for three consecutive days. The joint manager said that this behaviour needed to be stopped and proposed that the employee be asked to explain his behaviour. The manager counselled the joint manager to relax and avoid any action that might create conflict at the branch. In support of his advice, he told the joint manager that similar practices prevailed in the corporate and zonal offices. He went on to add that in his previous posting, the higher management had not supported his action even during a conflict situation arising out of the collective indiscipline of the staff.

During fieldwork, I witnessed another case of gross indiscipline by a minority union and lack of action by the management. One day, the Personnel Department received information that the activists of the minority union had installed a statue of a national hero in the main banking hall of the Mumbai main branch. The officer in charge of the branch sought instructions from the management on the Bank's response. The Personnel Department told the office to deal with the matter using its discretion.

In another case, a group of minority union leaders affiliated to the Congress Party occupied a vacant room which was to be allotted to an executive and declared it to be their union office. Apart from putting up the union banner, they also installed a photograph of the prime minister in the occupied office. The matter was reported to the central office, which deputed a very senior executive to enquire into the matter. It was decided in this meeting to lodge a criminal complaint against the union and take disciplinary action against those employees who were responsible for occupying the room without permission. Later, under the threat of a criminal complaint, the union agreed to vacate the room. The memos seeking an explanation from the employees, which were prepared by the personnel officers, were, however, not served on any of the activists of the union who had occupied the cabin. It was believed that the management decided to drop the idea of taking disciplinary action under the pressure of an influential politician.

A manager of a local branch in Mumbai later commented:

> The minority union has been creating problems for the last one–two years, which is known to the management. Neglecting to take notice of this and allowing their leaders to create problems in the branches have boosted their morale. The present incident…provided the right

opportunity for the management to take action against erring members of this union, but once again the management has compromised on principles. The message is loud and clear that we must live with the situation.

This statement seems to agree perfectly with the general perception of the managers about the management policy in dealing with union militancy.

It is thus evident that the top management followed a cautious policy in IR, often avoiding conflict situations by not confronting the unions directly even when they indulged in highly provocative activities. The management also remained indifferent to the activities of the union leaders during working hours. This was indicative of the low priority that the top management accorded to the hard-core aspects of IR, such as maintenance of discipline and dealing with union misbehaviour.

Survey Findings[2]

As part of my research, I had undertaken a survey of managerial perceptions of IR in early 1985. A large number of managers (70.80 per cent) expressed dissatisfaction with the way in which the higher management responded in a conflict situation. More than 82 per cent of the managers expressed their dissatisfaction with how conflicts were resolved.

Although a huge majority of the managers (93.60 per cent) resented the unions' interference in day-to-day administration, they did very little to control it because they felt that they were powerless to enforce any discipline. They felt helpless in improving IR due to the absence of proper communication on the management's IR policy (74.40 per cent), lack of support from the top management when IR matters were referred to it (67.60 per cent), lack of authority (74.60 per cent), lack of top management

---

[2] An analysis of IR climate was undertaking using interviews and a structured questionnaire covering 250 branch managers. Interviews were also conducted at different levels covering top management and operating managers at the zonal, regional, and branch levels. The survey was mainly about recording the respondents to questionnaire covering 250 branch managers. Interviews were also conducted on the functioning of the Personnel Department.

support in initiating disciplinary action (76 per cent), lack of recognition in effectively dealing with IR matters (63.20 per cent), and lack of consultation in decisions regarding employees' transfers and punishments (77.60 per cent).

A significant proportion of managers (65.60 per cent) expressed dissatisfaction about the way the Personnel Department functioned, and an almost equal number of managers (62.40 per cent) expressed their dissatisfaction with the specialists in the Personnel Department. Even senior executives like deputy general managers and general managers expressed negative feelings about their counterparts in the Personnel Department, whom they considered to be 'non-assertive and incompetent' and responsible, as one general manager said, for all the mess in the personnel/IR management in the Bank.

Three-fourth of managers surveyed (74 per cent) stated that the structured meetings functioned under pressure from and to the sole advantage of the unions and contributed to strengthening union power. A majority of managers (68 per cent) expressed dissatisfaction with the level of consultation by the top management with them for various matters discussed in the union–management meetings. Over 65.60 per cent of the respondents also believed that the top management did not care to understand the problems they faced at the operating level. This overwhelming feeling among the operating managers affected their initiatives in IR.

Thus, my fieldwork observations were supported by the survey findings about the reality of IR management in the Bank. It is argued here that the quality of workplace IR depends to a great degree on the manner in which IR policies are formulated and executed, and the extent to which the top management is willing to enforce a particular policy.

* * *

The period under discussion was marked by the pressures and tensions created by two major fraud cases that came to light in the immediately preceding period. Embarrassed by the government's action of sending both the CEO and the executive director home rather prematurely, the most urgent task before the management was to improve its image in the banking sector as well as its business performance.

The IR climate at the operating level was a major impediment in any effort of the Bank to improve its image, promote growth, and extend quality customer service. This climate had turned chaotic in the last few years due to the failure of successive managements to focus on operational problems, thereby allowing mounting insurgency of the unions at the workplace, indiscipline by employees, restrictive practices, and continuous challenge to the management's authority. The operating managers felt demoralised, more so in the absence of higher management support in initiating any steps for maintaining discipline, and they considered the murky IR to be a major constraint in improving the functioning of the branch.

It was interesting to observe during fieldwork that everyone—unions, personnel specialists, and the operating managers—complained about the total breakdown of the personnel decision-making system that contributed to chaos in the workplace and wanted the top management to take corrective measures.

Significantly, it was not that the source of major problems was not known to management, as it was their own creation. As mentioned earlier, a set of factors contributed to the prevailing frustration and cynicism, including disempowerment and ambiguous role of personnel specialists, committee-based decision-making even in routine personnel matters, and so on. All this cumulatively contributed to delays and indecision in employee issues leading to perpetual conflict at the workplaces.

Yet, the successive CEOs ignored all pleas to take any initial steps that instilled confidence in the management's concern for better IR at the workplace. For the management, it was business as usual, except that trade unions were distanced, their interference in day-to-day administration curtailed, and the officers' association was sidelined. The existing structure of personnel decision-making continued to be bureaucratic and time-consuming, decisions of structured meetings were not implemented, and there was no initiative from the top to improve discipline at the workplace. The impression one got at that time was that management handled IR in a piecemeal manner, on an issue-to-issue basis, and there was no effort to reach out to either employees or the operating managers. Resultantly, the staff motivation was at its lowest ebb.

While the management and especially the CEO, Premjit Singh, were able to assert and restore the credibility of management at the top, the high reliance on short-term solution to IR problems could be directly attributed to its failure to take a 360 degree view of the reality at the operational level and initiate any worthwhile steps to reconstruct the IR/HR function. A golden opportunity to restore the confidence of operating managers and staff by taking any confidence-building measures that could bear rich dividends was therefore missed.

It was revealed during my fieldwork that IR reforms or an urge to improve workplace IR did not figure on the CEO's agenda.

By this strategy, the present CEO also toed the line of his predecessor and perhaps remained in the illusion of 'being in control', while in reality, this was a mirage as, in the real sense, the control of the trade unions in the workplaces was total. Helplessness, that is, the belief by the trade unions that they were not able to influence legitimate changes in the interest of effective resolution of grievances, was manifested in increasing militancy at the operating level. Similarly, most operating managers' way of demonstrating their frustration with corporate office against non-response to references made to them on employee matters was manifested in non-action in performing even their basic role in managing staff. It was evident how structural ambiguities can lead to a certain behaviour by the trade unions, management personnel, and employees across the organisation. It also showed as to how CEOs can ignore the organisational need for effective decision-making in personnel for resolving grievances of the employees, just to pursue their own agenda to marginalise the trade unions. Cut and dried actions by the management, instead of engaging with real problem-solving and creating alternative approach in union–management relations, and a spirit of mistrust can lead to more complicated situations at the operating level, as is evident in the present case.

It is noteworthy that although the unions were sidelined at the top, they shifted their field of action from corporate office to branches where the situation deteriorated into complete chaos, especially in large branches in the urban and metropolitan centres. The staff came late and left early after doing the basic minimum routine work. Mounting housekeeping problems manifested, such as long-standing irreconciliation of inter-branch accounts, unreconciled entries in suspense account, poor record management, non-submission or delayed submission of control returns to the controlling office, irregular monitoring of advance accounts, and poor upkeep of the branches. Neither the workmen nor the officers were enthused to improve things and the unions, of course, were least concerned. The atmosphere of apathy compounded by the helplessness of the operating managers was palpable, affecting both the customer service and business of the Bank.

Reforms in IR can be triggered by any of the principal actors in IR or under some environmental pressures. In this particular case, both the management and trade unions failed to initiate reforms for different reasons. In the case of management, it was because of its obsession to keep unions at bay and deny them any reasonable role in decision-making. It failed to see in the crisis an opportunity to bring in the much-needed reforms in IR, especially at the operating level. Trade unions, although directly affected, failed to mount any counter-pressure on the management to improve the existing situation. Trade unions nurtured by management largess had to undergo the ignominy of such inertia of managerial action. Trade unions which effectively nurture their constituency can put up effective counter-pressure by mobilising their members to force the management into action. This obviously was missing in the BoB trade unions.

The CEO's apathy towards reforming IR, thus, was a significant factor for the chaotic IR at the operating level.

Chapter 8

TRADE UNIONS RULE THE ROOST (1990–2000)

Although I had completed my formal research, I continued to observe, in a manner akin to participant observation, the IR events that unfolded at the BoB under three subsequent CEOs from 1990 to 2000. During this period, I held various positions at the Bank, among them Principal of the Bank of Baroda Staff College in Ahmedabad, Assistant General Manager (Training) and Deputy General Manager (HRM) at the corporate office in Mumbai, and zonal manager in two line assignments in Meerut and Kolkata.

During this period, the three CEOs of the Bank were: A.C. Shah (1990–92); S.P. Talwar (1993–94); and K. Kannan (1995–99). In this chapter, I have briefly outlined the IR strategies followed by each of these CEOs and my experience of the impact of these strategies. In my various roles, I had a ringside view of how managerial strategies in IR were shaped and played out; how the top management responded to crisis situations in IR; how the management responded to IR referrals by senior operating managers; how CEOs and personnel functionaries socialised with or ignored union leaders; how CEOs used personnel specialists mostly as whipping boys; how management politics affected strategies; how trade unions leveraged their strength under the patronage of the CEOs; how trade unions interfered in administrative matters; and finally, how the management strategies led to workplace tensions and affected customer service.

This chapter also brings out the similarities and differences in the managerial styles and strategies of the home-grown CEOs (Shah and Kannan) and the outsider CEO (Talwar). We will see how egregious honeymoon at the top between the unions and the management had dysfunctional consequences at the lower level and how this was leveraged by both sides for short-term gains.

A Cosy Nexus with the Unions

A.C. Shah, an economist who joined BoB in the early 1960s, became its CEO in 1990. Shah had a long association with the Bank, joining it before the nationalisation of banks as an economic advisor and moving to a board-level position as Executive Director in February 1986. As Executive Director, Shah maintained a low profile because the then CEO, Premjit Singh, offered him only a limited role. Singh was suspicious of Shah and did not involve him in any major policy decisions. Singh told me that Shah was parochial and had leanings towards the officers' association. Shah nurtured a grievance against Singh for the treatment he received at his hands; he was also upset about Singh's general style of functioning, which was auto-cratic and in complete contrast to the pro-employee and pro-union style that had come to characterise the Bank. Shah held Singh responsible for the business stagnation that the Bank suffered during Singh's tenure during 1986–89.

When Shah took over as CEO a year later in 1990, he placed great emphasis on engaging the trade unions in helping him to improve busi-ness. He seemed to value the influence of the union functionaries on their members. He cultivated the general secretary of the Association in particular, because the general secretary had also been hostile towards Singh, who had kept him at a distance and did not consult him for transfers and promotions.

Shah began his tenure by demonstrating immense faith in the employ-ees and initiated some steps to reach out to them with a view to mobilizing their collective energy in giving push to business development. This was in complete contrast to his predecessor Singh, whose interactions with the staff had always been limited.

Shah approached the Bank of Baroda Staff College to design an Awareness Development Programme, including an audio recording of his message to the employees, to improve customer service and the deposit base of the Bank. Principal K.K. Verma and some of the faculty members, among them me, spent a great deal of time designing a strategy to take the CEO's message to thousands of BoB employees across the length and breadth of the country. We developed in-house trainers who would go to various locations, play the audio recording, and based on the CEO's message, start discussions with employees about how to improve business. Operating managers were also involved in this exercise. Overall, the impact of the programme was much beyond our expectations, so enthusiastically did the staff respond. It also strengthened my belief that directly engaging staff in the business can produce unexpected results.

Later, Shah gave another assignment to Staff College to study the Bank's personnel policy and suggest changes. We worked on this project with great passion and submitted a report. The main recommendation in our report was reform in the workplace, which entailed enforcement of basic discipline such as ensuring attendance and punctuality of the staff and curbing union interference in day-to-day work. These were sensitive areas which would have invited adverse reactions from the unions, which, it seemed, Shah was not willing to take on. Instead, he concentrated on building his rapport with the union leaders, who, in turn, leveraged their clout with him to enhance their own influence in the Bank.

Shah also appointed a leading management consultant, Professor S.K. Bhattacharya, to suggest organisational changes to align the Bank for many of the fast changes the industry faced. I was a member of an internal task force which helped Professor Bhattacharya. Bhattacharya's report suggested far-reaching changes in many aspects of the organisation. It was, however, not well received by the Association and therefore, Shah shelved the report. Thus, both the study reports—one done on personnel function reforms by the Staff College and the Bhattacharya report—were shelved as the Association opposed any reforms. Apparently, Shah did not want to annoy the Association leader and instead relied on his cooperation.

In an astute move, Shah reached out to the general secretary of the Association, seeking his cooperation in achieving the Bank's business goals. Aware that he was on a fixed tenure of three years (as after that he was to reach his superannuation) and anxious to accelerate the tempo of business at the Bank, Shah placed his complete trust in the general secretary of the association to win through him the commitment of the officers. The Association, which had been sidelined by Singh, was more than willing to take up this opportunity to revive its sagging image and regain the officers' esteem. In keeping with their track record, the Association leader bartered cooperation to obtain facilities for the Association as well as additional perquisites for the officers.

To further his aim, Shah did not mind giving the Association leader visibility and power, so much so that he asked him to visit the various zones and regions and motivate the officers there to increase business growth. The Association leader gladly accepted this role as the CEO's emissary. He visited the various zones and held meetings that were attended by the entire executive team. During the meetings, he talked the language of business and discouraged the raising of any grievances by the officers. As one middle-level officer told me, 'We have lost our secretary to the management.'

Shah's complete support of the Association manifested itself in many ways. The Association leader was consulted in all matters of transfers and postings of executives, even foreign postings, and he was nominated on various committees such as the Flat Allotment Committee and the House Journal Committee. The Association was given facilities such as fully furnished office space at more zonal centres. All these gestures symbolised Shah's increasing reliance on the Association. Shah's strategies sent a quick signal about the importance of the Association. Other sections of the management were quick to follow the top management's lead, and so the Association was soon able to influence the operating managers as well.

The visits of the Association leader were accorded no less importance than the visit of a top management executive from the corporate office inasmuch as some zonal managers and their executive teams would personally go to the railway station to receive the Association leader, even during working hours. Many executives cultivated the Association leader by calling on him during his stay and seeking his favour in their placements and promotions.

Local activists of the Association took the opportunity of these visits to brief their general secretary about the problems they faced in dealing with those executives who did not toe their line in regard to appraisal ratings of their members and, in particular, the office-bearers and the activists. If some executive did not accede to the local Association leader's demands about transfers and postings or if a particular executive was a hard taskmaster and did not succumb to the pressures of the Association, he was marked out. The top management, under pressure from the Association or as a quid pro quo for its members' cooperation, was ready to replace such executives with more pliable ones. In this environment, most executives behaved like 'good boys' so that they could avail promotions and plum postings.

Most executives like the regional and zonal managers did their best to keep themselves on the right side of the Association leader. At the operating level, the zonal and regional managers cultivated the zonal secretaries of the Association to ensure that they did not complain. Postings and transfers of managers and officers at the operating level were done in consultation with the zonal secretaries. The activists of the Association were the biggest beneficiaries under this regime and officers who had genuine grievances were often ignored. The message was that you had to be close to the Association to get choice postings, foreign postings, good appraisal ratings, and promotions.

Many talented and ambitious officers preferred to take up active roles in the Association because it was clear that if you were not on the right side of the Association, your career would not take off; being a prominent office-bearer in the Association guaranteed you were on the fast track in your career. It was no coincidence that three of the principal office-bearers of the Association became CEOs of PSBs. It was as if there was a parallel management in the Bank. Many executives grumbled privately about the state of affairs, but found themselves helpless to do anything about it. All this led to demoralisation in the ranks of officers as they felt that only those close to the Association received promotions and favoured postings. This considerably diluted the motivation in the ranks of officers in the Bank.

The general secretary of the Association was habitually critical of the training faculty as they generally kept away from active participation in the Association activities. I was perhaps among a handful of officers in the entire Bank who was not a member of the Association and I was therefore a target of the Association, which never missed an opportunity to criticise HRD as they saw in me a heretic talking the taboo language of employee development.

During Shah's tenure, the attacks on the training system increased manifold, so much so that under the instigation of the Association leader, training activities were suspended for about six months in June 1992 and all the trainers in the various zones were asked to report to their respective zonal offices to undertake routine work. Shah, despite being an academic himself who often articulated the virtues of staff training, succumbed to the tendentious propaganda unleashed by the Association against the training system. Such was the influence of the Association on the CEO! The Association rode high and usurped executive authority to influence Shah in matters of senior-level promotions, and many senior executives therefore took care to remain on his right side.

The role of HR Department was marginal. The General Manager, HR, Tandon, put up all the proposals for transfers and placement of the senior executives to CEO after discussions with the Association leader. Tandon merely worked as a pawn in the hands of the Association as a quid pro quo for the promotion he received with the help of the Association leader. He exploited his closeness with Shah to the hilt in influencing career decisions of senior executives. Shah also consulted the Association leader before releasing promotions of the executives. It was during this period that the Association managed to get major facilities from the Bank, like a fully furnished office in the prestigious Parliament Street building of the Bank at New Delhi.

Shah's mollycoddling strategies towards trade unions helped contain the union militancy to some extent especially from the officers cadre and helped the Bank to break the stagnancy in the business, evident from the fact that BoB registered the highest deposit growth in any single year in the entire post-nationalisation period. But this success was not without its consequences for the IR climate in the branches.

The workmen's unions, although they criticised Shah's proximity to the Association leader in private conversations, remained inactive as no check was put on the rampant indiscipline of their cadres in the branches. The workplaces remained preoccupied with their own little problems in managing business and the managers continued to complain about the increasing tension and loss of authority in managing day-to-day work and rendering customer service.

As a faculty member in the Staff College, during my training programmes for branch managers on effective management of IR, I faced the fury of the managers about the chaotic IR environment in the Bank; they laid the blame for this squarely on the top management and its clandestine understandings with the Association leader. They also blamed the Association leaders for hobnobbing with the management and ignoring their genuine problems. I could clearly see disconnect between the Association's members and its leaders in spite of the latter's overall power and influence with the management. The leaders were far removed from the problems of the workplaces as experienced by their members. This vindicated my research findings. I also learnt that with such bonhomie prevailing between the management and the unions, the members had started seeing their leaders as offshoots of the management, who became increasingly less visible and accessible, heightening the disconnect even further.

Shah's short-term strategy of enlisting the cooperation of the officers' association was a clever ploy to suppress the legitimate articulation of grievances by officers and employees. He played on the Association leaders' penchant for seeking personal favours to enhance their own position. This cosy arrangement at the top between the CEO and the leader of the Association delivered quiet times on the IR front at the top, but the workplaces were seething with discontent. Although Shah was able to register the highest deposit growth in any single year in recent years, the credit for the feat was grabbed by the Association and the balance of power tilted in its favour. The Association leader became a new power centre with the help of Shah, who appeared obliged to him. Thus, Shah left a legacy that became a major challenge for his successor, S.P. Talwar.

* * *

Driven by his anxiety to accelerate the tempo of business at the Bank, Shah crafted a new IR strategy which put the unions at the centre stage in pursuing a developmental agenda. He hoped this strategy would yield him the business growth he desired to see at the Bank. But the unions' support came with a price tag for the management.

The IR were conducted in a highly centralised and personalised manner with the complete exclusion of the personnel specialists. The IR were seen in terms of personal interactions between the key union leaders and the CEO. The Association leader, in particular, bartered his support for more concessions and favours to the Association. This perhaps well-intended strategy of the CEO was fully encashed by the Association to strengthen its own power and hold on the officers and executives, thereby holding a virtual veto for any reform proposed by the management.

This further explains Shah's reluctance to implement outcomes of a study on personnel management in the Bank undertaken by the Bank's Staff College at Ahmedabad and a report by Professor S.K. Bhattacharya (a leading consultant) on various organisational issues.

Even though the Bank could broadly achieve its business targets by pandering to the Association's demands and need for consultations in various key issues relating to careers of even senior executives, it was not without its pernicious consequences in the branches. In a certain way, this was the golden period for the officers' association in the Bank and it leveraged its power over the executives to influence several HR decisions and develop veto power in major policy matters.

It is pertinent that a side effect of such relationship was the weakening of both the management and the Association, both of whom tended to hide their real issues under the garb of mutual bonhomie, lest it created tensions in the relationship.

Shah's period can be described as a period of Opportunistic Cooperation between the key actors in management and trade unions. In this pattern, both management and unions exploit each other and leverage their position to achieve their short-term goals. Management goes out of the way in cultivating trade unions and making them feel important. The unions, in return, lend their support to management in their endeavour to improve business growth and also contain grievances of their members. Both the parties focus on their temporary goals and exploit each other to the hilt.

Winds of Change (1993–94)

In April 1993, after Shah retired, the Government of India appointed S.P. Talwar, a veteran banker and CEO of the Union Bank of India, as CEO of BoB. Talwar came without the baggage of an insider. He had risen from the ranks in the Oriental Bank of Commerce (OBC) to the position of CEO. From OBC, he moved to the Union Bank of India as its CEO. Talwar was known for his humanistic and pragmatic approach in dealing with employee problems. His affable style in dealing with colleagues won him instant acceptance at BoB. He brought in fresh air by way of his hands-on style and speedy decision-making. He soon won the confidence of the senior and top management with his warm and practical attitude to problem-solving.

Talwar's appointment in 1993 coincided with the replacement of the restrictive economic regime by the process of liberalisation, which heralded a new era in the Indian economy. The financial sector too was swept by the winds of change. In August 1991, the government had appointed a high-level committee on reforms in the financial sector under the chairmanship of M. Narasimham, former Governor of the RBI. The committee was asked to look into all aspects of the financial system and make comprehensive recommendations to reform the financial sector. Major changes brought about by the implementation of the Narasimham Committee Report (1991), which enabled banks to run on professional lines, included deregulation of interest rates, raising the capital adequacy ratio to international standards, allowing PSBs to raise capital from the market, and introduction of new accounting norms, asset classification, and prudential norms. The economic liberalisation thus brought in its wake challenges and opportunities for the Indian banking sector.

The BoB was well poised for the transformation. Talwar was, however, worried about the succession gaps in the senior and top management cadres. Out of eight general managers, six were due to retire in the next two years. Thus, one of his first major initiatives was to undertake a promotion exercise in the executive cadre and fill the vacancies in the senior management cadre. The promotions were done without much time for speculation and without consultations with the Association, a marked departure from predecessor Shah's strategy. Talwar promoted executives on merit and after taking inputs from the general managers on the performance and potential of the various eligible candidates.

Talwar was a CEO rooted in real world of problems. His intense connect with people helped him to understand their problems and initiate remedial action on an accelerated pace. Although an outsider, he wanted to connect with people and their problems as the top priority. Therefore, after taking over as CEO, Talwar visited the various zones and regions and met the executives there. He discovered that the Bank, despite its good brand equity in the market, experienced a number of problems like a difficult operating environment, delayed decision-making, poor housekeeping, and the excessive influence of the unions, especially the Association, on many senior executives.

Most operating managers complained about the prevailing IR climate and the interference by the unions in day-to-day management, which prevented them from providing good customer service and undertaking new business. As an outsider, Talwar had known about the good reputation of the Bank, but he was shocked at what he uncovered about the functioning of the branches. In one of the meetings with the executives, he was frank: 'I am quite disappointed looking at the functioning of the branches. There is so much mess around, housekeeping problems, delayed customer service, staff indiscipline, etc.' He advised the operating managers at the various levels to take quick measures to improve working conditions and promised them his support. The initial reaction of the unions was to 'wait and watch'. It was, however, clear, as one general manager put it, that 'Talwar is no pushover. He will change the way things are done.'

After about six months, Talwar visited Ahmedabad and I had a brief interaction with him when I narrated to him the problems with the Bank's training system and ways to improve it. I conveyed to him the overwhelming feedback from the participants of the various training programmes about the need to improve the climate at the branches for business growth and customer service. He soon posted me to the corporate office as Assistant General Manager (Personnel) to fill the vacancy caused by the sudden death of I.P. Mendonca, the then Assistant General Manager (Personnel). My appointment came as a big surprise to me for I had generally prepared myself for a longer tenure in training and HRD as stipulated by the terms of my appointment as a 'core faculty' at the Staff College.

I reported to the corporate office, but within 48 hours was informed by the General Manager (HRM), J.N. Tandon, that the board had deferred my appointment. He indicated to me that the decision had been taken on the insistence of the general secretary of the Association who himself was a board member (representing officers). Apparently, the Association leader had questioned Talwar's decision to shift me from training to the mainstream of the Bank. This clearly indicated that the Association wanted to continue interfering in senior executive placements and it was a signal to Talwar to fall in line with previous practice of consulting the Association in executive appointments. Within 24 hours, before I could leave Mumbai to resume my position at the Staff College in Ahmedabad, I was recalled and asked to report to the corporate office as Assistant General Manager (Training). Although the internal training function was managed from the Staff College, a new position had been created to accommodate me in Mumbai. This was an astute move by Talwar to assert his power and ensure that I was retained at the corporate office. With this move, he also met the objection that I could not be moved to a function other than training. My return to the Staff College would have been greatly embarrassing and loss of face for the CEO.

I remained virtually jobless for the next six months, merely looking after some sundry training matters. In fact, I created work for myself by attending to training issues such as streamlining training arrangements in consultation with the principal of the Staff College. While positioned in the Personnel Department, I could observe and learn a great deal about union–management dynamics, the influence of the trade unions in personnel decision-making, and the daily issues that the unions raised with the personnel executives. Not knowing what was in store for me, I maintained a low profile. Though unhappy with my nebulous role as Assistant General Manager (Training), I was determined to maintain my composure and refused to complain.

During my stay at the corporate office, I observed that Talwar was a straightforward CEO and was humane in his approach. His style in HRM was hands-on. Cutting across the bureaucracy, he would directly phone regional and zonal managers to enquire about the issues and problems and solve them without loss of time. This was a completely new experience for the operating managers. In the shortest possible time, he had complete grasp of the Bank and its culture. He showed deep interest in knowing the senior executives. Before undertaking any promotion exercise, he would hold several sessions with senior executives to discuss the prospective candidates. He involved me as well in these discussions. I think I received his attention because I always gave him a fair assessment of people based on data and he seemed to trust my opinion. This was his way of integrating me into the mainstream HR function.

As mentioned earlier, Talwar did not consult the Association about the transfers and postings of senior executives, a practice that Shah had started and a privilege that the Association seemed to value more than engaging with the real grievances of the officers. He also communicated directly with senior executives and took prompt corrective action. Talwar was quite clear in his mind that the Association should confine its activities to its members and that it should not engage in matters relating to the senior and top management. Clearly, there was a shift in IR strategy and the IR climate remained unsure.

In spite of Talwar's clear guidelines to eliminate the influence of the Association in managerial decisions, General Manager (HRM) Tandon continued to interact as closely as before with the general secretary of the Association. I observed that the Association leader would meet Tandon almost everyday in the evening, and Tandon did not invite either me or any other functionary of the Personnel Department to these meetings. Subsequently, we would get to know that the Association leader had provided inputs to Tandon recommending transfers and postings of the executives and other matters that benefited the Association. Tandon's proposals to the CEO on postings and transfers would often reflect the Association leader's recommendations. In this way, Tandon kept alive the influence of the Association, albeit in a clandestine manner, and he often ensured that nothing was done within the management to upset the Association leader. Some regional and zonal-level executives who had been favoured by the Association during Shah's tenure continued to support it both overtly and covertly. They passed on important and confidential information to the general secretary and the zonal secretaries of the Association and stealthily carried out their diktats.

Talwar was aware of Tandon's soft corner for the Association and he tried to neutralise it by discussing various proposals for placement of executives in a larger group comprising other functional general managers. Talwar, being an outsider, was aware of the handicap of not knowing the background and affiliations of the various executives and he often called me to get data on them. He had the habit of collecting data about individual executives from several sources and would take decisions about their careers only after due diligence. The Association's influence on critical matters was reduced to a great degree. Many in the top management were happy with Talwar's strategy to restore credibility of management decisions and instil a sense of confidence in the executives about fairness in career decisions.

In June 1994, the Bank undertook a promotion exercise from assistant general managers to deputy general managers. What followed encouraged me immensely. I was not only promoted as Deputy General Manager (HRM and General Administration) but also topped the list. I was aptly rewarded for my patience. Within one year, I was firmly placed in the mainstream HR function in spite of the initial problems I had encountered. Patience under humiliating circumstances has its own rewards. By this time, Talwar's hold on the Bank was total and the influence of the Association had been reduced to marginal at best.

Into the Mainstream

From the first day that I took up the post of Deputy General Manager, Tandon began delegating a lot of responsibility to me. He also gave me an opportunity to conduct corporate-level union meetings independently. Occasionally, I was asked to visit challenging zones like Kolkata and UP and represent the top management in the zonal union meetings. These experiences boosted my confidence. In my new role, under a CEO like Talwar, I thought we could do a lot to improve IR at the operating level, but Tandon did not want to do anything to get into the bad books of the Association.

Once a zonal manager referred an issue to our department about whether a regional secretary of the Association could be transferred from one region to another in his zone. I replied saying this was possible because all officers are transferrable as per their service conditions. When Tandon came to know about this communication, he promptly recalled it. Thus, despite a CEO who wanted to streamline the IR situation, the General Manager (HRM) was able to sabotage it in a subtle manner. In fact, Tandon told me, 'CEOs come and go, but we have to maintain our relations with the trade unions.' In spite of previous CEO A.C. Shah's antipathy towards Tandon, he had survived and been promoted at the behest of the Association. This was his time to return the favour. It also demonstrates how some members of the top management were more loyal to the Association than to the Bank. In fact, it is evident that management politics has played an important role in shaping IR strategy at BoB at different points in time.

Tandon always hesitated to take a stand on matters of indiscipline or violations reported by the operating managers, unless forced to do so by the CEO. On his own, he was king of the status quo. If an issue arose at the regional or zonal level, it was not uncommon to call the zonal personnel managers and unions to the corporate office to sort out the issue with the intervention of the General Manager (HRM) and the general secretary of the union concerned. This clearly indicated that Tandon did not want to take on the unions and improve workplace IR despite the CEO advising him to be business-like with the unions and streamline IR. This also explained the antipathy of the senior line managers towards the personnel specialists.

Talwar was not happy about the prevailing pattern of union–management relations. He was a humanist, polite and suave, and often shared with me his feelings about the extraordinary influence of the unions in general, and of the Association in particular, on the General Manager (HRM). Once he told me about an incident when he undertook an exercise for promotion from deputy general manager to general manager immediately after joining the Bank as CEO. Tandon advised him that there was a tradition in the Bank to consult the general secretary of the Association before announcing the results. Talwar invited the general secretary to his office, got up from his chair in a dramatic manner, and asked the general secretary to occupy it, as the Bank could have only one CEO at a time! The embarrassed general secretary got the message and left. He strongly believed and shared with me as much, 'You cannot have two drivers at the steering wheel—the vehicle will crash.'

Talwar frequently interacted with the regional and zonal managers and gave them the confidence to act without any fear or favour. Talwar's efforts to change the prevailing culture had to contend with a major handicap, however—he was new to BoB and many of the general managers and senior executives, being products of the Association's largesse, were sympathisers of the Association and in fact worked for it. He also had to contend with his General Manager (HRM) being very close to the Association and unwilling to take any major steps to disturb the status quo.

Talwar's efforts to infuse a sense of confidence and independence among the executives met with some initial success. During the one-and-a-half years of his tenure in the Bank, the IR scenario was quite subdued. The unions, including the ever-demanding Association, maintained a low profile. Talwar did not consult them on matters relating to promotions of senior executives or on important transfers. As there was no constitutional validity to such favours extended to the Association, the management could withdraw them without attracting protest. But, apart from the withdrawal of such visible favours, the management could not initiate any major reforms in the conduct of IR because of an unwilling head of HRM who had himself benefited from the Association in accelerating his career and survived in spite of scathing criticism from the operating managers.

Unfortunately, Talwar's tenure was cut short before he could make a real impact. He was elevated by the government and asked to take over as the Deputy Governor of the RBI. Talwar's exit in November 1994 was widely felt within the Bank, and more importantly by the customers, because in the short span of one-and-a-half years, he had infused new life in the Bank with his dynamism and humane attitude. He was also able to sideline the trade unions which had acquired unbridled power during Shah's tenure.

Talwar's departure was a great personal loss. His leadership style had taught me a lot: effective leaders are hands-on, visible, accessible, and courageous enough to change the status quo. And these qualities I imbibed and learnt on the job. But for his decision to call me to the corporate office, I would have been deprived of witnessing such an effective leadership role in action. Never before in my memory had the organisation experienced such a professional and business-like environment as during Talwar's leadership.

* * *

Talwar came at a time in the Bank when his predecessor, Shah, had been able to revive the business tempo but left a messy culture at the branch level, which led to frequent problems at the branches affecting customer service adversely and huge piling up of housekeeping problems, like arrears in balancing of books and pending inter-branch reconciliation for a long time. Talwar inherited an indulgent IR culture, with pampered unions who were accorded undue importance. Talwar was people oriented, and his strategy in IR was clearly a reversal of Shah's strategy. Talwar took charge of the 'management functions' and brooked no interference from the Association in areas of management function such as promotions and transfers. He maintained a business-like approach towards the unions and did not continue with the past legacies of pampering the union leaders or extending any favours or concessions. The IR during this period were tepid and shorn of the bonhomie that had existed in the past between the CEO and the union leaders. But Talwar's moves were not enough to establish a tension-free environment in the branches of the Bank. The General Manager (HRM), Tandon, in a tactical mode, maintained a low profile and did not do anything that could even remotely be interpreted by the unions as implementing Talwar's policy aggressively.

Thus, Talwar's efforts to regain control and rid the Bank of the undue influence of the trade unions in managerial matters was, in some ways, sabotaged by Tandon to perpetuate his cosy relationship with the Association. As Talwar was settling down, his tenure was cut short by his elevation as Deputy Governor, RBI. Talwar's short tenure witnessed a period of adjustment to the process of change after liberalisation, streamlining of internal machinery for inspection and recovery, implementation of new prudential norms, improving operational efficiency, revival of executive morale, building up of management bench strength, and a general sense of well-being in the organisation.

In spite of his efforts to rid personnel decision-making of the influence of the Association, Talwar's ambition of institutionalising and carving out a long-term strategy in IR at the Bank remained unfulfilled. With his departure, the Bank's IR situation became uncertain once again. Talwar's short tenure can best be described as 'paternalistic constitutionalism' because he was intensely people oriented without diluting managerial authority and operated within the framework of existing rules and regulations.

Surrendering before the Unions (1995–99)

K. Kannan, an old BoB hand, replaced Talwar as CEO in January 1995. Kannan was an insider, having joined the Bank in 1965. He had served the Bank in many capacities, but his most notable contribution was the implementation of the programmes and schemes pertaining to the priority sector. He was out of BoB for a short period of three years from April 1992 to January 1995 when he was with Dena Bank (a smaller-sized PSB), first as Executive Director and later as Chairman and Managing Director. He returned from there as CEO of BoB. Kannan was known as an enthusiastic executive. He was also known for his close relationship with the general secretary of the Association as both had worked in the same office early in their careers.

Kannan took charge of the Bank at a time when financial sector reforms continued to gain momentum, leading to a fully market-driven environment marked by greater autonomy in many critical fields, such as product development, pricing, and mobilisation and deployment of resources, and increasing challenges in the area of HR to improve work culture and productivity. The Narasimham Committee Report of 1991 on financial sector reforms gave a further boost to the process of deregulation of the banking sector, making a strong case for reducing the government's role in the management of PSBs. The Indian banking scene witnessed revolutionary changes with the arrival of some private sector banks like HDFC Bank and ICICI Bank, which offered significantly superior services, including anytime–anywhere banking.

These developments put immense pressure on the PSBs, and BoB was no exception. Kannan drew up an ambitious Corporate Strategic Plan (1996–2000), which envisaged doubling of business and a more than five-fold rise in net profit. One of the biggest challenges before the Bank was to prepare to meet the ever-growing competitive pressures and accelerate business growth. The Bank had to improve its work environment and work culture and move towards total computerisation of its branches. To implement this vision, Kannan seemed to rely heavily on his informal relations and goodwill with the workmen's unions and officers' associations, the leaders of which, he believed, would be useful to mobilise the energy of the staff in improving the Bank's business.

Kannan was generally self-righteous and unpredictable and people in the management were cautious about offering any suggestion to him. The lack of team spirit and an environment of mutual suspicion that prevailed at the top at that time could be attributed to Kannan's leadership style.

Unions Back in Business

With Kannan at the helm of the Bank, the unions were back in business. The Association celebrated Kannan's return to the Bank because its general secretary enjoyed a great personal rapport with him. It was common practice for the Association to felicitate CEOs who toed their line and Kannan, after his appointment as CEO, received a warm felicitation from the Association.

As Deputy General Manager (HRM) for about eight months at the corporate office during Kannan's tenure, I witnessed a chaotic environment in which the trade unions (which had maintained a low profile under Talwar) suddenly became active. Many legitimate actions against delinquent staff by the operating managers were resisted and challenged by the unions and finally stayed.

At the operating level, managers experienced intense inter-union rivalry which affected customer service. In the corporate office, we received complaints about instances of indiscipline in the branches, such as lack of punctuality, misbehaviour of staff with customers, union leaders abstaining from work and doing union work during working hours, harassment of officers, and work being left incomplete by the workmen staff.

The General Manager (HRM), Tandon, often ignored such complaints. In extreme cases of indiscipline, he called the union leaders and sought their help to counsel their delinquent members. Similarly, if an issue pertained to the officers, he would take it up with the general secretary of the Association. Instead of taking timely managerial action to arrest indiscipline, patchwork and Band-Aid solutions were offered, giving rise to more violations.

As Deputy General Manager (HRM), I emphasised on the need to take action in a case of serious behavioural misconduct in one of the branches in Mumbai. This case relating to gross misconduct on the part of an employee was referred to corporate office for seeking our permission to suspend the staff concerned. Tandon was quick to counsel me that any action on our part was likely to aggravate union problems, which would displease Kannan. He advised me to call the top leader of the union and sort out the issue. In this case, on my insistence, the union agreed for the shifting of the concerned staff member to another branch and issue caution, although the case called for severe action. The operating managers and personnel managers doused such fires almost on a daily basis. General Manager Tandon wanted us to maintain a low profile and desist from taking any firm stand or advise any tough action to the operating managers for fear of the unions creating bigger problems and inviting Kannan's wrath on the heads of the personnel functionaries.

It was Kannan's style to listen to the unions' biased reports without checking back the facts and criticise the HRM functionaries. The executives in the HRM Department felt demoralised because Kannan would never stand by any firm action. He did not want any IR problems anywhere, and that discouraged the operating managers and personnel executives from initiating any action against erring staff. In April 1995, there was an agitation in the Eastern Zone, in Kolkata, and without getting into any discussion about the problem, Kannan instructed me to go to Kolkata by the next earliest flight. I was totally at a loss in the absence of any briefing about the strategy to be adopted but had to proceed.

The Association Regains Its Influence

The general secretary of the Association took full advantage of his personal relations with Kannan, who seemed to believe that through the Association, he could motivate officers and drive them to go that extra mile. The strategic ploy of the Association was the same as during Shah's time: 'issue circulars to members [the officers] to activate business development, impress the management and leverage on their own power'. The mechanism was to move around the various zones and regions as the new messiah of business development, influence the local management to favour local activists in transfers and placements, and target managers who acted on merit and refused to toe the line and get them transferred, or start agitations. The Association lost no opportunity to demonstrate to Kannan its power and control over the officers. It was like a repeat of Shah's tenure for the Association after the brief interlude under Talwar. As Deputy General Manager (HRM), I observed my immediate boss, Tandon, surrender completely to the Association and do nothing that would even remotely hurt it. Every evening, the Association leader and Tandon had tea together and decided crucial issues such as postings and transfers. The various proposed

HR policy revisions had to be discussed with the Association before being put before the board. This extraordinary influence on the career of even senior executives resulted in considerable dilution of managerial authority at the operating level.

An example clearly brings out Kannan's dependence on the Association: in 1996, the Bank came out with its first public issue. In the first few days, the response to the public issue was tepid. Kannan was worried and instead of galvanising the internal machinery, asked the general secretary of the Association for help thereby abdicating his responsibility. On Kannan's prodding, the leader of the Association travelled from centre to centre to appeal to the officers to ensure the success of the public issue. Finally, thanks to the efforts of everyone, the public issue was successful and Kannan publicly attributed the success to the last-minute help from the Association. Kannan was thus willing to reciprocate and oblige the Association.

The strategy of the Association was to demonstrate that unless it gave the call, the Bank would find it difficult to achieve its targets. In this quest, the general secretary of the Association was invited to the Business Development Committee meetings convened by the corporate office with senior operational functionaries like the zonal and regional managers. He was seated next to CEO Kannan at these meetings and would participate like any other member of the top management, sometimes even berating an operating manager for his poor performance and announcing that the performance was poor because the local association leaders' cooperation had not been sought.

Having attended such conferences as a zonal manager (one of my later roles), it was embarrassing to hear the union leaders hold forth on how to conduct business when it was their own members who were creating problems by resisting transfers and launching agitations. It was also interesting to observe how an apparently unique mechanism of union–management cooperation could be reduced to a sham if it was used to leverage union power!

In its extreme form, union–management cooperation can degenerate into an unethical quid pro quo, as exemplified by CEO Kannan's attempts to induct the general secretary of the Association on the board of the Bank through the backdoor, as a shareholder-director. The government later issued a notification to remove the general secretary from the board because the appointment was found to be irregular and against the norms. This reflected the kind of union–management relationship in which the CEO and the general secretary of the Association unabashedly colluded to run the Bank, weakening in the process both the management and the Association, as later events would show. It may be pertinent to mention here that the general secretary had completed two tenures on the board under the employee director scheme applicable to nationalised banks, so he was not eligible for renomination after two tenures.

Kannan did not seem to be aware of the impact of his favouring the unions as no executive would dare to argue with him about the prevailing culture which originated in his own policies. When the top management shuts its ears and eyes, and lacks the sense to check on the impact of its policies on sensitive issues like IR in the organisational strata below it, especially in hierarchical and geographically dispersed organisations, operating managers devise their own survival strategies through alliances and understandings of their own in order to avoid conflict and ensure peace. Most branch managers reconciled themselves to staff indiscipline, avoided exerting managerial authority, and gave in to union pressures to ignore acts of indiscipline by the staff. In the prevailing inter-union rivalry, this made life very difficult for the managers and officers.

As Deputy General Manager (HRM), I endeavoured to work within the bounds of the rules and regulations and did not go out of my way to favour or maintain any clandestine contacts with the union leaders. Although my immediate boss, Tandon, maintained a low profile and would not respond to complaints by the operating managers for fear of adverse reactions from the unions, I would put my opinion in writing fearlessly. The unions were not happy with me because I did not toe their line. My views on reaching out to employees through employee engagement programmes and developmental interventions were interpreted by the unions as an effort to distract the employees from the unions. My extensive background in the training system and HRD was considered a disqualification by the unions. They did not want anyone in management to reach out directly to the employees. What a paradox—the champions of the employees were restraining the management from reaching out to the employees!

In this scenario, my future appeared uncertain. I knew that my days in the corporate office in Mumbai were numbered. Rumours floated in the air about my next posting and these strengthened my fears further. Soon I was handed over a line assignment as head of banking operations in Meerut, the headquarters of the Western UP Zone. Later, after his retirement in 1999, Kannan confided in me that he had transferred me to banking operations because the unions were targeting me and he wanted to help me by keeping me out of the corporate office.

I had little idea at that time that the Meerut posting would prove to be the biggest blessing of my career. I could not have imagined that my subsequent performance in operations would catapult me to board positions as Executive Director and CEO, positions that would provide me the opportunity to eventually streamline IR in the Bank and empower the managers to manage the workplace without the interference of the unions.

* * *

Once Kannan became CEO of the Bank, IR took an about-turn from the time of S.P. Talwar. Kannan's IR strategy harked back to Talwar's predecessor Shah's time. The unions were back in business with renewed vigour and confidence. There was some degree of commonality in Shah and Kannan's managerial strategies. Both of them isolated the personnel specialists, centralised IR decision-making, gave the unions new visibility, allowed the Association to interfere in transfers, promotions, and placements of executives, and extended new facilities to them like offices at some zonal centres and unlimited travel for the general secretary of the Association. As a quid pro quo, the unions would issue circulars to their members advising them to facilitate efforts in business developments. Members of the unions took such calls by their leader rather casually. Sometimes officers' association held meetings for business development with their members. The management engaged the unions, in particular the Association, in business development by inviting them to zonal managers' business conferences and involving them in the selection of marketing teams for business development. Emboldened by the encouragement received from the CEO, the Association leader would often visit zones/regions and hold rallies of officers, apparently for business development, but such rallies would invariably turn into grievance sessions against the senior operating managers; and in some cases, the

Association leader, through his clout with the CEO, ensured shifting of some operating managers.

Involvement of the officers association may have been initiated with good intentions but it had serious adverse organisational implications. The official visits of the association leader to various regions and zones under the guise of motivating officers for business development had two implications. First, it diluted the authority of the senior operating managers like regional managers and zonal managers in monitoring officers' performance and second, it gave a handle to the association to meddle with the placement of officers, which is a management function. This created confusion in the minds of the senior operating managers. In this system, the association would always take credit, if a particular region/zone performed well and would discredit the operating managers, if the performance was not up to the mark. Thus, the strategy of the CEO to associate the top leadership of the association with business development had proved to be counter-productive in as much as the association leveraged on the opportunity to further the career prospects of their activists, much to the dissatisfaction of the general officer fraternity.

This merged identity of the Association/union with the management became a major source of disconnect between the members and the unions on one hand, and between the top management and the operating managers on the other hand, which made IR more complex and twisted at the operating level.

With this strategy to buy peace, Kannan (who called in sick for most of his tenure) could still achieve business results and managed the public issue of the Bank successfully. The Bank registered better growth than the industry average, and the net profit more than doubled. Also by 2000, the Bank regained its number one position among nationalised banks in terms of global deposits and advances—a position from which it had slipped during 1997–99. The Bank also reduced its non-performing assets and improved its capital adequacy. But while business improved, the housekeeping problems in the branches piled up. Too much alignment and excessive cooperation with the unions can never be without a price for both the management and the trade unions. Moreover, such cooperation is fragile in nature as change in the context and in the leading actors on either side can create extreme hostilities and unstable IR, as we have seen in the earlier chapters.

This period too can be compared to Shah's as a period of 'opportunistic cooperation'. However, in spite of a full tenure of five years, Kannan could not initiate any long-term measures to streamline IR and failed to craft any durable IR strategy, leaving the Bank enmeshed in IR problems at the branch level. Kannan's strategy proved to be just as dysfunctional in meeting the new challenges after liberalisation and led to a major turmoil in union–management relations, as the subsequent events in the Bank reveal.

Part II

FROM RESEARCH TO EXPERIMENTS IN THE FIELD

The chapters in this part cover the period when I moved from the BoB's corporate HRM Department and worked as business head of two geographical zones. These roles provided me first-hand experience about top management strategies in IR and how they played out in the field on a daily basis, as also how they impacted operating managers' efforts to develop new business. The two postings were akin to a nursery where I could test my ideas and all that I had learnt about human processes in management. It was challenging to experiment with new ideas and thought patterns in the ongoing culture of the Bank, as detailed in the last chapter. What was it like to be 'A general manager in the middle'? How does one cope with the corporate culture and create a subculture in the middle and extend it to the lower levels? These line assignments and the experiences gained through them, fraught as they were with tensions and stresses, nevertheless enabled me to look forward with hope and optimism about the potential of human processes (IR and HRD) to create a new future for the Bank.

This section describes my first-hand experience in dealing with IR issues in the field and how the IR strategies and policies of the top management impacted the actual conduct of business on the ground.

Chapter 9

NEW EXPLORATIONS AND INITIATIVES (1995–97)

I was transferred to a line assignment as zonal head of banking operations in western UP at Meerut in August 1995. The politically sensitive state of UP, though largest in the country and having given successive prime ministers, was quite backward on various economic indicators and posed numerous challenges. The working in the banks was besieged by poor work culture and restrictive practices, protected by militant trade unionism, which adversely affected the overall performance of banks in the region.

Although CEO Kannan told me that this line assignment would boost my career prospects, everyone at the Bank, however, seemed to know that the unions had instigated my ouster from the corporate office. The unions did not approve of my focus on HRD, employee engagement, and formalisation of union–management relations, as evidenced by my professional academic writings and my own exhortations at the various banking conferences that I liberally attended. I was considered a sort of heretic in the prevailing corporate environment. Many officers close to the unions told me, informally, about how CEO Kannan had been pressurised by the unions to transfer me from the corporate office. Many of them believed I was being dumped into an operational role as a punishment. All of a sudden, I felt like a stranger in the corporate office in Mumbai. Finally, though reluctantly, I decided to go and take up the operational role. It was a very difficult personal decision, but I decided to take up the challenge.

I truly believed that the management has a basic responsibility to manage the HR side of an enterprise in terms of maintaining the motivation levels of their staff, engaging them, and demonstrating fairness and respect in dealing with them. I did not want to surrender to the existing pattern at the Bank, which mainly revolved around informal understandings with the Federation and the Association to barter the cooperation of their members in exchange for personal favours to the leaders of these organisations. Although I had respect for unions as legitimate organisations whose job was to articulate the collective issues of their members, I was not willing to abandon my own responsibility as a senior management functionary in this area. I believed that HRM cannot be outsourced to employee unions.

As I took my first step into operational banking, I was firm in my belief that it was only through the process of reaching out to branch managers and officers and other employees that I could improve the tempo of business. Both at the corporate office in Mumbai and earlier as a faculty member at the Bank of Baroda Staff College in Ahmedabad, I had often heard about the difficult IR climate at the Bank's branches being cited as the main impediment in conducting business. I now wanted to diagnose the actual situation on the ground and take steps to create a facilitative climate at the branch level for the efficient conduct of business as I believed that business growth was hampered not only by external events but, in a larger measure, by internal factors. My aim in my new posting was to improve the internal environment at the workplace.

I believe that in each role and in each new environment, an executive needs to redefine his role according to the challenges he faces. As a zonal manager, I defined my role as a facilitator and as a problem solver—my goal was to help resolve the branch managers' problems and facilitate an environment in which they could act with confidence and work without constraints in pursuing their business roles.

The state of UP, with over 500 branches, was crucial to the Bank's operations. Two zonal offices, the western and eastern UP zonal offices, headquartered at Meerut and Lucknow respectively, controlled the Bank's business in the state. Of the two, the Western UP Zone was relatively younger, having been established in 1988, and contributed about 5 per cent of BoB's total business. In terms of importance and attention from the top management, it ranked at the bottom, possibly next only to Kolkata. Very rarely did senior executives from the corporate office visit this zone. The Western UP Zone had 198 branches, of which 114 were in rural areas.

The zone managed the operations of its branches through three regional offices, each headed by a regional manager, each of whom supervised around 50–70 branches. Thus, the branches reported to the regional managers, who, in turn, reported to the zonal manager.

Western UP was traditionally considered the rice bowl of the state. Besides rice, the principal crops in the area were sugarcane, potato, and mentha (mint). The area had many rich and prosperous agriculturalists and traders, but very few medium and large industries. The BoB had played a key role in rural development in the six districts of this zone. Its area of operations covered some important districts such as Agra, Bareilly, Nainital, Ghaziabad, and Noida, of which the latter two were part of the National Capital Region (NCR). The Western UP Zone also had two RRBs, one each in Bareilly and Shahjahanpur. On the whole, IR in the zone were by and large satisfactory, except in large branches in some urban centres where discipline, productivity, and customer services were not up to the desirable levels and it affected growth of business. Further, the regional and zonal offices responded in a lukewarm fashion to the problems referred to them by the branches and made no special efforts to improve the climate for business growth.

Getting the Basics Right

I have always believed that in order to set up a plan for/make a plan for improvement, one needs authentic diagnosis of the issues after interacting with people on ground. With this intent, I planned an ambitious travel schedule which included visits to rural/semi-urban and urban branches. Visits to these branches were a great learning experience about the problems faced by them. Visits to some difficult centres in hilly areas of Nainital and Garhwal areas, after travelling sometimes the whole day to reach a particular branch, were, in particular, very emotional as the branch managers concerned broke down after meeting me and shared the misery created by lack of communication and apathy of regional/zonal offices in sitting over their problems. In some cases, I was told that it was the first time that any executive had visited these branches; also, some of these managers had not been able to visit their home town for a long time as no relieving arrangements could be made. I was touched by their plight, caused by their isolation, difficult physical environment, and lack of empathy by administrative offices.

My branch visits were revealing in many ways. Laxity in supervision and lack of responsiveness in responding to their problems on the part of controlling offices were the key issues. Most rural and semi-urban branches that I visited reported problems relating to seating arrangements, lighting and drinking water, and shortage of infrastructure like note-counting machines, calculators, and safe deposit lockers. The branches operated much below their actual potential because of many incompetent persons posted in the branches who daily commuted from district headquarters, where they stayed. On account of these factors, the Bank was not able to seize new business opportunities as most managers remained occupied with day-to-day administrative problems. The regional managers who supervised the branches had a somewhat casual approach to administrative issues. They often soft-pedalled important problems and tried to pass the buck on to the zonal office.

In some cases, the laxity of regional offices was startling. For example, during one field visit to a medium-size branch, I found that a permanent branch manager had been absent from work for several weeks without authorisation. It was common knowledge that he had taken up a job with a customer's firm in Delhi. Despite the regional manager knowing this, he had not initiated any action against the branch manager, nor had he brought the issue to my notice. I was told by many colleagues that under pressure from the officers' association, the regional manager did not initiate any action even on such an issue of gross violation of discipline by a branch manager. Had I not visited the branch, the branch manager would have gone scot-free. This is but one example of the many cases of mal-administration that I discovered during my visits to the branches.

In many cases, I discovered that managers heading the branches were merely passing time and did not contribute to any growth of the branches. They failed to demonstrate exemplary behaviour, leading to deterioration in overall discipline in the branches. Many of such managers and officers managed cushy postings near their home towns with the help of the officers' association and felt assured about immunity from any action. Under the patronage of the Association, some managers took it for granted that they would be conveniently placed and enjoy guaranteed career progression. In my meetings with customers, they reported a restrictive and non-responsive work culture, which led to delays in sorting out their problems. In some cases, managerial apathy was the key issue, with this having a cascading effect on the junior staff such as the clerks. No one wanted to enforce discipline at the branches.

One of the key problems that I also sensed was the ineffectiveness of the branch leadership and this was attributed to the many 'misfits' posted in these positions on the recommendation of the Association. The Association would often get its activists accommodated as branch managers according to their convenience of posting and grab important centres for their candidates, irrespective of their suitability, to give them an edge in undertaking the Association work and networking with other officers in nearby branches. There was an unwritten understanding that the zonal and regional managers would take the zonal secretary of the Association into confidence before posting managers and officers. This was a sensitive issue, but crucial because it directly impacted the business performance of the zone.

Thus, it was evident that in urban branches, their suboptimal performance was mainly due to HR issues. The HR problems and lax administration were not unique to this zone. Operating managers at all the levels in the Bank were generally reluctant to initiate any strong measures to improve productivity and enforce discipline for fear of union problems. Most of them believed that the top management would not support them if a problem arose. Their perceptions were not entirely wrong. The immediate bosses of the branch managers (regional managers) preferred peace in the branches to avoid inviting the ire of the top management, which was the general pattern in the Bank. Everyone wanted to remain on the right side of the unions.

Meerut was my first operational assignment and I was anxious to make it successful. Many among my peers were sceptical about my chances of success due to my lack of operational experience. Notwithstanding my limitations in operational banking, I tried my best to understand the sources of problems that inhibited business growth and made a sincere attempt to resolve them. I believed that the job of a leader is to create a climate for performance and be an aid to managers in helping them achieve their business goals. This is what I did.

One thing was very clear: my nature did not allow me to sleep over the problems. It was not in my genes to be part of the status quo. The choice before me was only about the speed of the change. Changing the prevalent order overnight would have had dysfunctional consequences both for me as well as for the zone. I wished to effect not the change itself but the processes that inhibited growth and unleashing the business potential. Abruptly replacing one system with another does not yield a new order. My approach, therefore, was determined, but diagnostic and persuasive. I believe that it is the methodology of change that delivers the functional or dysfunctional output. I wanted to cause minimum disturbance in the system. I was conscious that, in my case, my obituary in operations could be written prematurely at the slightest turbulence. Therefore, I planned the direction of my change very consciously and diligently.

I believed that to achieve business results and better performance, the management should have complete freedom in choosing the right man for the right job. The convenience of an officer cannot be the sole criterion for his or her placement.

Therefore, in the next placement exercise of the managers, in complete departure from the earlier policy of consulting the Association and with a view to identifying the right person for the right position, I decided to meet eligible candidates and interact with each of them for about half-an-hour with a view to understanding their career highlights, special skills, potential, and aspirations before taking a decision about their placement. Accordingly, we selected 33 managers to be deployed in branches. The above exercise gave me a good idea about each candidate's career background, his achievements, special skills, and personal problems. The process was welcomed by the officers concerned and was hugely satisfying for me. It helped me connect with the officers at both the intellectual and emotional levels. The officers told me that this was the first time in their careers that the management had taken them into confidence and asked them about their expectations and aspirations for their career growth. During this two-way process, many officers volunteered to work anywhere as per the requirements of the Bank. I was amazed at this demonstration of flexibility. It was clear that the officers wanted to connect with the management for their placement preferences and career development. Wherever this was missing, the officers knocked at the door of the Association.

We also relocated non-performing managers to smaller branches to give them another opportunity and removed some of them as managers, placing them as second officers. Such managers were prima facie unsuitable but apparently under the pressure of the officers' association, accommodated.

The Association, however, reacted strongly to the changes initiated by me regarding placement of managers. Notwithstanding the protests, all the officers reported at their respective branches. The Association's efforts to exploit the issue blew up in its face. Due to overwhelming support for the process from the officers' community, the Association could not organise any protest in spite of a call by them for not reporting at the respective branches till the matter was resolved. My faith in human processes was vindicated.

A message was sent to the Association that henceforth, the placement decisions regarding managers' would be taken solely on merit and as per the requirements of the Bank, without any consultations with the Association. It was made clear that the officers and managers were accountable to the management for performance and their career decisions would be guided only by merit. Also, the way in which management authority was re-established, it could not be questioned by any person in the corporate office. My decision regarding placement of managers without consulting the Association, however, created ripples in the Association as this could potentially encourage other zonal managers to also ignore their interference in placement decisions. Clearly, my HR strategy focused on the 'officers' interests' and not on their 'leader's interests', a departure from the overall culture prevailing in the Bank

Improving the IR Climate

My next step was to improve the IR climate in the branches. Again, I avoided any abrupt action because I truly believed that in a situation of accumulated problems, abrupt actions can do more damage, unless, of course, the situation was explosive and called for such an approach. I believed in diagnosing the problem and planning my interventions accordingly. Consistent with my belief, I collected concrete data about the extent of the violations of discipline in some of the major branches, the frequency of the violations, the business growth pattern, customer complaints, and finally, the track record of the delinquent staff concerned. With this data at hand, I commenced discussions with the zonal secretary of the Federation; I shared with him my anxiety about the persistent acts of indiscipline by their members in some branches, giving him evidence of the violations of the rules of conduct. I also shared with him my determination to improve the functioning of the relevant branches and my willingness to give the identified employees an opportunity to reform. It must be said to the credit of the zonal secretary that he took my message very seriously and visited some of the large centres and suitably counselled the members there.

Pursuant to my quest to bring about substantial improvement in the difficult branches in my zone, I chose Agra (famous for the Taj Mahal) for more than one reason: it was a difficult centre from IR perspective; and I had a sentimental attachment to it as Agra happened to be my birthplace. The unions ruled the roost here and the managers were helpless before them. In spite of excellent business potential, the branches in Agra stagnated because the quality of customer service was very poor. I decided to take the bull by its horns. I visited Agra and addressed the staff from all the branches in the city and from those nearby. I shared with them my vision for the zone and unleashing the potential for business growth in the area. I made an emotional appeal to them to engage whole-heartedly in improving business growth. I also mentioned that the prevailing environment of indiscipline and intimidation was not acceptable and the management was prepared to deal with this, if forced to. In the same meeting, the zonal secretary of the Federation called upon the staff to cooperate fully and involve themselves in business growth. The staff were invited to share their concerns. My frank talk was very much appreciated by the officers and managers and conveyed the message, particularly to errant employees. The meeting gave me tremendous satisfaction.

The next day, I visited some key branches in Agra. I found that a branch in a high-potential centre had congested and dirty premises. In spite of good business potential, there was no way a customer would be attracted to the branch. I was informed that the manager and staff have been pleading for change of premises with their regional manager, but without any concrete result. After being convinced about the same, I set a deadline of six months to shift the branch to spacious premises with a modern look, which was accomplished. I inaugurated the new premises and could notice all-round jubilation in our staff and the customers. The staff of the branch felt highly motivated as their working environment had been transformed in a span of just six months. In a staff meeting after the inauguration, I called upon them to ensure that this branch became the showpiece in business growth and customer service. I proposed a memorandum of understanding (MoU) to be signed with the staff for achieving various parameters of business. We signed an MoU with them. It was gratifying to note that the branch not only achieved all the agreed targets but demonstrated a new service culture. Direct engagement with the staff in the problem-solving process can often bring dramatic outcomes. Most of the time, it is managerial apathy that leads to accumulation of hardened attitudes! Also, dealing with IR problems is a precursor to business efficiency.

Encouraged by the Agra experience, I visited other big centres in the zone, such as Bareilly, Ghaziabad, and Noida, and addressed the employees directly, shared my vision for the zone, and sought their engagement in the improvement of business and customer service.

Sensitising Administrative Offices

My extensive visits to the branches, especially in rural areas and far-flung hilly terrains, had given me deep insights about how administrative offices like regional offices or my own zonal office responded to their problems. Delay in response, apathy, vague instructions, lack of empathy, and occasional arrogance, all combined together, was the way administrative offices responded to branches. Their attitude resembled that of controllers who believe that their main job was to lord over the branches. No wonder, most managers ran to officers' association for help and that is how they became power centres. It was the perfect combination of hierarchy and bureaucracy acting in tandem. Commercial organisations could not be run and expected to deliver positive outcomes through this arrangement.

It was clear to me that one of the key reasons for suboptimal action on various parameters by the branches was because they did not receive timely response from various functional heads in regional office and my own office. The frontline managers are the ones who generate business for the Bank and they need quick decisions for customers' issues in business, and also on administrative and HR problems, from their administrative offices. This is why the administrative officers have to be responsive and problem solvers. What bothered me most was that many of these administrative officers had worked in the branches, yet when they came into the administration side, they were sucked into the culture of control and bossing. When functional heads operate as controllers instead of facilitators, the operating units' performance is hampered and the operating managers begin to fight shy of taking the initiative in any matter. This was an important issue for me to work on. We needed a collaborative and trustful relationship between our office and the branches on the one hand, and between our office and the regional offices on the other. We also wanted accountability from the people working in the administrative offices in terms of timely decision-making.

I took several steps to sensitise the staff of the administrative offices (the zonal and regional offices) about the need to accelerate the decision-making process and improve their responsiveness to issues referred by the branches. I have always believed that data is the best evidence to prove a point and I had collected enough of it during my visits to branches. I shared, in a combined meeting of all regional managers and all the departmental heads of regional and zonal office, all the data pointing to delays in response, arrogant way of written communication, and sleeping over small problems of rural branches, like sanctioning a water cooler for customer comfort in extreme heat or sanction of some additional chairs for customers. I also pointed out that I will personally monitor the response mechanism periodically and this would be a key responsibility area of performance for administrative staff. In some cases, I also relocated some inefficient officers from regional and zonal office.

In sum, my main aim was to impress upon our officers that their main role was to create a climate of performance for the branches on proactive basis and efficiently deliver the decisions. In addition, I initiated a system of monthly demi-official letters from key branch managers to me about the progress of business on various parameters, the support they required from my regional office/zonal office, and issues pending with the various departments in administrative offices. All these steps infused a sense of accountability in administrative staff and I had fewer complaints on this count from the branches. These steps also improved the communication between the administrative offices and the branches and created a new opportunity for collaboration and joint problem-solving.

It was because of repeated emphasis on certain core aspects of our working that we were able to bring the culture of accountability in the administration.

With all these measures in place, the branches were now better positioned to seize business opportunities and, overall, there appeared to be better alignment between the field and the administration. The three regional managers also demonstrated a proactive approach to solving the problems of the branches and in promoting efficiency in their own offices and effectively guiding the branches.

Focus on Building Managerial Skills

It was my assessment that while our senior managers were largely committed, they lacked the managerial abilities to operate in the emerging environment. One could not blame them for this because very few of them had had the opportunity for formal training in managerial effectiveness and they had largely focused on acquiring technical skills. Over a period of time, they had progressed in their career and now managed large branches and a sizeable number of staff. To address this issue, I organised a programme on managerial effectiveness for some select branch managers, and called in a leading expert, S. Chandra, former professor of the Administrative Staff College of India in Hyderabad, to lead the programme. The programme was just a baby step to trigger the need for self-improvement in the managers.

Many of these initiatives, such as improving IR climate by engaging employees, listening to the concerns of field managers, consultative process with managers in their placement decisions, and improving responsiveness by cutting bureaucracy and accountability in administrative officers, helped create a new work culture.

Meerut zone, which hardly ever figured in any discussions at the corporate level due to its low-profile business, was suddenly being talked about as it showed fast movement on some business parameters, like mobilisation of savings bank deposits (ranked number one), turning around negative-growth branches, zero arrears in housekeeping position, and crossing targets on priority sector lending. Nothing dramatic, but the zone showed promise to change its staid image.

In the context of the zone's overall performance, I was promoted to General Manager. It was a matter of personal satisfaction that in my first line assignment, I was able to create an impact. Personally, for me, it was a vindication of my philosophy that focusing on human processes was the key driver for business growth. It was also a confirmation of my long-held belief that each manager can take the initiative to transform a messy situation into an orderly one guided by his own commitment to the purpose and by mobilising human effort. The Western UP Zone was my laboratory for experimenting with a new style of managing business, which focused on an organisational development approach that included diagnosis of problems, designing people processes, and implementing a common vision. The fact that I was not a conventional banker helped me in some ways to practise a new style of management that was based on people-focused methodology.

* * *

According to Fred Borch, former CEO, General Electric (as quoted by Uyterhoeven, 1989), the transition from a functional role to general management role is the greatest challenge to one's managerial career. So was it for me in Meerut, which was my maiden foray into the realm of a major field assignment, and I was naturally apprehensive. However, I was determined to give it my best shot. My background in HRD and organisational development helped me to look at the zone as a social system with the avowed objective to serve the different strata of society—individuals, entrepreneurs, businessmen, and so on.

Unlike the conventional banker whose frame of reference centred only around managing opportunities for growth of business, for me, sustainable business development required a level of service culture that remained the centrifugal force to drive the business. I looked at my task as a facilitator, developing a well-oiled and responsive machinery at the controlling office and creating a culture that was conducive to improving service to our customers. In this endeavour, I concentrated on all such factors that contributed to delivery of service, that is, people, processes, systems, and so on. In this quest, I initiated many measures to build a culture of trust between controlling office and the branches, improving the channels of communication, speeding up decision-making, and resolving problems expeditiously. I respected the field-level managers and focused on empowering them. I paid special attention to resolving issues that hindered service delivery, developing motivation by selecting right man for the right job, improving problem-solving mechanism, making decision-makers accountable, improving the quality of our interaction with stakeholders, and above all, introducing innovative HR processes such as town hall meetings with staff members and introduction of signing MoU at the branch level.

My focus on these soft issues delivered business results and created momentum in the zone. Also, my belief in focusing on the drivers of change brought the desired outcomes.

The Meerut experience demonstrates that each leader brings to his role his unique abilities and has an opportunity for improving the existing culture to align the organisation for sustainable growth. It is the career upbringing and professional background that shapes the mental model of a leader. It was my firm belief that by building intangibles like culture and leadership, we create tangible outcomes, which has been vindicated in my subsequent career progression.

With heightened communication with the branch managers and focus on problem-solving and accountability at every level, the zone was able to achieve spectacular business results. My efforts to understand the legitimacy of the trade unions and work with them and simultaneously reach out to employees independent of our relationship with the trade unions were in some ways a departure from the prevailing corporate policy, which sought to only focus on building relationships with key leaders of the unions. We achieved excellent business results without any disruption of work, at the same time maintaining the integrity of managerial actions as well as formal but cordial relations with the unions. In spite of the dominant culture of cultivating the union leaders, the success of this model, which focused on internal process reforms, accountability, and employee development, was an affirmation of my philosophy.

My efforts to integrate IR and HR and get positive business results vindicated my belief that both are organically connected and one does not work to the exclusion of the other. A good IR climate based on a relationship with the union leaders by itself is not adequate unless buttressed by people-centric engagement of the management.

Box 9.1   New Explorations and Initiatives: Learnings from Reflection

1. Senior executives in the middle need to develop their understanding of issues by going around and meeting as many field managers as possible to generate agenda for change and create an enabling environment for business development. Engaging in open and transparent conversations with the field staff about problems can bring about significant insights about the business and can help authorities to initiate appropriate and right actions and enable field staff to excel in their job.

2. Credibility for change comes when leaders accept their own accountability in changing things around them and adopt a hands-on approach in attending to problems.

3. Successful role transition from specialist to generalist can be achieved by constant learning and a spirit of experimentation with new ideas.

4. Within their work domain, the managers and leaders can improve culture, unconstrained by the overall culture of the organisation.

5. Senior operating managers need to take responsibility for IR/HR management to pursue business agenda successfully. Abdication of responsibility on this count can lead to deleterious business results and demotivation of employees. Management of employees cannot be outsourced to trade unions.

6. Pandering to trade union leaders and their dictates dilutes administrative control and is not conducive to the interests of the organisation. Alternative strategies like reaching out to the employees produces effective results.

7. It is important to develop well-oiled machinery in the administrative offices to respond to field concerns with alacrity. Accountability should be fixed on the administrative managers for delays in response and failure to provide timely guidance to operating managers. Administrative offices should act as facilitators instead of as controllers.

8. In situations of accumulated problems, abrupt actions should be avoided unless the situation is explosive and warrants such action.

9. It is important to focus on human processes and drivers of change to achieve positive outcomes.

Chapter 10

DISLODGING THE STATUS QUO (1997–2000)

On my promotion to General Manager in mid-1997, I was offered yet another challenging assignment, this time to head the critical Eastern Zone, which comprised West Bengal, Sikkim, and the north-eastern states. I operated from the Bank's zonal office in Calcutta (renamed as Kolkata in 2001). Kolkata had traditionally been a hostile territory for public service, especially for CEOs and HR professionals. Work stoppages, slowdowns, strikes, agitations, and protest marches were rampant there. The environment of agitation created rampant unionism and an alternate power structure. Kolkata was also the headquarter of three PSBs, namely, Allahabad Bank, United Bank of India, and UCO Bank. All these banks figured in the list of weak banks in the country and one of the major reasons for their subdued business growth was attributed to the prevailing IR climate in these banks. The major trade unions in the banks in Kolkata owed their allegiance to the communist government in the state and pursued militant and obstructive tactics in furthering their agenda.

The BoB's Eastern Zone was full of unionism and union-inspired indiscipline. Intense inter-union rivalry and the general environment of defiance had made severe dents in the Bank's business growth and customer service. This is perhaps why the Bank was slow in expanding its branch network in this zone. Under the patronage of the ruling Marxist government, the trade unions frequently used strikes and gheraos as the main weapon of exercising pressure on the managements. And Kolkata was the epicentre of IR activities in the zone.

The ERC, the majority union of the Bank's workmen in Kolkata, was affiliated to the Marxist-backed BEFI and had a hostile relationship with the Bank's recognised workmen's union, the Federation. Traditionally, the Bank avoided any formal bipartite discussions with the BEFI and dealt with the problems in the Eastern Zone on an ad hoc basis. The Federation had always prevailed upon the Bank not to develop any bipartite relationship with the ERC. This led to a situation where the ERC used the agitation mode and created many new practices in defiance of the all-India agreements with the Federation. For example, a new category of employees called 'canteen boys' emerged in the Eastern Zone to serve tea to employees and visitors. In no other zone of the Bank did such a practice exist. The top management's 'lack of engagement' with the BEFI and its attempts to improve the business environment in Kolkata only worsened the situation.

The IR climate was a prime reason of stagnant business growth for several years. Although Kolkata was a metro centre like Mumbai or Delhi, its performance compared poorly with that of these centres. Customers often complained about poor service and the non-cooperative attitude of front-line staff. The internecine war between various unions often led to go-slow and restricted output. No wonder as many as 26 of the zone's 50-odd metro branches were stagnant. While the average productivity (business per employee) in the Bank was Rs 11 million, the corresponding figure for the zone was just Rs 7 million. In some large branches in the busy hub of Kolkata, productivity per employee was a mere Rs 4 million, obviously due to overstaffing and stagnation in business. On account of prevailing scenario in IR, the Bank did not undertake any further branch expansion in the region and the market share of the Bank was nothing to talk about.

The local unions, on the smallest pretext, created an issue and would engage authorities in endless discussions during working hours, paralysing the customer service. If during exigency, a manager allotted a particular department to a staff member, his union would make an issue as to why member of another union was not given that job. It was a herculean job for the branch managers to run the branch and they often surrendered to trade union pressures. The housekeeping in the branches remained pending with attendant risk of frauds. The hands-off approach of the corporate management made Kolkata an 'amputated leg' in the corporate body of the Bank.

The union culture in Kolkata was totally different from that in Mumbai. As seen in earlier chapters, the Mumbai unions thrived on the favour of the management and could seldom mobilise a worthwhile protest even when they were slighted and sidelined. They compromised members' interests to promote their own self-interest. This had led to a weak connect between them and their members, as revealed by my research. In Kolkata, the trade unions in general and the BEFI-affiliated union in particular, however, always agitated militantly to seek resolution of the grievances of their members and safeguard their interests. The union–member connect was very strong here. The unions nearly always managed to put the management on the wrong foot. In fact, as far back as in 1984–85, the Bank had witnessed a 56-day strike, held to protest against the job rotation of staff—a classic example of the union's militancy and its strong hold on its members.

The complicated IR situation in Kolkata needs to be understood in the context of the management strategy to contain and confine the ERC's militancy to Kolkata and maintain its generally peaceful relations with the Federation by not developing any visible structured relations with the ERC. The Federation strongly resisted the ERC's attempts to seek a structured relationship with the management. Thus, the members of the ERC were not allowed to come to Mumbai for any discussions with the management; all meetings on local issues were held in Kolkata. An unintended consequence of this strategy was that the ERC and the BEFI increased their hostility towards the Bank management by violating the all-India settlements and forcing the local management to extend new facilities beyond the settlements. It was small wonder then that most executives were reluctant to be posted to Kolkata, especially in a position of such responsibility as zonal manager, and postings there were considered to be punishment postings.

It was against this backdrop that I was sent to Kolkata. It was to be the biggest challenge of my professional career, but I truly believed that I could make a difference in Kolkata in view of my understanding of IR issues and my orientation to engage with people issues. My Meerut experience had convinced me that engaging with people issues genuinely and resolving problems can considerably soften the environment and create a climate of trust. I was, however, aware that I was entering a new and difficult territory. As IR was the most important factor that had obfuscated the growth of business in the Eastern Zone, I wanted to engage with it as my first priority. So, I decided to plunge first by diagnosing the issues, with an intent to develop an authentic approach to bring about a transformation in the existing pattern. The problem was so humungous that I had to devote almost 80 per cent of my time to sorting out pending IR issues. After several meetings with the officials of the ERC and the representatives of the Federation and the Coordination Committee (the Bank's other workmen's unions) in the zone, I collected a litany of grievances: structured meetings were not held with the unions; decisions that had been agreed upon were not implemented; policies were implemented discriminatively; personnel decision-making was ad hoc and inconsistent; and working conditions were abysmal, including poorly maintained premises.

While at the corporate office for my research fieldwork, I had myself observed that the top management avoided engaging with the ERC, affiliated to BEFI, and that the problems referred by them were ignored, usually at the behest of the Federation. There was no forum to discuss the problems of a sensitive zone like Kolkata. Often, the ERC had to call an agitation to force the Bank to focus on issues relating to its members. There was a huge trust deficit between the local trade unions and the top management. The source of this underlying, mutual distrust between the local unions and the top management can be traced to multiple factors, such as lack of engagement of the top management with the zone and the absence of any forum for the redressal of the grievances of the aggrieved employees. Added to this was the failure of the management to abide by its own assurances given to the ERC. For example, it had been agreed that General Manager (HRM) from the corporate office would visit Kolkata every six months to meet with the local unions and solve their problems, but he rarely did so unless forced to visit by a call for an agitation by the trade unions. Thus, the credibility of the top management was a big issue. From the perspective of the management, the source of their lack of engagement with Kolkata was an 'agitation culture' adopted by militant unions in Kolkata, unlike their experience elsewhere, where they could manage trade unions and combat their militancy.

Confidence-Building Measures

Against this background, my first priority was to build trust as I was firmly convinced that this was the foundation for any further initiative to improve the climate for business growth. I diagnosed the problems by meeting the leaders of the various unions, the branch managers, and other

officials. In these meetings, I listened to each group carefully and identified the common problems they faced. I learnt, among other things, that
there were issues pending decision at the corporate level, delays in the
sanction of loans to the staff of the zone, non-implementation of decisions
already taken, non-recognition of staff with long service as per the policy
of the Bank, and sports club activities not being held. I realised that it was
important for me to take some quick measures to initiate positive action
on these issues at my discretion. I initially focused on issues affecting the
staff as a group. For example, sports activities (which were suspended due
to inter-union problems) were resumed under the supervision of a neutral
sportsman of repute acceptable to unions and a function was organised to
present silver salver to 200 eligible recipients who had completed 25 years
of service. Also, a schedule of structured meetings with the unions was
drawn up, grievance resolution machinery was honed, and through vigor-
ous follow-up, many pending issues at corporate level were resolved.

I advised T.K.M. Das, Chief Manager (Personnel) of the Eastern Zone,
to attend to individual grievances promptly. I deputed him to the corporate
office in Mumbai to expedite the HR issues referred by the zone and pending for decisions. I also personally followed up on pending staff matters with
the corporate office. For example, I took up with the Executive Director,
P.S. Shenoy, a matter relating to the regularisation of part-time daily wage
workers, which had been a sore point with the unions for a long time.

All these steps went a long way in softening the stance of the unions
in subsequent bipartite discussions. In a difficult IR environment, initiating confidence-building measures prepares the ground for more serious
engagement on critical issues. Symbolic gestures undertaken by one or
both parties often reinforce, or occasionally initiate, the progressive spiral
of trust. The trade unions openly acknowledged their satisfaction with my
initiatives to resolve long-pending issues in the zone.

Business Development Committee

I not only wanted to set up a system of regular interaction with the trade
unions to resolve pending issues but also to engage them collectively in
the developmental agenda for the zone, which had stagnated for a long
period of time. However, one of my biggest challenges was to bring all

the trade unions on a common platform as they had always refused in the past to sit together to protect their ideological identities. They suggested that discussions could be held with each union separately, but I did not agree as that would not have achieved the purpose of building consensus on the developmental agenda of the zone. After about four months of persuasive efforts and my assurance that this forum would not discuss IR issues, the unions finally relented and agreed to participate together to discuss developmental agenda. With the trade unions now willing to trust my intent, I set up a Business Development Committee (BDC), which comprised representatives of all three workmen's unions, the Association, and the management (regional managers and myself). The BDC met once in every two months. With the unions coming on board, I worked on bringing the representatives of the management and the trade unions together to discuss strategies to develop business in the zone. I intensely believed that as locals, they understood the potential of various areas better and could provide useful insights to kick-start the developmental agenda in the zone.

The focus of the BDC was purely on business growth and included issues such as: business development opportunities; issues in customer service and how to improve it; how front line can help service improvement; introduction of technology; how to develop differentiation in service; expansion of branches in potential areas; review of performance on various business issues related to customer service; steps for improving housekeeping in the branches; technology implementation; strategies for turnaround of stagnant and negative-growth branches; and branch expansion by identification of new centres. In these meetings, we also discussed many issues of immediate concern to the management, such as the low productivity of employees in the zone and ways of improving this.

I was quite amazed to see the level of enthusiasm amongst the members of BDC in freely discussing the issues relating to business growth of the zone. The people who earlier could not see eye to eye mingled and spoke with the same fervour in suggesting newer ideas, such as Sunday banking in certain semi-urban centres and expansion of branches in some potential districts. I could clearly see a common concern for improving customer service and front-line service. We often talk of mindset change but fail to design mechanisms to pursue it. The BDC clearly showed that the union leaders, in their discussions and in the background of business data presented, were ready to look at the issues afresh and not from their union lenses.

Opportunity to discuss issues in a trustful environment helped in breaking the impasse on account of stiff attitudes on both the sides and set the stage for sorting out some critical issues which had always been an Achilles heel in moving the zone ahead. I was amazed to see how the union leaders, who were once known only for slogan shouting and leading agitations, participated enthusiastically in the meetings and took an active interest in understanding the problems and finding solutions. They were as concerned about business growth as the management. Gradually, there emerged a unanimous chorus from these meetings about the need to improve customer service and improve the Bank's business through aggressive marketing. The union representatives not only offered support but also made a number of constructive suggestions, which were found to be useful and implemented.

One such critical issue that affected customer service in the branches was staff absenteeism and lack of punctuality. Different practices prevailed in different branches and employees often came late, ranging from 15 minutes to an hour. The general reason cited for the delay was the chaotic traffic in Kolkata city. We raised this issue in a BDC meeting and appointed a task force of the general secretaries of all the unions at the zonal level to study the problem and work out an acceptable solution. The management team explained to the union representatives the consequences of absenteeism and lack of punctuality on customer service. I realised that it was a sensitive issue for the trade unions and was aware that no decision could be taken in a hurry.

After about three months, the task force presented its report to the BDC and, amongst many things, it pointed out with data that about 20 per cent staff came late on a habitual basis. There were views and counter-views to tackle the problem. After much debate, I emphasised that as a service organisation, we should all try to come on time and demonstrate a sense of responsibility. I was aware that consensus mattered in Kolkata more than the majority view. Any small union could derail the process in a multi-union environment. After some postponed meetings, we finally decided through consensus that for six months, the staff would be given a concession of 15 minutes on three occasions in a month; if anyone misused it, the concession would be withdrawn. It was also decided that the concession would be discontinued after six months.

In the circumstances, I think it was a great achievement that we developed a consensus on such a critical issue. We implemented the concession decision immediately and uniformly throughout the Kolkata city branches. A monitoring committee comprising the regional manager and personnel manager oversaw the implementation and all violations were reported for action. It must be said to the credit of all the unions in Kolkata that they stood by their commitment. This greatly contributed to the smooth functioning of the branches.

Gradually, the BDC evolved into a forum which helped to achieve many objectives. An atmosphere of trust was created which in turn contributed to promoting a harmonious environment for business growth. The consensus on issues involving the different unions promoted good-will across cadres. All these resulted in an amicable work climate in the zone. I could clearly experience some degree of mindset change in the key trade union leaders in my subsequent dialogues even on IR matters. Trust building is key in IR and it builds when management invests time and energy in building it. Business pressures and reliance on shortcuts often prevent trust building. Engagement of management in solving critical issues is a precursor to getting employee engagement. It encouraged me personally to engage with the unions and trust them. It also taught me some lessons in building consensus and displaying patience in a difficult situation, which was a great learning as, at a personal level, I was quite task-driven and impatient. This experience provided me new insights about functioning in a real-life difficult environment.

Speaking the Language of Business

The free and frank atmosphere in the BDC meetings centred around growth of the zone, with occasional lamentations by the unions about top management's step-motherly treatment by not undertaking any expansion for a long time. I explained to them that agitational culture, low productivity, lack of computerisation, and overstaffing have been the key factors in preventing any new initiatives and that we will have to be pragmatic in removing these barriers in the interest of progress of the zone. I promised to start branch expansion provided unions agreed to computerisation at least in these new branches and had an open mind for implementing it in other branches. I also prevailed upon them to agree to redeploy surplus staff from surplus branches to these newly opened branches. With heightened level of understanding, the ground was prepared for laying foundation for moving the growth agenda without any protest. We could open branches with computerisation from the very first day, without any additional staff. This was a major breakthrough.

Following this, the unions contributed vitally in helping us to identify growth centres where we could open new branches. These inputs were further discussed with the regional heads and we worked out a commonly agreed upon plan of branch expansion. The BDC developed a blueprint of the growth centres for branch expansion in the zone.

I persuaded the corporate office to allow us to expand the branch network and finally, we opened seven new branches at potential growth centres. The response from the general public in these centres was unbelievable, and in some of them, like Aamtala, Kestopur, and Brahmapur, we garnered deposits ranging from Rs 100 million to Rs 150 million in the opening week. All the BDC members were invited for the openings and I was amazed to see the enthusiasm, both among the union leaders and the employees.

The rush for opening new accounts on the first few days was so phenomenal that we had to erect canopies in front of the branch premises to accommodate the customers and also send in staff from the administrative offices to cope with the workload. Even the union leaders jumped into the ring and counted cash and participated in the account-opening activities.

This enthused the staff and unions alike, and we channelised this enthusiasm by involving the union leaders in more business-related activities by inviting them to speak to the employees in various forums. For the first time probably in the history of the Eastern Zone, all the trade unions addressed the employees at various meetings, forums, or through their circulars, and asked them for their whole-hearted support and involvement in business development.

The level of enthusiasm amongst the union leaders in the BDC meetings was great and on their suggestion, we started Sunday banking facility at our branch in Barasat, a Kolkata suburb, which received an overwhelming response from the local population. Similarly, the BDC identified the need for a specialised housing finance branch to cater to the housing loan requirements of the fast-increasing middle-class clientele. This led to BoB opening a specialised housing finance branch in Kolkata, which did brisk business.

In various meetings of the BDC, the unions gave a number of suggestions about improving the productivity, marketing and customer service, and issues related to business development. Some of the suggestions were as follows:

1. The idea of working in shifts should be explored in some branches in the business district to meet the special needs of the traders.
2. The various deposit schemes of the banks should be prominently displayed in a central area of the banking hall.
3. A database should be created on segment-wise customers.
4. Branches in residential areas could start operations from 9.00 a.m.
5. Marketing teams, including employees, should be formed at the branch level.
6. A 'customer meet' system should be introduced, and a cluster of customer meets can be organised for a cluster of branches.
7. Union leaders with first-hand knowledge of customer problems should be invited to the customer meets.
8. Attendance and punctuality must be improved.
9. A study should be carried out to diagnose the problems of branches with low productivity levels and branch-wise action plans developed to achieve a turnaround.
10. Redeployment of staff should be considered (suggested by some unions).
11. The Bank could open more branches in the developing centres.
12. Regular staff meetings should be held at the branch level to discuss business-related issues.
13. Steps must be taken to loosen the grip of fear to facilitate decision-making in the sphere of credit.
14. The image of the Bank should be improved through renovation and better upkeep of the premises.
15. Participation in fairs in rural centres should be encouraged.
16. There is a need to improve liason with government officials.

We took each of these suggestions made by the unions in the BDC very seriously and undertook steps such as renovation of premises, opening of new branches, improving interface with customers, and organising regular staff meetings. In fact, the zone undertook to renovate the premises of 40 branches and 14 branches were air-conditioned.

The regular meetings of the BDC helped build trust between the management and the unions on the one hand, and among the unions themselves, on the other. Branch managers reported fewer cases of inter-union rivalry and staff indiscipline. The management was able to focus on the turnaround of negative-growth branches; and for the first time, it appeared that the zone could move forward to seize new business opportunities. As per the decisions in the BDC, more and more branches were opened.

This experience of joint problem-solving helped to open new vistas for taking forward the dialogue on more serious problems afflicting the operations, like job rotation of staff from one branch to other and computerisation of branches.

This meeting of minds from different constituencies helped in discussing issues in an uninhibited manner and in taking steps for reforming workplace IR.

Implementing Job Rotation

In an environment of trust, many contentious issues can be resolved and the BDC gave me that confidence. In union–management relations, personal credibility of 'Actors' on both sides is very critical in achieving desired changes. I was confident that as long as my personal credibility was not doubted and I was not considered to be 'crafty' or 'exploitative', the unions in this communist territory would be willing to engage in sorting out the more serious issues. They had by now experienced my relentless pursuance of the corporate office to resolve outstanding problems, in particular the absorption of daily wage workers in the regular cadre, and my quest to improve the problem-solving process.

An issue that had generated intense resistance in the past, including a 56-day strike in the branches, was the issue of job rotation of staff from one branch to another. While this was a policy that had been implemented across the Bank's branches in the country, it faced severe resistance from unions of all hues in Kolkata. In the environment of doubt and suspicion that had existed earlier, the unions suspected that the job rotation would be used to divide the union movement by shifting staff as per the management's whims and they felt it could be used as a reward and punishment strategy. One senior ERC functionary told me, 'the majority union at the bank level (the Federation) could in connivance with the management use this opportunity to punish our members and create cracks in our union.'

With relations with the unions easing on a daily basis, I now felt confident enough to bring the issue of job rotation to the discussion table. Accordingly, I had a couple of sessions with the different trade unions and finally, a combined session with all of them. I listened to them with great attention and told them that I looked on job rotation as a developmental intervention, rather than an instrument of punishment. I appealed to them that in the changing banking scenario, it was important for bank employees to work on different desks and different types of branches—large, small, and specialised. This was necessary for their own career growth and motivation. In order to allay suspicions and build consensus, I suggested that we form a task force under the Chief of HR at the zonal level, Das, which would have representatives from all three unions. The job of the task force was to come out with norms of job rotation that would ensure that no discrimination was practised at any level in implementing the scheme both within the branches and outside the branches. My suggestion was accepted by all three unions and I was happy to find that the task force worked out criteria for job rotation that were quite similar to those the management had visualised. After some rounds of discussions, we were able to rotate more than 600 employees in the branches in Kolkata without any problems. This too was a breakthrough of sorts. Our success in implementing job rotation caught the attention of the corporate office, which generally was oblivious to the initiatives in Kolkata.

On account of the fact that we consistently worked with the trade unions on many contentious issues and solving many outstanding problems, the IR tensions in the Eastern Zone were considerably reduced and the process of business growth and development picked up. Kolkata emphatically demonstrated that if you genuinely engage with trade unions and employees and involve them in problem-solving, you can establish enduring peace. Common wisdom suggests that difficult situations require more attention and engagement by the management. The pity was that there had been a total absence of managerial initiatives, both at the corporate level and the zonal level, to deal with the problems in Kolkata.

While corporate-level support is crucial and sometimes a precondition for pursuing change at the local level, more so in a hierarchical PSB, my own experience demonstrated that the local change agent has to demonstrate initiative and passion in pursuing change.

Improving Managerial Effectiveness

Not all of Kolkata's problems could be attributed to the trade unions. I could sense that the managers' motivation and competency were as big a problem. Working under union pressure with hardly any recognition for their pains and stress had taken a toll on their motivation, and this could be seen in their performance. There was no fire in the belly that demonstrated any proactive initiative in engaging with problem-solving or in canvassing new business. The daily frustrations of dealing with employee issues and handling militant trade union representatives seemed to have demoralised the managerial workforce. Against this background, some of the recent steps, such as the implementation of the job rotation plan and the improved system of attendance, had considerably improved the work environment. It was also perhaps the first time in several years that a good number of managers were promoted by the higher management on my recommendation, thanks to the changed perceptions of the Eastern Zone. Cumulatively, these developments created a better environment for focusing on business growth. But it was still my firm belief that many gains could be sustained in the new environment only when our managerial staff were exposed to new orientation in managerial effectiveness and continuously improved their skill sets, especially in credit area.

The time seemed just right for building managerial talent and grooming our managers. We took the help of IIM Kolkata and arranged a programme on managerial effectiveness for the branch heads of the key branches in the zone at the IIM's Centre for Human Values. The programme focused on improving self-awareness, interpersonal relations, and leadership skills. The three-day programme was well received by all the participants; and it made a positive impact on their overall functioning, which was evident from their work.

We experienced a new zeal in our branch heads to take initiatives in developing business. Softening of IR environment in the branches was a major factor in seeing a new enthusiasm among many Kolkata managers. Some of them took the initiative to hold meetings with the staff. The staff which was earlier divided on their union affiliations now responded as staff members to discuss the growth prospects of their branches.

Many business-related problems were discussed at administrative offices, with managers and their bosses brainstorming on the issues of extricating their branches from housekeeping problems, mobilisation of low-cost deposits, and turning around stagnant branches. Some task forces were formed with officers of the branches and administrative offices on key issues. All these initiatives helped creating a new culture of working together and creating harmony between branches and administrative offices.

The effects of these efforts percolated to the level of branches too. These managers, on their part, worked towards changing the work culture to one based on mutual trust and respect. Periodic meetings were organised at which the staff members were encouraged to contribute their ideas for business development. At the level of the controlling offices, bi-monthly meetings were held to track the progress of the branches and remove the impediments to their growth, while building consensus on plans and programmes.

Small groups of officers from the controlling offices and the branches were formed, mandated to discuss and suggest plan of action in respect of critical issues like reduction of non-performing assets, mobilisation of low-cost deposits, and turn-around of stagnant branches, among others. These groups produced good results in the identified areas.

Considerable emphasis was laid on training of officers on key areas of branch functioning, especially credit. With a view to improving both the quality and magnitude of the credit portfolio, I organised specific programmes at Kolkata by inviting faculty members from our Staff College at Ahmedabad. This way, we could impart training to a larger number of officers as compared to nominating a limited number to the training establishment and succeeded in having a bigger pool of trained credit officers, well equipped to manage this crucial area of working of the Bank.

With a view to bringing about attitudinal change in the front line to make them sensitive towards customers and their own peers, I invited Kakoli Saha, a behavioural science trainer at the Staff College, Ahmedabad, who conducted a number of programmes, titled 'Growing Together', for the front-line staff. The programme was based on experiential learning and was appreciated by the participants. Those who attended the programme appreciated the insight it provided them on their own attitudes and behaviour. Some branch managers confirmed to me that there was considerable change in the attitude of the staff who attended the programme. Several multi-level programmes were conducted on marketing and customer service. All these programmes brought about a new perspective in the front line towards customer service.

Effective Communication

It is never enough to only take trade unions or their leaders on board. My research revealed as to how focusing on unions or their leaders is important, but not enough. No management can abdicate its responsibility in reaching out to employees in general, and foot soldiers in particular.

I wanted that employees of the zone should understand the problems of stagnancy and how it affects everyone. I was keen that they should be partners in change and prime movers in changing the image of the Bank. I made a special effort to reach out to them and have face-to-face conversations on some of the critical issues, and also take inputs while designing our policies. My own assessment after visiting many branches was that there were suboptimal conversations between the managers and employees about the customer service issues. Trade unions always had smarter communication and engagement with members than the management. We needed to connect with the employees directly and engage them.

Improving Internal Communication

Considering that the average person in West Bengal is intellectually inclined and is more articulate with his/her opinions/views, I conceived the idea of bringing out an internal newsletter for the zone to improve communication with our employees. It would highlight the trends in business,

list the recent happenings, and discuss important developments or challenges faced by the zone or the Bank.

With this in mind, a small team of officers in my office and I worked on
bringing out an eight-page quarterly publication titled, *The Eastern Spirit*. I
sought the then CEO Kannan's introductory message for the first issue. In
the very first issue, in my message, I mentioned about the great traditions
of eastern India philosophers and social workers, like Vivekanand, Mother
Teresa, and Rabindranath Tagore (all icons of Bengal), to serve the society,
which defined the spirit of the region. The very first issue had a blockbuster
impact. It caught the attention of intellectually and culturally inclined average employee in this part of India.

The Eastern Spirit soon became so popular among the staff that we
received requests to make it into a monthly newsletter. Time constraints
unfortunately prevented this, but *The Eastern Spirit* remained an eagerly
awaited publication by the employees. All the unions in the zone welcomed
the starting of this publication and advised their members to enhance the
standard of customer service.

Simultaneous to this effort, we also took several steps to improve our
connect with the customers and organised interface sessions between
them and our front-line managers.

Role of the Corporate Office

Even though Kolkata was the epicentre of our numerous initiatives, the
results could be experienced even at the other centres in the zone as
reflected by the improved business levels and smooth industrial relations
climate. The changed perception of the staff and unions indeed contributed significantly to this. But the corporate management did not use this
opportunity to demonstrate its commitment for long-term change. It generally appreciated my handling of IR in Kolkata, but never discussed any
game plan to build on what we had achieved or any long-term IR strategy
based on my experience.

The overall environment in the Bank was that of mollycoddling the
Federation and the Association, with little thought to working out a
strategy to engage with the BEFI on a long-term basis. Although, by and
large, the corporate office did not meddle with my efforts, occasional

interference was experienced under the instigation of the Association. In one instance, after the visit of the general secretary of the Association to Kolkata, I received transfer orders for two of my executives from Kolkata to Mumbai. Apparently, the transfer orders were issued by the corporate office under the instigation of the general secretary. It was well known that these two executives were not in the good books of the Association because they acted with complete neutrality and did not oblige the local leaders of the Association. I immediately took up the matter with CEO Kannan, arguing for cancellation of these transfers as these executives were basically competent and contributed a great deal to pushing forward change despite the many odds. Obviously, the effort of the general secretary was to weaken my authority and demonstrate that he called the shots. After my lengthy communication to Kannan about the contribution of these executives to the ongoing process of change in the zone, I managed to stall their transfers. Although Kolkata was mostly left on its own, such occasional turbulences disturbed peace of my mind.

During this time (see Chapter 8, 'Trade Unions Rule the Roost (1990–2000)'), the Association's hold on the top management remained very strong and its leaders used it to build relations with executives at different levels and to influence transfer and promotion decisions. The Association leader also cultivated General Manager (HRM), J.N. Tandon, who shared all important and strategic information with him. The Association leader remained the main carrier of information on transfers and promotions. A case will illustrate this point. One morning, I received a phone call at 7.00 a.m. from my Regional Manager, M.L. Rathi, to tell me that he had been promoted to the deputy general manager cadre. On enquiry, he informed me that he had received a phone call from the general secretary of the Association about his promotion. As the General Manager of the zone, I had not known about Rathi's promotion officially. No one from the corporate office had informed me about the promotion of a senior executive who reported directly to me. This is how the Association built relationships with the senior executives and used the relationships to increase their hold on the executives. This is also an example of how the Association leveraged career information of senior executives to maintain their hold over them.

My research findings confirmed my belief that the Association leaders built their empire by taking an interest in the career decisions of the executives. They made sure that they came to know about such decisions earlier than other members of the senior management and used the information to leverage their power. This is how the system operated during the tenure of CEO Kannan.

Business Outcomes

Many initiatives undertaken to build trust and credibility created a facilitative climate for performance. In the very first year, the zone leapfrogged into dramatic growth in various key parameters of business. For example, it achieved 31 per cent growth rate in savings bank deposits, 30 per cent growth rate in current account, and 22 per cent growth in core deposits, which was an all-time high in the zone's history; and this performance was symbolic of the zone's potential to improve further. The zone broke from its past stagnancy and showed movement. During my tenure of three years, the total business increased from Rs 19.86 billion to Rs 31.45 billion, and credit increased from Rs 6.37 billion to Rs 9.05 billion during my tenure of three years from March 1997 to March 2000, thereby shaking off the stigma of stagnation which had hung over the zone for quite some time. The zone doubled its savings bank portfolio in these three years and even registered the highest growth in savings bank deposits in the entire bank in 2000. The number of branches in arrears of housekeeping was brought down from 38 to just three. Eighteen of 22 negative-growth branches were now positive and had joined the growth trajectory.

Resolution of outstanding problems through engaged attention and problem-solving methodology considerably softened the environment, and from the management perspective, it was a breakthrough in union–management relations in Kolkata that had looked impossible sitting in the corporate office in Mumbai. With the logjam on critical issues such as job rotation, computerisation, and indiscipline being sorted out with consultations with all the unions, Kolkata looked poised for growth.

* * *

After my first experience in Meerut, Kolkata provided a still bigger challenge in terms of prevailing IR climate, a long-standing adversarial relationship of the unions in Kolkata with the top management, and a kind of stalemate that affected the business in this territory. While I had no specific mandate from the management, I had expectations from myself. It was going to be the biggest challenge of my professional career where responsibility exceeded authority. I was to be a player and a coach combined (Uyterhoeven, 1989), similar to that of any 'General Manager in the Middle'. The only difference was that here in this role, the playing field was difficult and uneven. I had the challenging task of nurturing a new paradigm of relationships with trade unions, the line managers, and general employees.

Kolkata, however, turned out to be a school of new learning and experimentation, which provided me new insights about the behaviour of collectives affiliated to the Left parties and how to engage with them. Part of the challenge in Kolkata was to deal with the BEFI and AIBEA-affiliated unions, which competed with one other to develop members' loyalty, resulting in daily on-the-job skirmishes in matters such as work allotment, punctuality, attendance, and levels of output. Strong union–member connect in Kolkata, unlike in the rest of India, manifested itself in the daily protests by the unions in some of the branches at the slightest exercise of authority by the managers, which complicated IR management.

The environment in the branches had to improve if business was to be restored to healthy levels. In spite of many challenges and the absence of a clear mandate from the top management to confront the key issues of non-implementation of computerisation and many other guidelines, my strategy was one of persistence in pursuing reform of the workplace by continuous dialogue with the unions, listening to their concerns, and sharing data about instances of indiscipline and restrictive practices by their members. For the first time, management issues were highlighted in both structured as well as informal meetings with the trade unions. It made the unions seriously reflect on and engage with the management on such issues.

Multiple initiatives, such as the creation of the BDC—a joint forum of the representatives all the unions and the management—to discuss business development issues, resolution of some long-standing IR issues, training of both managers and front-line employees, and image-building measures for the zone, all helped remove the logjam in the union–management relationship and paved the way for improvement in the overall climate of performance in the workplace. Discussions and dialogues on key issues replaced the culture of protest to a great degree. The new trustful environment helped us to implement job rotation (which had been pending for a long time) and computerisation (which had been fiercely resisted earlier) and enforce strict norms for attendance and punctuality (a major issue that had hindered customer service).

The experience taught as to how an environment of deep mistrust can be converted into one of trust using only the weapons of authenticity and candour. Although Kolkata posed a challenge in terms of complexity of IR, alienated unions and employees, and a moribund business situation, trust building was a key aspect of our strategy with the unions and employees. Our focus with the staff was on improved direct communication, competency building, and a humanistic orientation to their problems. Besides, our relentless engagement with the trade unions and with the employees simultaneously improved the business climate and the zone delivered improved performance on all business parameters.

Kolkata also provided me with new insights in developing IR strategy. Each area of operation provided a new context and challenges that were not always amenable to treatment under the overall policy framework and sometimes even required out-of-the-box thinking. I also learnt that in an IR-sensitive zone, organisations need a different breed of senior management staff who can engage with unions and staff as a matter of faith. Throughout my Kolkata experience, the corporate office never gave me any brief or promise of support in my endeavours. If I took initiatives to improve IR, they were purely my personal initiatives and the risks were entirely mine. The unwritten message was that as long as you do not create problems for the corporate office, it will not interfere in your working. This confirmed the understanding I had developed during the fieldwork for my doctoral research, wherein I had observed that most regional managers and zonal managers did not take any initiative in improving the IR situation in the Bank for fear of lack of support from the top management. However, our initiatives in engaging with the trade unions in Kolkata in a militant multi-union environment opened new hope for conducting IR with engaged dialogues and understanding. This helped Eastern Zone in general, and Kolkata in particular, to witness fructification of new initiatives, such as expansion of branches, computerisation, customer-centric initiatives, and improvement in workplace discipline and productivity.

It is personally gratifying that despite initial apathy towards my initiatives, the palpable change in IR situation in Kolkata brought accolades from the CEO himself. During his visit to Kolkata in late 1999, he was startled to find unions of all ideologies coming together on the same dias to felicitate him. He shared that this was something he had always wished and openly acknowledged his happiness with the new spirit of cooperation and trust in union–management relations in Kolkata. Later, I was told by my peers at the central office that the CEO always quoted Kolkata spirit and how he felt inspired by this new winds of change.

There is always a temptation to attribute our lack of initiatives or shortcomings to an absence of enabling environment. In case of organisations, such a thinking is generally widely prevalent. In our own context, lack of top management support in improving IR was widely cited by line managers as a major impediment in improving the existing pattern. In some cases, it was also used as an alibi for not taking any initiatives. My own experience, both in Meerut and in Kolkata, convinced me that while the support of the higher management was important for a line manager to facilitate change, absence of the same by itself cannot be the only reason for lack of initiative. In many situations, positive action for change in the workplace can also enthuse the senior and top management to lend their support. Even in the most difficult situations, like initiating steps to maintain workplace discipline, I undertook many modest initiatives to lend support to my line managers and engage with them in the problem-solving process. Together, we could enter into a new era of mutual trust and pilot many reforms that improved discipline, customer service, and eventually business in the branches. I have a feeling that Kolkata was a typical case of Pygmalion effect.[1] During 1997–2000, we were able to break the trap

---

[1] The Pygmalion effect refers to the phenomenon that the greater the expectation placed upon people, the better they perform. The effect is named after Pygmalion, a Cypriot sculptor, in a narrative by Ovid in Greek mythology, who falls in love with a female statue he has carved out of ivory. The Pygmalion effect is a form of self-fulfilling prophecy and in this respect, people with poor expectations internalise their negative label and those with positive labels succeed accordingly.

of this effect by successfully working out an agenda of change and implementing it, with encouraging results.

My experiences at Meerut and Kolkata strengthened my belief that good IR can be built on the edifice of trust and credible management initiatives. Short-term strategies to buy peace by pampering the unions would be fragile and fraught with the risk of alienating the employees. My initiatives and experience clearly suggest that a durable and sustained system of IR can only be built on the foundation of employee engagement and HRD and not relying on buying the cooperation of the trade unions alone. Kolkata, in many ways, taught me many leadership lessons which helped me in my journey ahead. It also provided me a major breakthrough in my career.

I had no idea that I would soon have the opportunity to weave my beliefs and convictions for architecting a system of IR in my future roles at the BoB.

Box 10.1 Dislodging the Status Quo: Learnings from Reflection

1. Senior managers in the middle can bring about significant positive changes in union–management relationship in their area of operation. Support of top is not always a prerequisite unless, as a result of one's initiatives, major disruptions are expected. Feeling comfortable with inaction and avoiding criticism cannot be our measure of success. Line managers and managers in the middle can be source of 'Reverse Inspiration'. The process of inspiring can be hierarchy neutral.

2. Creative problem-solving is at the core of managerial work, which requires diagnosis of the context as also a deep emotional and intellectual engagement of the leadership in the middle.

3. The most difficult union–management situations require relentless efforts in building trust and credibility by the management through engaged dialogues and problem-solving. Dramatic results can be achieved with patience and resilience, irrespective of the overall culture in the organisations.

4. Personal credibility and sincerity of efforts of the leader is a prerequisite in initiating any efforts for change and transformation.

5. In a situation of legacy-driven culture and deep mistrust in union–management relations, the leaders have to take a number of confidence-building steps, as also experiment with innovative mechanism, to break the logjam and seek unions' involvement in the issues germane to business growth of the bank.

6. Even in a highly unionised environment, the leaders cannot abandon their responsibility to motivate and develop employees through effective communication, grievance-handling mechanism, and training. Trade unions are not a substitute to employees, each requiring different treatment.
7. In situations of alienation of employees, the critical role of leaders is to boost their morale and raise their aspirations.
8. Difficult situations in IR require engaged attention and relentless effort of management to sort out issues and reach broad consensus on key issues.

Part III

TOWARDS A NEW PARADIGM

This section deals with my experience in two strategic roles at the board level with the BoB: first, as Executive Director; and later, as the CEO. My experience in the field in Meerut and Kolkata had given me enough insights into many dimensions of the actual operation of IR and their impact on customer service and business development. As head of the Western UP and Eastern Zones, I had experienced the constraints of improving staff productivity and customer service amidst internecine conflict between the trade unions at BoB and their potential to disrupt service whenever any managerial action was taken. Worse still, I had experienced the apathy of the management at the top, which had remained oblivious to the constraints we at the operating level faced and pandered to the workmen's and officers' unions. Despite these constraints, I had managed to not just survive but actually transform the existing situation through a process of personal engagement and by taking modest risks in undertaking changes. I now had a better sense of IR reality and a deepening awareness that the Bank needed to be extricated from the guerrilla-like warfare that took place at the operating level.

In my role as executive director, I initiated changes in the course of IR management in the Bank with a view to empowering the operating managers to do their jobs without fear. It meant the creative destruction of the legacy IR and initiation of a system of formalisation that clearly defined the domains of the unions. In spite of resistance from the unions, we could transform the pattern of IR at the Bank through a number of major reforms and by restoring institutional mechanisms for union–management relations. In my subsequent role as CEO, we accelerated the process of reforms, mainly focusing on employee engagement, new capability building, and fair and transparent mechanisms for problem-solving, thereby moving from union leader-focused IR strategies to employee-focused ones. This part examines the stresses and tensions inherent to regaining control of the personnel and IR functions. The changes brought about in IR, with their focus on empowering the operating managers and engaging the employees and developing them professionally, proved to be a game changer in terms of efficient conduct of business and helped the Bank achieve enviable stature among its peers in the industry.

Chapter 11

REFORMING IR

My efforts as zonal manager in Kolkata, especially in implementing computerisation and job rotation and enforcing punctuality in attendance, were a subject of discussion amongst the managements of various banks. I was promoted to board-level position by the government in September 2000 and posted as Executive Director in BoB.

During this period, P.S. Shenoy was the CEO. A career banker who had earlier worked in Bank of India, he joined BoB as Executive Director in the year 1998 and was elevated as CEO in May 2000 after Kannan's retirement. Shenoy, a robust banker with more than three decades of banking experience was, however, a status quoist and somewhat bureaucratic in his approach to issues and problems. He was also known to be conservative and generally averse to taking risks. At a time when competition was hotting up in Indian banking and change, especially the introduction of new technology, was the key priority, BoB needed to transform itself in many areas if it was to hold on to its number one position in the nationalised bank sector.

After being appointed Executive Director, however, my immediate anxiety was about how I would cope with my new professional role. I had the immediate task of developing some understanding, if not expertise, of the hard-core areas of banking, such as corporate credit, treasury, and the working of the board, to which I had no prior exposure. It would be accurate to say that I found my new role daunting. But despite these challenges, I was determined to make a difference in the conduct of IR in the Bank by initiating reforms, including clearly redefining the role of the unions, reducing their interference in 'management matters', and moving towards a more formalised IR structure. I was aware that the road ahead was bumpy, but I was determined to give it my best shot. As a member of the top management team, and because I was known to be an HR specialist, people in the lower echelons, especially the thousands of operating managers, expected me to change the existing culture of IR which was severely constraining the conduct of business at the Bank. The operating managers were fed up with the daily IR problems at the workplace and the unethical compromises they were forced into because they could not be sure of support from the top management. My field research had also thrown up similar revelations from the branch heads and senior operating managers. As a full-time board member, I felt it was my duty as a leader to design and pilot changes in IR that were long overdue and that would pave the way for more constructive change in the new, more competitive environment.

Around the beginning of 2000, banks faced myriad challenges on account of technologically driven, new private sector banks such as ICICI Bank and HDFC Bank. The migration of customers from PSBs to these private banks was rapid, and BoB was no exception. As a progressive bank, it had to quickly adopt technology and reorient itself to serve these new-age customers. This would require a complete change in the product design of its offerings, extended hours of service, and moving to a new technological platform that would enable it to offer 'anytime–anywhere' banking.

Given the existing culture in the Bank and the pampered unions who saw change and transformation as opportunities to claim their pound of flesh, it was difficult to even think of piloting change. If we had to seek the assent of the unions at every stage of the transformation process, change would not happen. The alternative was to take charge of the situation and vigorously pursue the changes we needed so urgently to effect. But in order to do that, the management had to be very clear of the direction in which it wanted to take the Bank and stand unitedly together to take it there.

CEO Shenoy did not carry any baggage from the past and he did not demonstrate any intention of handling IR matters in the way his immediate predecessor Kannan had, at least initially. While he did not display any leanings towards the unions and the Association, he did not want to rock the boat. He gave the impression that he wanted 'change without pain'. As long as he did not pursue a collusive–collaborative relationship with the unions like A.C. Shah and Kannan, some of us in the management were committed to bringing about significant changes in our policy towards the unions.

An important initiative by the government in 2001 gave us an opportunity to experiment with our new approach in dealing with important employment-related issues. This initiative was the voluntary retirement scheme (VRS) for employees of PSBs, and its time-bound implementation provided an important context for change in management policy to plan, design, and implement a new HR policy. The government gave broad guidelines for designing the VRS. The Bank took on the task of designing the VRS and implementing it within the parameters of government policy. It was a challenging task, given the resistance it faced from the trade unions.

The initiative had major HR implications. CEO Shenoy specifically asked me to guide the HR functionaries in implementing the VRS in the Bank. The work involved undertaking a manpower planning exercise, identifying surpluses and shortages, explaining the rationale of the scheme to the employees, dealing with the anxiety of the trade unions, disposing off promptly the pending vigilance cases against those who sought voluntary retirement, and finally, dealing with the anxieties of senior functionaries in the management with regard to expected gaps as many senior staff intended to avail of the VRS. The management also had its apprehensions about IR consequences. We commenced discussions with our trade unions and impressed upon them to be pragmatic and accept the scheme with grace. Although both officers' association and workmen unions were opposed to the VRS, they were aware that many senior staff wanted to opt for the scheme. We discussed with them the staff deployment post VRS and assured them that maximum staff will be deployed in the branches even if it needed pruning of administrative offices.

For about three months, I was intensely involved in this exercise, coordinating within the Bank, with the government, and with the IBA. Finally, we implemented the scheme successfully, with 6,521 staff members opting for the VRS. This included 3,094 officers and 3,427 workmen staff. The total outgo over a period of five years was Rs 6,500 million. In fact, BoB was the first bank to implement the VRS and its success emboldened other banks to follow suit.

Once the VRS had been implemented, the Bank faced immense problems from its operating units on account of mismatch of staff positions in various regions and branches and many staff members were relocated to address these problems. There were also special problems with regard to relocation of workmen staff, as the industry-level settlement governing their service conditions restricted their transfer to within a certain distance limit. Post VRS, we also became aware of our weaknesses in the manpower planning process. Accordingly, we planned new initiatives to build competencies to fill the gaps in various functions.

A Mini Reorganisation

Given the acute shortage of manpower in the branches post VRS, it was imperative for the Bank to undertake a reorganisation of its administrative structure (Figure 11.1) to ensure leaner administrative offices, more so when there was duplication of work between the regional and zonal offices. However, the period immediately after the VRS implementation was not considered by the management to be the right time to undertake such a major reorganisation because it would affect the smooth running of the Bank's operations. Therefore, a mini reorganisation of the administrative units was undertaken internally, which essentially involved truncating

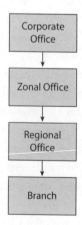

FIGURE 11.1   The BoB's Four-tier Administrative Structure

the zonal offices and enlarging the area of operations of regional offices by empowering the senior management in these offices. This led to a reduction in the number of regional offices from 59 to 44. Around half of the staff in the zonal offices was reduced by closing down departments that duplicated the work of the regional offices.

The regional offices were empowered for decision-making by providing them with an executive at the level of assistant general manager as their head and creating a new position of deputy regional manager to provide support. An elaborate checklist of activities to be undertaken by the zonal and regional offices was developed to create role clarity in the new set-up.

Notwithstanding the many problems faced both internally as well as from vested interests like trade unions and local politicians, the Bank was able to successfully truncate its zonal offices and close down 15 regional offices, thereby making available surplus staff that could be redeployed in branches. Besides this, officers from corporate office were also relocated to branches. This helped strengthen the staff position in the affected branches.

The management responded to trade unions' reservations by meeting them and generally sharing the strategy of moving surplus staff from administrative offices to branches by truncating the zonal offices and reducing the number of regional offices. Although the Bank's officers' association wanted elaborate negotiations on the issue, like which regional offices will be wound up and what new structure will be provided in regional offices, we refused to make this mini reorganisation a subject matter for negotiation in view of Bank's earlier experience with the trade unions in such matters. We, however, examined many suggestions offered by the Association with an open mind.

Thus, the entire process was handled by the management without any formal negotiations with the unions, in particular the officers' association, in a clear departure from its earlier policy of consulting the Association at every stage. Although the Association expressed considerable displeasure about this decision and formed a united front of unions in the Bank to oppose it, this had no impact on the successful implementation of the mini reorganisation. The reason was simple: in the past, the officers' association had always opposed any proposal for new initiatives. For example, in 1990, they opposed the implementation of an internal report on improvement in personnel management; they opposed the implementation of S.K. Dutta

Committee[1] Report in 1996–97; and in 1999, they resisted the implementation of flexi-banking, 7-day banking, and so on, and started a smear campaign against the General Manager concerned, V.G. Subramaniam. The Association also had the temerity to demand disciplinary action against him for issuing the circular to branches about this. Consultation would, therefore, have meant elaborate negotiations and the slowing down of the process of implementation with many changes being demanded by the Association. Here was an instance when a determined top leadership speaking in one voice was able to successfully weather all resistance—both from within and outside—and ensure implementation, that too within a record time of 45 days.

The successful implementation of the VRS and the reorganisation of the administrative offices apparently rattled the Association as this was perhaps the first time in many years that the Bank management had implemented important changes without negotiations or at least a nod of approval from its leaders.

From the day I assumed charge as Executive Director, the Association was quite apprehensive because its leaders suspected, perhaps rightly, that I would seek to reorder hitherto established patterns by introducing systems and processes in the conduct of IR and HRM, rather than cultivating and pampering them, a trend that had become the sole survival strategy for some earlier CEOs. In fact, the Association requested Shenoy to directly handle HR and they ignored my existence as the second-highest functionary in the Bank.

One of the key insights from my research was that most IR problems at the workplace occurred on account of the delays in personnel/IR decision-making, delayed response in the matter of indiscipline by staff and union activists, failure to support branch managers and other operating managers in IR matters, and pampering union leaders and granting them many favours and concessions. This was the main reason for workplaces remaining in perpetual conflict obstructing customer service. My intention was to

---

[1] S.K. Dutta, a former top executive of State Bank of India, was engaged as a consultant to study the systems and processes and suggest changes to make the Bank more market and customer savvy.

restore order in the workplaces by clear policy pronouncements, support to branch managers, and being responsive to their problems.

Accordingly, I took several initiatives to empower the operating managers and give them the confidence about management support in improving discipline at the operating level. I hastened the resolution of pending disciplinary cases and responded to hundreds of pending references on HR issues from the zones/regions. I also initiated steps to improve the decision-making in personnel/IR and vigilances cases, and also drastically improve the speed of response. These initiatives to improve the overall functioning of the branches by supporting managers and empowering them to enforce their authority to improve discipline and productivity were greatly appreciated at all levels and boosted the morale of the operating managers who, for so long, had remained under siege by the trade unions.

In a subtle manner, the influence of the Association in promotions and placement was also removed. Steps were taken to discontinue past informal understandings and practices. For example, there was a tradition to hand over the list of promotions of executives and officers to them one day in advance before the declaration of formal results. This was used by them to inform selected officers and executives in advance thereby leveraging their influence on them.

Over a period of time, the Association leaders considered themselves to be sole influencers to motivate officers and, as seen earlier, used this to their advantage. I initiated certain steps to restore management credibility in HR matters. One such step was to ensure that the list of promotions or transfer was not given to the Association leaders in advance at the corporate level and it was only after declaration of results that formally a list was sent to them for information for their records. In case of promotion of senior executives, I personally phoned the executives concerned to give him/her the information about promotion.

Thus, the news of promotion emanated from the management first. This won huge goodwill from the general cadre of officers and executives. By these steps, the management quickly restored its credibility. Further, being an insider, most of the senior executives confided in me the problems they faced in the management of IR at the senior operating levels, like at the level of zonal managers. I consulted them about the changes in placements of executives (chief managers heading large branches) under them and by this process, I developed a very good rapport with the senior executive cadre.

It had a cascading effect, and most zonal and regional managers too stopped consulting the Association at the zonal level about transfers of branch managers and officers. They now felt confident about deciding postings of officers on merit and suitability, instead of pressures from the Association. In hierarchical organisations, what is done at the top level flows down to the lower levels. Thus, culture change at the top is essential to give a push to culture change at all other levels.

The Association was quite peeved at this as it considerably reduced their clout in influencing decisions on placements of executives and senior officers. They perceived me to be the mastermind behind these changes and thought they could pressurise Shenoy to go back to the earlier practice of consulting them in such matters. As their interference in 'management domain issues' had no rational basis, they could not formally agitate on such issues. So, they chose instead to personally target me and started creating a wedge between Shenoy and me. The general secretary of the Association continuously instigated Shenoy against me, spinning lies about my style of working and claiming that I was disturbing industrial peace at the Bank.

He would often meet Shenoy to report on what I had said in a particular place while addressing branch managers. My calls for business growth and productivity enhancement were interpreted as threats to operating managers. Shenoy tried to broker peace between the general secretary and me, but his efforts failed because the Association's intentions were not honest. All that the general secretary wanted was to return to the traditional practice of influencing management decisions in the garb of participative management; and I was firmly opposed to this as it was misused to divide executives and leverage the power of the Association leaders.

Roadblocks in Technology Implementation

Although the Bank successfully implemented both the VRS and the mini reorganisation exercise, a more challenging task awaited it: of kick-starting the information technology (IT)-enabled business transformation programme sometime in early 2000. The Bank had commissioned the services of Gartner Inc.[2] to help the Bank reposition itself as a lean, agile, and technologically driven bank ready to face the competition. This was a huge project which required a high degree of multi-skill expertise and coordination internally.

Our consultant, Gartner, presented a blueprint for the Bank's proposed IT strategy and a schedule of implementation to the board. The board approved Gartner's proposal for the deployment of a centralised solution at Bank's metro and urban branches (numbering around 1,000), with real-time online connectivity, as also integration of the Bank's international and subsidiary operations, laying the foundation for a global treasury, and integration of general ledgers for all domestic and international operations. Gartner had to also select the technology system integrator that would implement core banking.

The consultant also submitted reports on other areas key areas like marketing, group corporate office structure, HR, control systems, and the performance management system. Many of its recommendations had long-term implications and the entire management was excited about the projected future of the Bank.

The Association, which had always boasted about its commitment to the Bank and promoted its 'Grow with the Bank' policy, now resisted the Bank's move to hire Gartner for its technological transformation on the flimsy pretext that Gartner was a foreign company and did not have experience in the field of formulating and implementing business strategy in the Indian banking scenario. One of its circulars read:[3]

> The Bank has sufficient in-house expertise available for such tasks. The Bank reached the premier position in the Banking Industry in the past only through them and not through any 'Gora' consultant. Even if the Bank feels [it] necessary to engage a consultant, there are many with proven capabilities within India who could have been engaged for the purpose...

[2] Gartner Inc. is an American research and advisory firm providing IT-related insights for IT and other businesses.

[3] Circular dated 22 January 2002, issued by the AIBOBOA (Greater Mumbai Zone), the Bank of Baroda Employees Union (Greater Mumbai and Thane district), and the Bank of Baroda Employees' Association.

The management held meetings with the Association and the workmen's unions to brief them about the Bank's ambitious plans to implement the technology-driven business strategy. Gartner made presentations before them. But there was no let-up in the Association's tirade against the Bank on the issue. With a view to blowing the issue out of proportion and confusing the employees, it released a booklet titled, *East India Company Comes to Bank of Baroda*. The main plank of attack was that the Bank had not acted wisely in hiring a foreign consultant. In an interdependent, globalised world, it was difficult to accept this logic. The Association created confusion across the Bank, spreading rumours about the wholesale closure of administrative offices, retrenchment of staff, and inconvenience to customers, if Gartner report was allowed to be implemented. Apparently, the Association's aim was to stymie the technology-driven business transformation programme, and it instigated the workmen's unions also to protest the move to change the way in which business was being conducted at the Bank.

When all this could not bend the Bank, a vilification campaign was started by vested interests alleging serious charges of irregularity by the top management in selecting Gartner, including complaints to the government and to investigating agencies. A white paper was released by the Association on Gartner's appointment. The Association also gave a call for protest rallies against the appointment of Gartner and sought support for its agitational programme from the United Forum of Bank Unions (UFBU), which consisted of various unions of officers and workmen at the banking industry level. It launched a campaign through leaflets, posters, press releases, and public meetings, and also organised demonstrations and dharnas[4] before all the regional offices. The Association also put the question before the government about the Bank's wisdom in hiring a foreign consultant. I was summoned by the then Minister of State for Finance, Government of India, Anandrao Adsul, to explain the background of the Bank's decision in hiring a foreign consultant.

---

[4] A dharna is a non-violent sit-in protest, which may include fast undertaken at the door of an offender, especially a debtor, in India, as a means of obtaining compliance with a demand for justice.

The Association's repeated pleas for consultations and bringing back the culture of participation only indicated that its main grouse was not Gartner's appointment, but the management's refusal to restore the status quo ante in its relations with them.

The continued resistance from the Association-led group of trade unions soon began to rattle CEO Shenoy; his style was non-confrontational and he was ready to settle for some degree of compromise in most conflict situations. He often said to me: 'If certain practices have been in vogue in the Bank for a long time, how can we change them?' This was practically an indication to me to halt the reform process. My views, however, were different. During my fieldwork, I had personally witnessed and heard horror stories of indiscipline in the branches, union dominance, and the unwillingness of the senior and top management to rescue the branches from the daily onslaught of the trade unions. From my operational experience in Meerut and Kolkata, I knew that it was not impossible to change the existing reality and all that was needed was that the management be prepared to engage with the problem.

My empathy with the operating managers was heartfelt and I owed it to my current position in management to make a difference in their working lives and to create a bright future for the Bank by dealing with its problems head-on and, if necessary, take short-term hits for long-term gains. During my field research, I got a clear sense that majority of the officers resented the clout of their leaders in administrative matters and more so in their career decisions. Therefore, I felt that it would be very difficult for the Association to mobilise any protest against management initiatives in creating a new transparent culture in the matters of placement and promotion. Later events, narrated in the following pages, vindicate my belief. Everyone appreciated the new system of meritocracy where each stood a fair chance based on one's performance and not their closeness with the Association.

Restoring Control

I have always believed about the importance of credibility in leadership. Accordingly, we were conscious of the necessity, first and foremost, to improve the functioning of the Mumbai-based offices. Significantly, the

Mumbai branches were generally characterised by sluggish business growth, poor levels of customer service, and staff indiscipline.

Thus, a number of the Association activists and office-bearers, who held branch manager positions in key branches and often moved from one branch to another in a particular area, managed their offices as per the diktats of the Association leader and often spent their office time doing the Association work. It was widely speculated that these managers acted as a conduit for collecting donations for the Association from the Bank's customers, even though this was a misconduct, and the government, time and again, exhorted the PSBs to put an end to this practice. Their acts of omission and commission were often overlooked under pressure from the Association. During my fieldwork, I had observed that some heads of key branches (who were office-bearers of the Association) moved around during working hours with impunity. They managed to have in their branches adequate number of staff and officers of their choice, while managers who did not have the protective umbrella of the Association often had to run from pillar to post for additional staff or management support in administrative matters.

The management now took note of the Mumbai situation and initiated several steps to create a business facilitation climate. We posted one K.K Agarwal, General Manager, as zonal manager of Mumbai. An unassuming but a no-nonsense executive, he initiated several steps to restore disciple, including transferring some non-performing branch managers who had continued in their positions on account of their closeness to the Association leaders. Agarwal, in spite of resistance from the Association, was able to restore management authority in a short time and enforce a business-like environment. The management's efforts were interpreted by the Association as harassment and victimisation. However, once it was clear that the management was determined to restore control and introduce meritocracy in promotion and placement procedures, senior operating managers like the zonal and regional managers were emboldened to report unethical and corrupt practices by branch managers, who had till now been sheltered by the Association. The management dealt with such cases effectively.

This, however, annoyed the Association leader who vociferously attacked me in his various meetings with the officers at various centres, accusing me of disturbing the industrial peace in the Bank.

Systemic Interventions

Large organisations are held in balance by suitable control systems and institutionalised policy frameworks. In the absence of institutional mechanisms, individual managerial initiatives can be effective only for a limited period. Also, it is not only the top management but also the management at all levels that has to own the responsibility to effectively manage their people. This has to be a key responsibility of the operating managers. I was of the view that union militancy and its capacity to interfere had a direct correlation with the prevailing demoralisation amongst branch managers, who avoided taking any initiative in improving the situation at their level.

A trigger for systemic intervention came from several inspection reports in various geographical areas of the Bank, which threw up glaring cases of excess payment of ex-gratia and terminal benefits to VRS optees and the general breakdown of implementation of staff rules and regulations on account of the intransigence of the unions which supported their members irrespective of the merits of their case. The Inspection Division of the Bank pointed out the following:

1. Abuse of the profit and loss account—large numbers of erroneous and unethical payments of claims.
2. Excess/erroneous payment of allowances and short recoveries.
3. Large-scale appointment of subordinate staff on temporary basis despite a blanket ban on such recruitments by the Bank.
4. Large-scale habitual absenteeism/unauthorised absence in around 200 cases.
5. Non-implementation of orders of disciplinary authority.
6. Very poor discipline management affecting customer service.
7. Non-compliance with statutory guidelines.
8. Large number of non-payment of credit card dues by the employees.
9. A host of other irregular practices against the rules, undermining the interests of the Bank.

The Inspectors also reported that verification of sundry charges and repairs and maintenance expenses revealed that the sundry charges account was being treated like a till without any check from the authorities. This explained the reasons for Bank's profit and loss expenses being the highest in the banking industry.

It was not that this was the first time that the Inspection Division had pointed out such irregularities. The Association complained regularly against the inspectors who pointed out irregularities and tried constantly to impede their career progression. In such a culture, the Inspection Division hesitated to comment on staff matters.

The problem was symptomatic of a complete breakdown of branch manager's authority in exercising control over staff, who, under the protection of their unions, had a field day in the branches. It may be recalled that during the tenures of both Shah and Kannan, the unions had leveraged their power to the extent that no operating manager dared to assert any authority to control irregular practices at the branch level. Trade unions wreaked havoc, especially in the large branches in urban areas. No one was made accountable for any wrongdoing and things drifted at the operating level. In the name of garnering cooperation of the unions in business development, operating managers were discouraged from doing anything that irked the unions.

I was of the firm belief that it was necessary to restore managerial authority at the workplace if the Bank were to progress, and that needed cleaning up the administrative mess and getting rid of day-to-day interference by the unions. This was one part of the problem; the other part was the sheer incompetence of the many of the branch managers and failure to assert their authority in enforcing discipline. So, while we needed to create a climate that instilled some fear in the recalcitrant staff for violation of authority, equally important was to fix accountability among managers for ineffective personnel administration resulting in failure to enforce their authority with regard to allocation of work and dealing with cases of indiscipline.

The Beginning of Workplace Reforms

On my suggestion, the Audit Committee of the board agreed to introduce a system of 'HR audits' in the branches with the objective of ensuring that the existing rules and procedures with respect to staff management and workplace discipline were followed scrupulously. In addition, the audit would identify the policy gaps and advise on taking remedial steps wherever required. Lest the exercise got reduced to a checklist, we set up a task force of personnel executives to discuss and work out a system that could be implemented. This marked the introduction of a comprehensive system of HR audit in the Bank that initially covered the branches in the metros and the urban centres. It had the approval of CEO Shenoy.

The HR audit was a systemic intervention aimed at correcting maladies and restoring managerial authority at the operating level. The audit signified the need to urgently tone up the HR administration in the Bank. We immediately set up a task force under G.G. Joshi, Assistant General Manager in charge of personnel, who did a commendable job in institutionalising the HR audit.

Personnel managers in regional and zonal offices were trained to undertake the HR audit of large branches in a time-bound manner. The details of HR audit were meticulously worked out and it was drilled into the Bank's branch managers that this was as important as doing business and they will be accountable for any aberration in its implementation. The message was loud and clear that the managers have to now act and activate their efforts in maintaining discipline, productivity, and customer service and cannot ignore their own role in effective personnel administration of their branches. The HR audit focused on checking the utilisation of manpower; leave and salary administration; staff expenses, including medical expenses, leave travel concessions, and sundry expenses; perks; unauthorised absences; restrictive practices and discipline; job rotation; and implementation of the Bank's rules and regulations. Branch heads were made accountable for rectifying irregularities. This was the first-ever organisation-wide systematic attempt to control the staffing practices at the branch level.

The results of the audit surprised many of us in the top management. We had expected some irregularities here and there, but not of the magnitude that the HR audits threw up. It revealed to us a complete breakdown of managerial control: counters were being opened belatedly on account of lack of punctuality of staff; all sorts of unauthorised financial claims by employees; irregular employment of around 1,200 casual labour across the branches in the Bank without authorisation; 200 cases of long unauthorised absence of staff; a good number of officers who had not reported to their new place of posting with no follow-up action taken; salary payments were not checked at branch level resulting in wrong payments; staff-sponsored loans to their friends and relatives were detected; and a large number of union activists belonging to both majority and minority unions moved around disturbing the branches in the name of union work. In many cases, staff had taken advance payments under leave travel concession (LTC) without actually undertaking the trip; availed of leave without debiting their leave account; and availed of special allowances without performing the duties the allowances entailed.

The audit also revealed that a huge amount of money was due under the BOBCARD facility, BOBCARD being the Credit Card Division of BoB. Defaulting employees did not respond to notices issued by the department. This was a reality check about the Bank's tender-minded policy towards the trade unions and complete chaos that prevailed at the operating levels.

While I was not much surprised because I knew about the problems and had witnessed the state of affairs during my fieldwork, CEO Shenoy was completely taken aback, more so because the trade union leaders had always assured him that everything was fine and they were the ones supporting the operating managers in their endeavours for business development. Shenoy was so upset that he confessed that he was unaware of the extent of deterioration in the branches and wanted me and the Inspection Division to take quick steps to recover the amount from the staff, wherever necessary. It needed thorough overhaul of our administrative processes and building ownership for better HR administration.

Recoveries to the extent of Rs 20 million were made from staff who had overdrawn advances from the Bank for leave travel without undertaking any journeys, from unpaid credit card bills, and so on. Disciplinary action was initiated against those who were on long unauthorised leave and leave records were corrected. Post the HR audit, several guidelines were issued to streamline the administration, including clarifications on many issues. The HR audit was made a key responsibility area (KRA) for the regional/ branch and HR managers, with accountability to ensure the conduct of the HR function within the ambit of the defined rules and regulations. Without doubt, collapse of personnel administration in the branches was attributed largely to trade union interference in administration and lack of accountability on the part of branch managers. Not to mention the management failure at all the levels to fix the problem.

A number of steps were taken to remedy the situation:

1. Core management functions were clearly demarcated and the unions advised to refrain from interfering in these.
2. Discipline norms were strictly implemented in relation to attendance and punctuality, unauthorised absence, extraordinary leave on loss of pay, and non-payment of credit card dues.
3. Cases of long unauthorised absence, which were running into hundreds, were monitored and dealt with at lightning speed. Specific guidelines were put in place to deal with such cases in the future. Accountability was fixed on the regional personnel officers to quickly conclude such cases.
4. A large number of non-vigilance cases, which had been pending over a long period, were dealt with. Clear-cut accountability was fixed on operating managers like the zonal, regional, and branch managers to ensure discipline.
5. Recoveries were effected from trade union leaders who stood as guarantors to bad loans sanctioned to outsiders.
6. Loans to staff members and their relatives under government-sponsored programmes were curtailed.
7. Office-bearers and leaders of the Association and the other unions were also put through job rotation.
8. A number of restrictive practices at the respective branches were curbed.
9. Accountability for workplace discipline for branch managers was introduced.

The HR audit was a stark reminder about the fragility of the Bank's strategy of soft-pedalling the HR administration for fear of its IR consequences. Evidently, over the years, the unions had virtually usurped the administration, while the top management had been busy socialising with, and distributing favours to, a few union leaders with little consideration for how they rendered the operating managers incapable of tackling even day-to-day acts of indiscipline by union members. The operating managers were indeed the worst victims of the mutually feeding circle of CEOs and union leaders.

My fieldwork during research had clearly indicated the worsening of the workplace climate since many years as the focus of the Bank's IR strategy revolved mainly around managing, manipulating, or favouring key union leaders and ignoring the state of affairs in the branches. As a consequence, the unions protected and pampered the undisciplined staff and provided them immunity from any punitive action for their acts of misconduct. In this environment, most managers failed to assert their authority even in genuine cases for fear of reprisals from the trade unions and lack of support from the higher management.

The unions were completely exposed for instigating and encouraging mass indiscipline and irregularities. With the state of affairs in the Bank branches exposed after the HR audit and recovery of outstanding dues from the employees being initiated, the unions were on the defensive and cried foul. But it was clear that the management meant business. The operating managers felt quite encouraged by these moves and one of them summed up the feelings of many: 'One of the biggest gains of the HR audit was the restoration of the freedom of the branch managers to manage.'

The successful implementation of the HR audit resulted in substantial reduction of expenditure, apart from streamlining the administration at the Bank's branches and offices. It also signified the management's resolve to improve HR administration in the Bank. It was perhaps a first-of-its-kind transformation initiative, which created an impact at the grass-roots level and restored overnight the authority of the branch managers in the work-place. Tight monitoring and support from the corporate office yielded immediate results. It was also perhaps the first time that the pampered unions had to run for cover.

The HR audit signalled the new approach of the management and its intention of brooking no interference from the unions in administrative matters at the branch level and to empower branch managers to manage staff matters within the ambit of the rules and guidelines that had been laid down. While we recognised the role of the unions in representing the collective grievances of employees at the appropriate levels, any coercive action at the branch level and disruption of work at the branches by any staff member or union representative was dealt with sternly. The CEO and the board appreciated my efforts in implementing the HR audit in the branches, which sorted out the mess that had existed in BoB's administration.

It was perhaps for the first time in several decades that the unions felt challenged by the exposure of workplace realities and they experienced huge pressure from their members to defend the indefensible.

The most intriguing part of the rot that had crept into the system was that the inspecting officers had also been turning a blind eye, apparently under pressure from the unions, to many of the irregularities that prevailed at the branches, including the really serious ones in advances. This prompted us to issue letters calling for explanations to select inspecting officers in order to shake the system and discourage such malfeasance in the future. All the unions knew well that the HR audit would cost them dearly with regard to their influence on the staff if it remained unchallenged.

The Unions' Resistance to HR Audit

While most operating managers were happy about this strategic shift in the Bank's new initiatives in toning up the IR climate and restoring managerial authority, the Association was peeved and it had reason to be upset as its leaders faced an identity crisis as a result of the management distancing itself from them. Their action in resisting transformation of the workplaces was in sharp contrast to their oft-repeated pleadings to provide succour to branch managers and officers from the excesses of workmen unions. The Association scandalised the issue and instigated workmen unions and formed a united front jointly with them. Its main objective was to target me as the brain behind these changes and create a rift between CEO Shenoy and me.

A circular issued by the general secretary of the Association, along with the general secretaries of both the workmen's unions, inter alia stated:[5]

> ...Encouraged by the Executive Director, a section of management excels in creating a fear psychosis through its penchant for fixing staff

[5] Circular to all members, dated 15 August 2002, issued by the AIBOBOA, the AIBOBEF, and the AIBOBECC.

accountability at the drop of the hat. A reign of terror is let loose on employees and the threat of suspension is used as a tool to harass employees into submission.... He has been systematically demolishing democratic and participative traditions by crushing everything.... His ultimate aim is to drive the trade union organization to the wall.... The joint meeting makes an open appeal to our Bank's Chairman and Managing Director Shri P S Shenoy, the honest and experienced banker, in whose wisdom we all have immense faith to stop the tyrannical policies of persecution, threats, insults and intimidation pursued by the executive director and save our Bank.

In another circular,[6] he discredited me for initiating the HR audit. Soon thereafter, in a subsequent circular,[7] the general secretary of the Association questioned my professional recognition. When National HRD Network honoured me citing my outstanding contributions in the field of HRD, the Association leader wrote to president of the organisation to withdraw the award from me!

Never before in the recent history of the Bank had the Association targeted a top-level executive in such a blatant manner. Their acts of causing humiliation to me only heightened my resolve for reforms in IR. In real sense, I was undergoing my crucible[8] experience—an intense, traumatic experience that was a testing time but, in some ways, a time when I experienced a new resolve to continue the efforts to reform IR despite this massive attack on me personally.

I was only guided by a higher purpose to improve the life of operating managers who were daily bullied and humiliated by the trade unions, which hampered any new initiatives in business development and effective delivery of customer service. Ironically, pain and humiliation became a great source of personal motivation for me. It is never easy to undertake transformation in a highly unionised environment unless leaders have convictions and are driven by some higher-order purpose. The Association's

---

[6] Circular No. 23, dated 23 September 2002, to all members, issued by the AIBOBOA.

[7] Circular No. 25, dated 25 September 2002, to all members, issued by the AIBOBOA.

[8] A crucible is, by definition, a transformative experience through which an individual comes to a new or an altered sense of identity.

initiative to form the joint front with workmen unions was aimed at subverting the very foundation of workplace relationships and supervisory dynamics. Management could not accept this, nor bend on such an issue of principles.

Misalignment at the Top

Change management in a large organisation calls for alignment at the top to successfully pilot the change programme and deal with both its intended and unintended consequences. Much though we may wish so, it does not happen often. In BoB's case, the Association leader's main strategy after resignation of previous general secretary in 1978 (Chapter 4) was to maintain cordial relations with the CEO and get the work done and ignore everyone else. The Association also kept good relations with key executives of the Personnel Department. The Association leader played the same strategy and therefore, at the height of problems with the management, the strategy was to isolate me for attacks, and spare and applaud the CEO. Although the Association knew for certain that all the initiatives in HR had the approval of CEO, they, instead of protesting the actions of the management as an institution, targeted me personally and maintained cordial relations with the CEO. At the height of their smear campaign against me, the CEO, instead of chastising them for attacking me, maintained normal relations with them and even attended the Association's functions as chief guest.

Although all the actions to recover the amount from the staff and tone up personnel administration were initiated after Shenoy's written approval, his wishy-washy attitude in supporting my actions and advice to the Association against discrediting me was most surprising and hurting. In spite of my oral and written representation to him to take action against the Association for the tendentious campaign against me, Shenoy maintained silence and the Association was emboldened to continue their tirade against me. This was an extraordinary situation for me personally and sent confusing signals across the ranks of management.

My worry was that if the Association was allowed to get away vilifying the second senior-most functionary of the Bank, they will be emboldened to intimidate the others in management and it could have a demoralising impact on the executive cadre. It was the best bet for the unions to divide the management and come back with a bang. All our efforts so far in moving ahead with reforms would have collapsed.

I had no alternative but to seek the intervention of the Board of Directors, in spite of my friends' advice against my action, as there are times in the life of an individual when one needs to listen to one's inner voice. I realised that there was a lot at stake. It was less about personal humiliation and more about the future of the Bank and the honour of thousands of well-meaning operating managers and employees who wanted the freedom to operate and conduct business for the Bank. The Board of Directors endorsed my actions, appreciated the introduction of HR audit and other steps, and directed the CEO to initiate appropriate action against the Association and the workmen's unions for their resistance to changes and targeting the executive director. Resultantly, all agitations stopped.

The strategy of the Association to maintain clandestine relations with the CEO and target me personally, thus, boomeranged. The trade unions, which were part of a common forum created by the Association, understood the game of the Association and slowly pulled out from the influence of its general secretary. The president of the Association questioned his actions on this issue and even met me during the midst of the crisis to communicate his disenchantment from the actions of the general secretary of the Association. The general secretary's divisive strategy of not taking on the 'management' as an institution and personalise the attack against an individual was widely criticised within the internal forum of associations and was the major reason for the failure of the Association to resist any reform measures. More the Association targeted me, more the general secretary of the Association was isolated and criticised by various groups.

The Federation leader called on me and apologised for making me the target of their joint circulars and confided that it was under the instigation of the general secretary of the Association and in the name of trade union unity that his union had joined the agitation and targeted me in their circular of 15 August 2002. In a circular dated 9 November 2002,[9] the Federation leader said:

---

[9] Circular No. 13 of 2002 to all members/unit secretaries, dated 9 November 2002, by AIBOBEF (recognised).

These Mir Jafars[10] [hinting at the Association] would rather compromise with the management and indulge in treachery rather than achieving their goal by united struggle and sacrifice. Blowing hot and cold at the same time, while talking of united struggle, these elements were trying to pursue their own agenda rather than concentrate on the common issues.... Management policies normally evolved by collective wisdom and not by individual diktat, hence we do not share the view that any one individual was responsible for recent happening in the Bank and certainly we do not subscribe to personal attack on any individual.

Similar sentiments were expressed by the general secretary of the Coordination Committee. In a circular[11] to the members, he clarified the Committee's position, criticised the Association leader for 'Dividing the Management', and questioned the CEO as to why he was not standing by the executive director against the propaganda unleashed against the latter by the Association. It read:

> ... so and so (name of the general secretary of the Association) had issued two circulars against Executive Director [me] .... This was a futile attempt to divide the management. I expected that as CEO of the Bank, the Chairman would atleast make a reference to circulars issued by (so and so) [name of the leader of the Association] and appeal not to target one executive. But the CEO kept a studied silence and did not touch the issue.

A Delhi-based officers organisation, Bank of Baroda Officers Federation affiliated All India Bank Officers Congress (majority organisation of officers at the industry level), too questioned the motive of the Association leader. Its circular said:[12]

> It is known to everyone that our ED is totally committed to the welfare of the Bank ... the British policy of divide and rule innovated by the General secretary [of the Association] has miserably failed ... why he has issued such a nasty circular against ED who is one amongst us holding a very responsible position in the Bank.

[10] Mir Jafar (1691–1765), Nawab of Bengal, known as a betrayer in Indian history.

[11] Circular No. 14/2002 to all office-bearers, dated 3 November 2002, by the AIBOBECC.

[12] Circular No. GS/2002/40, dated 24 September 2002, issued by the General Secretary, All India Bank of Baroda Officers' Federation (affiliated to AIBOC).

No one was surprised by the behaviour of the Association leader. It was common knowledge that the general secretary of the Association drew his strength from relationship with CEOs and generally avoided confrontation with the CEO. He gave an impression of being the biggest well-wisher of the Bank and would occasionally issue circulars to officers to go an extra mile to develop business (Chapter 9). He would then leverage his position, interfere in postings and transfers, intimidate operating managers, all in the name of his closeness with the CEO. Whenever the management ignored the Association, as done by some CEOs such as Premjit Singh (1985–90) and S.P. Talwar (1993–94), the secretary of the Association maintained a low profile and did not organise any protests even to pursue the legitimate grievances of the officers. The Association survived on the favours from the CEOs whenever it could manoeuvre. My research had also revealed this.

In spite of an unhelpful and unsupportive environment, my main strength and moral support came from some personnel specialists whose commitment to reforms was exemplary. These middle-level executives, especially Chief Manager C.V. Chandrasekhar and an Assistant General Manager, G.G. Joshi, were pillars of strength in difficult times and shared my passion for IR reforms. Although Shenoy was hesitant to precipitate any further crisis, it is to his credit that at least on paper he did not stop any of my proposals for reforms.

These developments therefore did not deter me from pursuing further reforms as I strongly believed that leaving reforms half-done would be more disastrous for the Bank. I was committed to bring performance management, accountability, efficient customer handling, punctuality, and discipline to the centre stage in our new HR strategy. The quality of the HR administration and performance climate had to be improved at the operating level. We wanted a complete shift in our policies so that the operating managers were not at the mercy of the union leaders.

In consonance with the Bank's new aspirations, we set the following objectives to improve management control in IR:

1. Streamline facilities to trade unions, which were misused against the management.
2. Improve personnel decision-making and the system of redressal of employee grievances.

3. Clearly restrict the role of the Association in matters of transfer and promotion of executives.
4. Review the system of structured meetings to make them productive, and review all aspects, including discussing the management agenda, in structured meetings.
5. Initiate a business-like approach in dealing with trade unions and avoid any informal liaison or understanding on issues affecting service conditions of officers.
6. Develop a fair system for dealing with employees' grievances without any consideration of union affiliations, and withdraw all practices that were counter-productive to this intent.
7. Review long-standing practices in contravention of all-India settlements and government guidelines.
8. Craft a revised HR policy with a focus on new capability building, performance management, and employee engagement as its core agenda.
9. Reorient personnel specialists from an IR mindset to a developmental role.
10. Harmonise the various HR processes and systems to ensure development of HR.

In spite of the tension-ridden environment created by the unions, we continued our quest for reforms in IR. I have always believed that conflict need not be dysfunctional all the time. It all depends on how the conflict is managed. Procrastination when a conflict situation is inevitable is far more dangerous. I piloted many reforms of significance, as described next.

Major HR Reforms Undertaken

Unified HRM Function

As mentioned earlier, the split location of personnel function in Mumbai and Vadodara was at the root of delays in personnel decision-making leading to a number of problems (see Chapter 7). For more than 20 years, this arrangement continued in spite of both trade unions as well as operating managers experiencing severe problems. During my field-work, I had observed as to how the split location of personnel function contributed to internal bureaucracy, staff line conflict, passive attitude in personnel specialists, and ad hocism in decision-making at the operating level. I was of the firm view that easy access of the trade unions to Personnel Department in Mumbai and keeping them at bay cannot be the criteria to split this important function and the Bank needed to be guided by rational and logical considerations. We, therefore, shifted various departments like Recruitment and Promotion, Staff Administration, HRD, and a small unit of IR from Vadodara to Mumbai and created a unified HRM function at the corporate office under a senior general manager, assisted by a competent group of personnel specialists and also operational executives. The structure of HRM function at the corporate level is given in Figure 11.2.

This unified structure provided the top management a complete view of interconnectedness of various personnel functions and helped reviewing their effectiveness from time to time. I personally reviewed the functioning of the entire HRM function once in a fortnight and set strict deadlines for decision-making. Insight from the field during research helped me a lot to focus on the speed of decision-making, clarity of our communications,

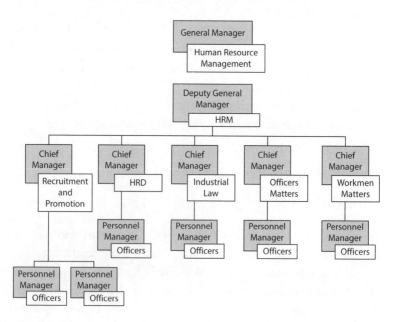

FIGURE 11.2   Structure of HRM Function at the Corporate Level, 2000–04

unambiguity in dealing with issues of workplace discipline, and sorting out many legacy issues in the smooth running of our branches.

Dealing with Some Legacy Issues

For quite a long time, the Bank was continuing with some practices in spite of government guidelines to the contrary as a part of mollycoddling policies pursued and fear of backlash from the trade unions.

One such issue was related to the date of retirement of the workmen staff. While the industry-level agreement (to which the Bank was a party) stipulated that a workman had to retire on the last day of the month in which he completed the age of superannuation, the BoB continued with the old policy of retiring a workman on the last day of the year in which he completed the age of superannuation. For example, if an employee reached the age of superannuation on 2 January, he would be allowed to continue in service till 31 December of that year. This was one example of pampering the unions with no regard for financial implications. No past management had even talked about this, fearing the adverse reaction of the unions. This was the right time to fall in line with the rest of the industry and correct this practice, and I put up a proposal to that effect before the board with its financial implications year after year. The board approved my proposal. A move that had been pending for decades was ready for implementation in minutes without any fuss. Interestingly, the first person affected by this decision was the president of the Federation, who was also the workman-director on the board of the Bank. The message was being sent out loud and clear that the unions could no longer influence the management to continue any facility beyond the realm of the rules and that the management was moving towards the process of formalisation of IR.

Restructuring the Structured Meetings

In 1982, the Bank had put in place a system of structured meetings with the Association as well as the workmen's unions at various levels, such as the regional, zonal, and corporate levels, to sort out employee grievances. The system stipulated quarterly meetings at the regional and zonal levels and half-yearly meetings at the corporate level. The corporate-level meeting discussed unresolved issues at the lower levels as well as policy matters. This was a good system for the orderly resolution of employee grievances in a large organisation. However, over a period of time, the unions had begun to leverage these meetings to strengthen their organisations and bully the managers, thereby preventing the meetings from achieving the purpose for which they had been created. Periodical meetings in more than 50 regional offices and 12 zonal offices on local issues made the environment excessively politicised with each union trying to demonstrate its supremacy over the others. The issues of workplace indiscipline and subsequent action were raised in these meetings, but under the threat of agitation, these discussions were compromised by the senior operating managers. In an environment in which the top management itself pandered to union demands, the tension at the operating level was palpable. My fieldwork in the Greater Mumbai Zone had already pointed to the prevailing insurgency that stemmed from the unions. These meetings were also abused by the union leaders for doing union work across the Bank on the Bank's time and at the Bank's cost, as hundreds of office-bearers of the unions loitered around the branches and harassed the branch managers.

Thus, another major initiative was taken, this time to streamline the structured meeting system. My fieldwork had revealed that over 500 structured meetings held in a year at 59 regional and 13 zonal offices with two workmen's unions and the officers' association (separate meetings with each union every quarter), and innumerable unstructured dialogues, kept our regional and zonal heads busy with union problems. It would not be an exaggeration to say that it was almost routine for the union functionaries to visit the regional offices and spend unscheduled time with the HR managers trying to gauge what was going on. All this was being done at the cost of the productivity of the branches where these union functionaries worked.

A well-intended structured meetings system was effectively being used by the unions to interfere in the day-to-day administration of the offices. It facilitated unlimited travel for the central-level leaders and days off for a big team from each union to attend periodical meetings at different levels. Worse, the meetings always ended with the unions emerging as the benefactors of the employees; as one senior executive commented, 'We bargained and the unions collected.' The system of structured meetings, which was started for the quick resolution of staff grievances, was therefore being leveraged by the unions to enhance their visibility and conduct union work during working hours.

A number of steps were taken to streamline the system of structured meetings and union practices. The aim of the exercise was to ensure that the structured meetings became business-like and productive.

1. The periodicity of the meetings was cut down from every quarter to twice a year at the regional level, and from twice a year to once a year at the corporate level; the meetings were discontinued at the zonal level. This freed a lot of time for the regional and zonal managers and enabled them to concentrate on business issues.
2. The number of participants from the union teams in the structured meetings was pruned.
3. The practice of giving a day's special leave to union functionaries before and after the meeting was scrapped.
4. Corporate-level general secretaries were no longer allowed to participate in the regional-level meetings.
5. The management's agenda was also to be discussed at all such meetings.
6. As a matter of principle, issues relating to disciplinary cases were not allowed to be raised during the structured meetings.
7. Special leave was no longer granted to the office-bearers of the Association to attend their central committee meetings.
8. The unions could no longer collect donations from customers.
9. The policy prescription that unions/Association office-bearers were not entitled to duty relief for union/personal work during office hours was reiterated and implemented without any exception.
10. Union and the Association office-bearers were also subjected to job rotation.
11. A settlement for the redeployment of workmen staff within 100 kilometres was signed and implemented, which facilitated the redeployment of surplus clerks from excess to deficit pockets.

Further, a principled stand was taken that the structured meetings would be held only with those organisations that did not indulge in vilification campaigns against individual executives and that did not oppose the Bank's transformation programme. After the two workmen's unions and the officers' association assured us of their support for the reforms and that they would not indulge in vilification campaigns against any executive, the Bank restarted discussions with the unions at various levels; these discussions had been suspended as a result of their opposing the introduction of new technology and Gartner's engagement as consultants.

Representation of Trade Unions in Committees Reviewed

Both the Association and the Federation were given representation on the Bank's House Journal Committee. Besides, the Association was also given representation on Flat Allotment Committee for senior executives and similarly, the Federation on allotment of flats to subordinate staff. The Association, in particular, leveraged these positions to project their visibility and influence. The management also invited general secretaries of both the Association as well as the Federation to share the dias with the top management during half-yearly business review meetings with senior operating managers like zonal and regional managers. In these meetings, the Association leader emphasised, to the operating managers, about the need to involve their office-bearers for business development at zonal/regional levels on the pattern of corporate office. Their representation in these forums sent a message about their closeness with the top management and in the process, many vulnerable operating managers allowed interference of these leaders in administrative functions. In the name of business development, the Association interfered in the postings and transfers of managers. The zonal/regional managers who resisted such efforts were marked out by the Association for non-cooperation and complaints to higher management. They, thus, abused their representation in these forums.

As a part of our strategy to sanitise the administration from their influence and restore management control in administration, we reviewed these arrangements and union representation in these forums was discontinued. At a time when we were formalising our relations with unions, we could not have continued any such thing that sent a wrong signal to operating staff, more so when such mechanisms were used to demoralise the operating managers.

Effective HR Administration

Together these steps signalled the management's resolve to streamline IR and improve HR administration. The management accepted its responsibility in managing these two vital areas and recognised its role in creating a facilitative business climate. After the introduction of the HR audit, these actions further reinforced our belief that the management at all levels must own its responsibility to improve productivity and discipline and act with fairness.

Sometime in the latter part of 2002, the corporate office moved from Ballard Pier to the newly emerging banking hub in Bandra Kurla Complex, Mumbai. In this new swanky office, we shifted with minimum staff in each function. We also did not allot any union or the Association office in this new place. Shifting to this new place gave us an opportunity to streamline administration and reduce the staff strength considerably.

Major HR Reforms Undertaken

Now that the HR audit, comprehensive review of structured meetings, and streamlining of various legacy-driven practices were successfully achieved, some more measures were initiated to reinforce the management's commitment to discipline and to simultaneously provide speedy solutions to employee problems. The aim was to reduce the internal bureaucracy that delayed personnel decision-making, make the system responsive to employee grievances, and provide structured solutions to day-to-day problems through the use of technology in HR administration.

Interestingly, the unions could not resist these changes. My sense is that the common employees did not endorse the power of their leaders who did not work and enjoyed perquisites such as immunity from work and security against mobility. The leaders were seen to be in connivance with the top management and as having lost touch with the ground realities.

Apparently, most leaders had failed to inspire the working class as they had aligned themselves too much with the management in order to pursue their own interests and to seek favours for themselves. This was in consonance with my research findings, which clearly pointed out the disconnect between the top union leaders and their members. These initiatives to reorder the union–management relationships in a more structured pattern were welcomed by the general employees and the operating managers. Reviving the credibility of the management, empowering the operating managers, and restoring the authority of the branch managers to manage the workplaces and discipline the employees gave me a great deal of professional satisfaction.

It was quite an experience to pilot these paradigmatic changes in the muddied IR culture of the Bank and to lay the foundation for the smooth implementation of the many dramatic changes that would take place in subsequent years. All the humiliation inflicted on me by the unions and lack of support by my immediate boss, and in fact his clandestine relationship with those who attacked my honour and confidence, was very hurting. Even as the odds were against me, I did not want to quit. I did not mind suffering for the larger purpose of creating a better future for hundreds of operating managers who expected me to improve their daily work life and rid the Bank from the clutches of the trade unions. Personally, I felt that the price I paid for it by way of tensions and turmoil was well worth it.

In my career of over 30 years at the Bank, no management ever put so much focus on improving the IR climate at the Bank; most learnt to live with the situation because they feared to disrupt business. It was rather a strange paradox that the members of the Association (the managers) were now happy about the diminishing role of their own leaders and the increasing role and authority they themselves would bear in managing the workplace. They clearly felt that their leaders had bartered their collective freedom for favours for themselves!

Crafting HR for the Future

It would be naïve to believe that weakening the unions' influence in IR would automatically improve the engagement of the employees. We had witnessed the naivety of predecessor managements' strategies of focusing on managing and favouring key union leaders in the simple belief that this would automatically translate into employee engagement. For them, maintaining a cosy relationship with union leaders was be all and end all of IR management. I was very conscious that the unions and the employees were two different entities and that the management needed to deal with both within separate policy frameworks. Good relations with the unions would not mean satisfied and engaged employees, just as good relations with the employees would not mean satisfied trade unions.

We now needed to craft a development-oriented framework for our HR policy. In our new HR strategy, the entire focus was on engaging employees and building new capabilities in them to enable them to meet the challenges of the competitive times we were now in.

I strongly believed that a new culture for performance and accountability could be accelerated only in an environment of greater emphasis on building HR. Therefore, in the pursuit of transforming itself into a vibrant and competitive universal financial service organisation, enabled by modern technology, the challenge for the Bank was to recast its human processes and align its HR to the new-order banking in order to fulfil its aspiration to remain an uncontested player in the public sector banking space.

An internal task force, under my direct supervision, developed an 'HR Vision 2010' document and presented it to the Board of Directors. The document had the following core objectives for HRD:

1. to adopt and pursue global HR best practices in our pursuit to become a bank of international standards and to become an employer of preferred choice;
2. to create a pool of entrepreneurial managers and business leaders for the future;
3. to create a performance-driven culture and an exciting workplace for employees;
4. to create an environment that maximised the performance and potential of employees;
5. to create a learning organisation for employees' intellectual growth and creativity; and
6. to inculcate a sense of self-worth, ethical values, and high professional integrity.

I also put before the board a proposal to form a board-level Steering Committee on HR, which would include HR professionals of repute from the industry and academics, in addition to the CEO, the executive director, and some of the board members. This high-level committee was to spearhead the HR agenda for the Bank right from the top.

The board readily approved our proposal. Pradip Khandwalla, a board member and a noted management expert, joined the Steering Committee. We also inducted two eminent HR professionals in the Steering Committee: Arvind Agrawal, President, HRD, RPG Group; and Professor B.L. Maheshwari, Director, Centre for Organization Development, Hyderabad. Under the guidance of the Steering Committee, we developed a blueprint on HR that envisaged a comprehensive review and reinvention of work processes, technology application, HR policies, front-line engagement, change management, and other processes. This was perhaps the first-ever written policy document on an HR vision in the Bank and, as per my information, in all of the Indian banking industry. It was strategic in nature, comprehensive in approach, and futuristic in vision, and covered areas such as enunciating an HR vision and model, talent management and development philosophy, a positive approach to addressing operating issues, a greater thrust on learning, and growth of the agenda of the Bank which would catapult it into the future.

Several initiatives were taken to build HR. Some of the key steps are mentioned here:

1. Development of a new HR resourcing policy after the closure of the BSRB.
2. Introduction of a performance appraisal system for the workmen cadre to encourage a culture of performance.
3. Building of a cadre of officers in the areas of credit, forex, and treasury management.
4. Building of a leadership in the senior management cadre by organising management development programmes at leading management institutes.
5. Framing of guidelines for grooming officers through job rotation, transfer on longer stay at one place, transfer from branch to administrative office and vice versa, transfer guidelines for lady officers, training and development, and specialised training for officers.

   • Management education programme called 'Tikshna' (Sanskrit origin meaning sharp, fast, and intelligent, having thirst for seeking fulfilment) was conducted for a core team of 500 identified executives, in association with internationally acclaimed business schools: IIM Ahmedabad and MDI, Gurgaon.

- Lateral recruitment of professionals with specialised skills and knowledge at senior levels.
- Campus recruitment of management graduates and other officers in different areas of banking.

Our focus on building leadership helped us realise our vision of fast-tracking executives with high potential and attracting professionals from the market. The Bank was turning a new page in its life to build a new future for its HR, who for too long had remained on the periphery and on whose shoulders the union leaders had enjoyed the perquisites of power.

As we moved to a more orderly conduct of IR and a better climate at the branches, I too moved from the Bank to assume charge as CEO of Dena Bank, a smaller-sized bank in a crisis and with a question mark on its survival. I had no idea then that I would return very soon to the BoB as CEO and that I would have the opportunity to further drive the transformation of the Bank.

* * *

This chapter describes, in some detail, the new competitive context for the Bank and the need for changing the prevailing culture of IR that was based on a 'participative-cum-accommodative culture', but worked in reality as a 'cosy–collusive–collaboration' between the management and the unions, which proved to be detrimental to workplace peace and smooth delivery of customer service. Based on my insights from the research, the IR strategies were reshaped to focus on employee relations (a clear shift from focusing on union leaders). The aim was to streamline the entire IR ecosystem and turn it around from the existing order. Personal relations are important in IR, but they have to be within the institutional framework of the union–management relationship.

The main plank of the management strategies was to institutionalise IR management, streamline unstructured understandings on various issues, reorder union–management relationship, debureaucratise decision-making in IR, and reform the workplace by restoring the credibility of the operating managers by supporting them in their endeavour to improve discipline and productivity. The strategy aimed at changing the existing culture in IR, reduce dependence on trade unions for business growth, and reach out to managers and employees.

In this endeavour, a number of well-crafted steps were taken, such as clearly defining role boundaries for the trade unions; reviewing the informal practices and withdrawing facilities and concessions over and above industry-level agreements; keeping the unions out of placement and promotion decisions; building efficiencies in the conduct of personnel/IR functions; unifying the HR function in the corporate office in Mumbai for a speedy resolution of issues; dealing with some legacy issues pending resolution for a long time; systemic intervention by introducing HR audit to bring workplace reforms; empowering branch managers for effective personnel administration and developing accountability in them; reviewing existing mechanisms of union–management interactions and streamlining the same; and developing a new HR policy encompassing building new competencies and capabilities.

As expected, these moves led to an unprecedented situation in which the unions raised the banner of revolt, but without much success. The management successfully transited to a new regime of carrying out its duties in a proper manner. The unions' efforts to block reforms in HR received a lukewarm response from their members as most members did not endorse their union leaders' practice of colluding with the management at the cost of ignoring their grievances.

In spite of a prolonged period of cold relations with the unions, the management was able to achieve major streamlining of the IR culture, restore the authority of the operating managers, and improve productivity. This demonstrates how formalisation can be achieved if management actions are consistent and fair. In the current instance, the process of transformation of the IR culture was also facilitated by the prevailing disconnect between the union organisations and their members, which in some ways demonstrates the fragility of IR based on collusive collaboration between the management and the unions.

This was clearly one of the most comprehensive reforms at the Bank after its nationalisation in 1969. The informality in the union–management relationship that had given the unions the power to block any reforms was replaced by empowerment of the operating managers, improvements in the HR administration, and better workplace discipline, all in sharp contrast to the earlier IR strategy. Formalisation of relations was considered a key strategy in the new IR set-up and the strategy pursued in IR was a shift from a 'spotlight on the union leaders' to a 'spotlight on the operating managers and employees'. These steps were in sync with our intention of creating a new culture of performance and HRD and our aim to lay the foundation for accelerated business development and hassle-free service to customers.

The turbulence in IR and the consequent delay in undertaking technology-driven business transformation was a price worth paying to save the Bank from daily hassles and to give the thousands of front-line managers of the Bank the freedom to run their branches without union interference. The actions and reforms at BoB were both comprehensive and multi-pronged in nature. Tinkering with ad hoc or half-hearted steps in reforming IR may not yield desired results. For sustainable impact of reforms, the entire ecosystem of IR needs progressive review and desired action plan. The result was that BoB was truly poised to regain its leadership position in the public sector.

It was the most risky and traumatic period of my leadership journey. Reforms in piloting IR was not without the risk of inviting the wrath of trade unions which, for decades, had flourished and ruled in the Bank in an atmosphere and culture of mutual survival and accommodation. The entire edifice of union–management relations thus sustained on the fulcrum of opportunistic alliance. My actions to go against the grain and rock the boat was considered a sacrilege by the trade unions, and I had to face the combined fury of all the unions which spearheaded the most vicious campaign challenging my professional integrity. Worse still, I was out on a limb and left to fight all these battles by myself. Except for the inputs from the personnel specialists in preparing issues for reforms and extending rock solid emotional support, there were very few in the management who understood the rationale of our conflict with the trade unions that could fundamentally alter the quality of life of our operating managers and preferred to remain as silent bystanders. I was being penalised for an initiative that held key to long-lasting peace at the workplaces.

Personally, for me, this experience unfolded my own potential to manage crisis situations to successfully achieve the goals of the organisation. What gave me immense professional satisfaction was that all this effort was worth the cost because it wrested management control in IR, empowering managers to function in an environment free of daily pinpricks and harassment at the hands of the trade unions. These reforms also prepared the Bank for undertaking a major transformation, as we will see in the next chapter.

Box 11.1 Reforming IR: Learnings from Reflection

1. Reforms in IR in a legacy-driven culture is one of the most difficult piece of top management work. A second-in-command, as a member of top management team, has an important role identity of his own. Hence, he can trigger major change initiatives in the best interests of the organisation.
2. Reforms in IR are a prerequisite for wider organisational transformation; and more so in a situation where trade unions are averse to changes and can effectively stonewall the transformation process.
3. Industrial relations is a complex function, which defies simple solution. A systems approach to look at IR can help. It is not something that can be fixed with some short-term measures like appeasement of trade unions. In fact, it can add to IR problems in the long run.
4. Leaders' biggest challenge in IR transformation is to break the status quo, including prevailing attitudes, structures, and legacy-driven processes, and take bold steps to change this. Cultural legacy can be dismantled by changing the existing attitudes, pattern of relationships, with professional competence and relentless engagement with the problem-solving process.
5. Leaders have an important role to challenge the mental models (of dependency and helplessness) of the operating managers by initiating positive action and demonstrating, with grit and determination, that they are committed to reform and transformation of the existing reality.
6. Leaders face both personal and professional vulnerabilities during IR transformation and can withstand all this if they remain focused on higher purpose and show resilience in the face of criticism or even isolation.
7. Undertaking reforms in IR needs a high degree of disciplined and professional approach in dealing with both the trade unions and the employees and requires intelligent diagnosis, use of judgement, risk-taking, and conflict resolution skills.
8. Conflict is an appropriate time to review the entire relationship and bring about desired changes, pending for a long time.

9. The focus of reforms in IR has to be on improving the workplace through empowerment and support to operating managers.
10. It is important to put in place an HR governance model both for IR/HR strategy and for other people-related issues to ward off HR risks and ensure consistency and fairness in employee matters.
11. The root of difficult problems is never a single factor but several factors acting in combination. Management must accept responsibility for their piece of mess.
12. There is inherent complexity in changing the existing pattern of IR based on favours and mollycoddling of trade unions and generally, a single-step solution is not the answer.
13. Often series of well-thought-out small changes can also produce a big impact.

Chapter 12

FROM IR TO HRD

In March 2005, the Government of India appointed me as the CEO of BoB, which was a sort of homecoming for me, and on a personal level, I was excited about this chance to lead the Bank in which I had begun my career as a junior officer, 34 years back in 1971. Yet, I was well aware of the enormity of the challenge that I was taking up.

During the period 2000–05, the performance of the Bank registered a sharp decline on several major business parameters, with the result its overall ranking among the nationalised banks slipped from the top position to the fourth position. There was a steep fall in the market share in both deposits and credits and significantly, in the most attractive business segments of current accounts and retail assets. For instance, in the crucial area of credit, as against the 20–25 per cent growth registered by peer banks, the same in the case of BOB was below 1 per cent. Resultantly, the Bank lost considerably on its market share in the business, with the performance below average in other key areas also, such as growth in total income and fee-based income.

A similar trend was witnessed in the Bank's performance in one of its traditional strongholds, Gujarat. This was despite the state's booming economy and Gujarat being one of the valuable parts of the Bank's franchise. The loss in market share in Gujarat was substantial, from 22.3 per cent to 20.1 per cent.

At the level of specialised corporate credit branches and other large branches headed by assistant general managers/chief managers too, the performance was far below potential. Despite their significance in the Bank's operation and contribution to the balance sheet, their overall performance registered a declining trend.

My own assessment of the general sentiment prevalent among the Bank staff was one of supreme complacency. They seemed to be ensconced in their own cocoons, oblivious to the realities around them. There was an imperative need to rigorously shake them out of their slumber if the Bank was not to become a dinosaur!

We have seen in the previous chapter the failed effort of the Bank to implement technology due to IR problems and more importantly, the leadership developing cold feet to push technology owing to union protests. Shenoy operated like a pilot who, in adverse weather, would rather return to the base camp than steer the aircraft through the journey. Thus, the technology project, which had been presented before the board several times, was postponed for one or the other reason, essentially because Shenoy lacked confidence and enthusiasm for it in the face of IR problems.

The lack of new technology tarnished the image of the Bank, which had hitherto been lauded for its progressive ways. The technology project team was both demotivated and directionless. Staff morale in general was low and managers complained about the high customer attrition rate, a result of the lack of alternate delivery channels such as core banking and ATMs. Customers showed their resentment, especially because other banks were ready with the new technology that made banking easier and more efficient. Customers complained, but were not listened to, and it was costing the Bank dearly in terms of its competitive positioning in the industry.

Financial analysts wrote the Bank's obituary, pointing to its sluggish pace of credit growth, low retail growth, low technology, and heavy reliance on treasury profits, and commented adversely on its performance. Phrases such as 'particularly weak on the core business front', 'a high-risk bank', and 'a bad apple in the public sector basket' were being thrown about freely and 'sell' was the unanimous recommendation for BoB's shares. We were deeply concerned about banking analysts labelling the Bank as an underperformer. In my first meeting of the Board of Directors, the board members unanimously promised their full support for fast-track decisions and gave me carte blanche for moving the Bank ahead. The government nominee on the board was especially reflective. He told me:

We have wasted enough time. Our credit growth has not picked up and technology implementation is lagging behind. Please accelerate the pace of changes. The entire board and the government will support your initiatives.

This was a huge push for our subsequent journey of transformation. We realised that we had a formidable task at hand and would need to fire on all cylinders from day one. It was imperative to act expeditiously to stem the loss in market position and reclaim leadership status.

The New Economic Scenario

The country had moved to a high growth trajectory, registering a gross domestic product (GDP) growth of over 8 per cent. The overall economic resurgence, rising exports, and the Indian growth story attracted worldwide attention and the country had become one of the most favoured invest-ment destinations. The significant demographic dividend, coupled with increasing incomes, substantially contributed to the rising domestic demand. All of these provided attractive opportunities to the banking sec-tor. The private sector and foreign banks established themselves firmly and Indian banking became highly competitive. The credit growth was robust, technology was increasingly leveraged to provide 24×7 banking, and sev-eral measures aimed at providing improved customer service were intro-duced. There was a new air of confidence and resurgence in the economy.

As we set out to hone our business vision and set our priorities, it was clear that some of our peer banks in the public sector had become aggressive in acquiring customers and driving business growth. In short, the rules of the game were being rewritten. The BoB had to catch up fast to bounce back to its pre-eminent position of bank of first choice for customers.

From day one, it was clear that we had to act fast. There was no time to be lost, every day mattered. We had to create a new growth momentum by energising people and creating an environment conducive for the imple-mentation of revolutionary technology and customer-centric innovations.

As we needed to work on several fronts simultaneously, it was my belief that we had several things to do, the first and foremost being: fast-track technology implementation; uplift credit growth; and restore the lost momentum for customer service. In a large organisation of our size, a set of top managers could never achieve all this unless our front line was on board and understood the context of our anxiety and deployed themselves with passion to achieve the desired goal.

I had the complete faith in the wisdom of employees whose career and future was tied to the growth of the Bank. We wanted to abandon the past policy of enlisting the support of union leaders for carrying out an essentially management function. I was very clear in my mind that employees would be the centre of our priority in terms of building their morale through transparent justice mechanism, listening to them, using field wisdom, building new capabilities, and affording them career progression. This was an uncompromising belief that guided us in our transformational endeavours.

First Thing First: Initiating Technology

Our top priority was rolling out core banking solutions (CBS) as the future of the Bank depended on it, for technology was fast becoming the key differentiator between a performing and a non-performing bank. A leading technology firm, Hewlett-Packard (HP), had already been selected as the system integrator for the project. The union opposition to Gartner's appointment as a consultant to technology-led business transformation programme and taking a foreign company on board was fading away under the overwhelming pressure for change from both customers and employees. However, many details and financials were still to be worked out.

Most obviously, it was time to take a judgement call and fast-track the initiatives that needed to be taken. This being the top priority, without any loss of time, we secured the approval of the board and signed the contract with HP on 15 April 2005, just six weeks after I had assumed charge as the CEO. This marked the beginning of the execution of core banking in right earnest. With a view to seeking everyone's cooperation for this huge paradigm shift in the Bank, we invited the general secretaries of the workmen's unions and the officers' association (all of whom had opposed Gartner's appointment) to attend the contract-signing ceremony with HP. Their presence at the ceremony signified a positive beginning for everyone in the Bank, and I was pleased when the union leaders congratulated me for kick-starting the technology implementation. The signing of contract was a great morale booster for everyone.

Our technology project was more comprehensive than that of the other banks because we were also putting all our global operations on the same platform. The project, when completed, would enable the Bank's customers throughout the world to access banking and financial services anywhere, anytime, through multiple delivery channels from Internet banking to call centres. The project was to span five years, but at the end of it, BoB would be on par with the most reputed financial service provider in the world. We planned to have the first sample branch ready by December 2005.

A Bold New Vision

We now needed to craft a bold new vision for the Bank so that we could revive its business culture and make it grow again. Even though, broadly, we knew the problems and perhaps even the solutions, I was keen to take on board all the stakeholders—to seek their involvement and learn from their experience. I started this process with the Board of Directors, discussing at board meetings the various issues relating to business and putting together a vision document with the help of the directors. Alongside business issues, I also presented a comprehensive strategic HR plan and a schedule of implementation. I was very happy to see their commitment in discussing the several position papers that had been diligently prepared by our team of general managers after discussions within the top management.

I invited late Udai Pareek, a well-known HR and organisation development consultant, to attend the board meeting and help us ensure equal focus on people issues, alongside business issues, in finalising the 'Vision 2005–10'. Pareek provided useful insights on various issues, like new capabilities required to implement the vision, succession issues in key functions, debureaucratised processes for customer retention, and need for an open and transparent culture in the Bank. The board immensely benefited from his insights and guidance and each functional head understood their role in building people processes within their function and take ownership. After two days of discussions with the board, the Bank was ready with a new vision document that would help it to transform itself into a multi-specialist sales and service organisation. The chief features of the vision document were:

1. doubling the global business of the Bank in the next three years;
2. placing renewed focus on retail so as to double the business segment;
3. transforming the top 500 branches into top-class sales and service centres through improved ambience, processes, people, and technology;
4. attracting additional customers from the Indian corporate world so as to bring at least 300–400 of the top 500 business groups in the country into the Bank's loan book;
5. initiating an aggressive overseas growth programme; and
6. developing an integrated HR plan encompassing new competencies and leadership bench strength for achieving the new vision.

Implementation Strategy

My long experience at the Bank had convinced me that development of a vision was a comparatively easier job than its implementation. The implementation required relooking at our existing ways of doing things—the internal bureaucracy that hindered decision-making, the silo-based working that created coordination problems, the lack of accountability that manifested itself in blame games—and learning how to weave in the new competencies and capabilities that were needed in our staff at various levels. The key questions that confronted me were:

1. How could we create a feeling of shared purpose in our top team about our emphasis on 'People'—engaging them, building their capabilities in the technological environment, and communicating effectively?
2. How could we inject a sense of urgency and sense of accountability for results across the organisation? How could we break the silos and work in a coordinated way?
3. How could we jointly solve problems in an effective way?
4. How could we facilitate and help the operating managers conduct their business smoothly by engaging people in the front line?
5. How could we learn together from the field insights?
6. How could we engage our 38,000 employees in working towards a common goal to rebuild the Bank?
7. How could we create a distributed leadership across the Bank that would guide and excite the employees and customers?

8. How could the top management be seen as a resource by the various business units so that they felt safe and confident about communicating their problems to us?

During my years at the Bank, especially my two tenures as Zonal Manager, I experienced a culture of top management merely issuing instructions to field functionaries without any interaction on the difficulties which may arise in implementation, based on the prevailing ground reality, which was quite dysfunctional. If there was one thing that I was committed to change, it was this culture at the top which sought accountability only from the lower-level functionaries without itself being accountable. I had found that this often acted as a dampener on the motivation and morale of the operating managers. We have seen in earlier chapters how such a culture in personnel management and IR demoralised operating managers in their endeavours to conduct business efficiently.

My professional training in HRD and organisational development (I am certified as a professional trainer in process work by the Indian Society of Applied Behaviour Science), and the fact that I had worked with some really outstanding HRD professionals like Udai Pareek, T.V. Rao, and Rajen K. Gupta in some training programmes as co-facilitator, ensured a strong commitment towards building human processes to navigate the organisation. For me, processes held the key to effective problem-solving.

I was of the firm belief that we needed to take strong foundational steps that would sustain the Bank in the long term and make it resilient against any setback. I was averse to short-term, Band-Aid solutions to both human as well as business problems and resolved to avoid this approach even if it meant sacrificing some short-term business gains. I also wanted to bring about a mindset change in the top management from an overwhelmingly 'commercial orientation' to a 'long-term value creation mental mode' in dealing with issues relating to employees and customers.

I felt that our chief focus should be on building 'intangibles' such as HR (capability building and engagement), leadership bench strength, governance, rebranding and image building, and customer-centricity and technology, all of which would help the Bank to develop resilience and grow as a vibrant institution. This kind of emphasis on intangibles could drive dramatic tangible results, as we saw later.

Changing the Culture

Morning Meetings

A School of Learning, Reflecting, and Execution

In the context of the Bank's prevailing culture of highly centralised decision-making, internal bureaucracy, interdepartmental conflicts, and control-driven communication (which I experienced in abundance in my role as zonal manager), as well as lack of responsive culture, my biggest challenge was to create a new culture of response, trust, and collaboration with high degree of field orientation. I wanted each one in top management to learn the new habit of collaboration and grow from controllers to leaders. In turn, my expectation was that each member of top management would engage their own staff and ensure their motivation and development. My main aim was to let go of the past ways of managing things and put the Bank in a continual learning mode by fostering systemic thinking among our top team.

My first move, therefore, was to constructively engage the top management in the organisation-building task. The top management in any organisation adds colour and tempo to change process. They would be the harbinger of change in our transformational journey. So, I introduced a system of daily morning meeting comprising all the general managers (about 15) at the corporate office to architect and be responsible for our transformation programme. The aim was to develop a collective stake in our proposed initiatives, solve problems together, build understanding and respect for each other, and set the tone for vigorously pursuing the mammoth transformation agenda which we had set for ourselves. Another key objective was to bring visible change in the top management behaviour vis- à-vis the operating managers in their day-to-day responses. I wanted top managers to be real problem solvers and not ivory tower monitors. One of my key concerns was to ensure a superior level of guidance from the corporate office to the field functionaries. We thus needed to initiate a new culture of timely response, mutual trust between the corporate office and field functionaries, and a hands-on approach to problem-solving.

The morning meetings were organised with strict discipline: they would start at sharp 9.30 a.m. and end at exactly 10.30 a.m. They carried no specific agenda because the idea was to help the group to interact comfortably and encourage everyone to raise issues in a spontaneous manner. Membership was initially confined to the general managers (though after some time, deputy general managers were also invited), two executive directors, one advisor, my executive secretary, and me. Attendance and participation were mandatory. Except on days when I was out of the headquarters on work, I made it a point to attend the meetings regularly. In my absence, the meetings were conducted by the executive directors.

We devoted time at the meetings to critique our existing processes, systems, communication styles, and how they could be aligned to the new expectations from all concerned employees and customers. The executive directors, or any other participant, or I brought issues considered necessary to improve our response time. We held open and productive discussions about the critical issues. We challenged each other on issues and eventually developed a healthy climate to openly discuss organisational issues. In this way, we could achieve a healthy respect for each other's point of view. In this forum, we could also discuss the merit and contributions of our operational functionaries, which provided good input in promotion and placement decisions. This considerably diluted the role of bureaucratic politics in career decisions of the senior executives.

Apart from issues identified as critical, we also discussed issues that were referred to me during my field visits or issues brought to our notice by customers that needed the attention of the top management. In many cases, our discussions led to reorganisation of work in a particular department, building new competencies in the executives, relocation of executives and officers, trimming of the number of layers required in resolution of problems, and so on.

Initially, for the first year, I did not emphasise discussions on the usual stuff—the charts and histograms of our business elements, how each region was performing on various business parameters, and so on—and get into monitoring/controlling. This would have meant doing more of the same thing. Instead, my main objective was to create a community of top functionaries and bring them out from their functional thinking to an understanding of the big picture and learning to think together, work together, and act synergistically. Leverage comes from new ways of thinking and therefore this emphasis. My other focus was: how to build a Bank that can innovate continually and connect with customers and employees in a significant way. During the first 100 days itself, we came out with many new initiatives, like rebranding of the Bank, initiation of 8 a.m. to 8 p.m. banking outlets, and 500 new ATMs. We also achieved dramatic growth in the first year itself in our important business parameters. My stand on focusing on the drivers of business was vindicated!

Once the immediate priorities had been sorted out, the next step was to think collectively about long-term plans. We had to prepare the Bank for the future. I could see twin challenges ahead of me. The first was to resurrect traditional business lines such as improving market share in deposits and advances, accelerating credit growth, and improving customer services. The second was to architect the Bank as a financial supermarket offering all kinds of banking and financial services under one umbrella. To meet these twin challenges, it was imperative to embark on process improvements and innovations.

There were many questions to answer. How different would Indian banking be in the future? What was the nature of the changes happening in the banking and customer universe? Which of these changes would have a significant impact on BoB? What measures would the Bank need to take to prepare it for these changes?

We initiated discussions in the morning meetings around the theme of future banking, competitors' ways of working, their marketing strategies, bottlenecks in our style of functioning, and many other things that needed to change in our internal processes, as well as building new competencies and capabilities in our people. We discarded conventional wisdom and aspired to build a culture of performance, accountability, and collaborative working. Our main theme was always around building a new culture of response and creating fusion of operations and administration. We needed to bind everybody into a single enterprise and break the silos that characterised our top management.

The morning meetings became the forum for setting in motion the spadework that was needed for the vision exercise, 'Vision 2005–10'. Initially, the functional heads developed a vision for their function by involving their key managers. Then each general manager presented his vision paper in the morning meeting and, after clinical analysis, the paper was given final shape, ready for presentation to the board. In this discussion process, each member had the opportunity to contribute and participate in finalising the vision paper for each key function. This positive alignment helped in raising the bar of discussions at a qualitative level and enabled everyone to see the larger, holistic picture. After a series of in-house discussions and drafts, crack teams were commissioned to fine-tune and align the individual function-wise vision with the overall larger vision of the Bank. Through this process, the ownership of the new vision was ensured.

The morning meetings helped us to find creative solutions to many problems during implementation, in particular anytime–anywhere banking. In the initial period of migration to the new technological systems, especially the core banking system, a large number of problems started pouring in from both the branch offices and the customers. Nobody in the top management had anticipated some of these basic customer service problems. Collectively putting our heads together, practically on a daily basis, we solved the issues. In addition, we also discussed a number of key issues referred to us by field managers, using our collective wisdom to find solutions to specific problems. I often brought emails from customers to these meetings and discussed the issues raised by them. Every person in the group knew about the problems and issues we faced in the context of our processes and was involved in trouble-shooting. A problem was never that of a functional general manager, it was a problem of the Bank. This helped break the silos and created alignment across functions. It also created an opportunity for daily learning through real-life problems.

Another priority in the morning meetings was to promote strategic thinking. We laid great emphasis on diagnosis as the starting point for problem-solving because lack of diagnosis, or faulty diagnosis, itself can become a major problem. When we discussed a live problem, we asked ourselves these diagnostic questions: the root cause of the problem; examining the problem from the lens of customers; need for long-term solution; and steps needed to prevent recurrence and for equipping the operating managers to appropriately address the issues.

Business was not all that we discussed at the morning meetings. We talked about, among other things, emerging issues in leadership and developments in the global economy. I would often circulate good articles that I had read. All of this resulted in new and creative thinking and helped in the implementation of new initiatives. One example of the creativity our discussions sparked could be seen in the names we came up with for our product offerings and innovations: Retail Loan Factory; SME Loan Factory; Gen-Next Branch; and Happy Hour Banking.

Towards the second year, after I was encouraged by the level of collaboration amongst various functional heads and the palpable change in the level of thinking, we began reviews of various parameters in business, such as deposits, advances, low-cost deposit growth, recovery, retail growth, SME growth, and growth in agriculture credit. We also reviewed the patterns of growth in the rural, semi-urban, urban, and metro areas. Our products were analysed critically to see how they compared with the offerings of our competitors, and suitable changes and modifications were suggested. Of course, process issues remained our priority. We also discussed various strategies such as international expansion and joint ventures for mutual fund and insurance and card business.

The morning meetings were intense and I personally benefited a lot from the arguments and counter-arguments in the group. There was an increasing openness among the group members. An occasional touch of humour added the necessary spice. Overall, the meetings became an important forum where anyone could table a business issue, a process problem, a customer complaint, or an HR issue.

A Forum for Execution

In a dynamic business environment, our capacity to execute vision was a key theme. Best of the vision could fail without an accelerated execution machine.

My tenure as the CEO coincided with the centenary year of the Bank. While planning various activities to suitably commemorate the event, we visualised an ambitious project, Vision 2010. This envisaged doubling of the Bank's business during 2005–08, implementation of CBS, expansion of the ATM network, launch of new product lines, expansion of international operations, restructuring of the Indian subsidiaries, and most importantly, rebranding of the Bank. All these required meticulous planning and diligent execution.

While the technological initiatives were proceeding at breakneck speed, we had to kick-start new business strategies, design new business models, and put them on the fast track to implementation. I busied myself mainly with building a new culture (of performance, service and collaboration, people processes), rebranding, international expansion, and technology push and customer-centric innovations, apart from focusing on board matters and external relations, including with regulators and the government. My two Executive Directors, A.C. Mahajan and Santhanaraman, were experienced bankers who ran the operational side of the banking. Our General Manager, IT, J.K. Chander, a gifted and home-grown technology enthusiast, guided the technology team with extraordinary zeal and delivered the first core banking branch in just six months. This greatly boosted everyone's morale demonstrating a new resolve to perform and excel.

We had to come up with strategies to double the business size and especially raise the credit portfolio. Subhash Kalia, General Manager, a quintessential credit expert, passionately worked to revive the credit portfolio and surprised everyone when the first-year credit growth touched over 40 per cent. Our all-purpose advisor and a former General Manager, V.G. Subramaniam, with his insightful conceptual thinking and restlessness, supervised the overall transformation project and worked with consultants. Similarly, our other General Managers, late M.M. Gadgil, Asit Pal, V.B.L. Saxena, K.K. Agarwal, B.A. Prabhakar, Subhash Mundra, Santhanam, late Dipankar Mukherjee, and others, did excellent work in their respective functions, brilliantly supported by their respective functional colleagues. Each one surprised everyone else. On the administrative side, my talented and meticulous executive secretary, Usha Ananthasubramanian, effectively coordinated my priorities, external interface, and board matters. Additionally, C.V. Chandrashekhar, Deputy General Manager, HRD, did a remarkable job on strategic initiatives in IR and HRD. Prakash Ranjan and later Joydeep, HRD managers in my secretariat, contributed significantly in designing some innovative programmes for the employees. In the morning meetings, all these and other colleagues collectively discussed the implementation details of each project, identifying the owners of the project, the support required, and the implementation schedule. In a trusting environment, everyone discussed issues relevant to their work, and this helped bringing interconnectedness in various functions.

But there was still a lot to be done. We needed to restructure internally and we also needed to pursue new revenue streams, for all of which we needed expert advice. So, we hired a globally acclaimed management consulting firm, McKinsey and Company, which had the market knowledge to help us design new business models and in internal restructuring wherever necessary. The transformation project was code-named 'Project Parivartan'. We regularly reviewed McKinsey's work in the morning meetings.

Over a period of time, our morning meetings became a forum where our functional heads ventured to come out of their silos to participate in a larger dream to see the big picture, cooperate and collaborate with other colleagues abandoning their bureaucratic ways of playing ping-pong game, and create a new environment of pushing the flywheel of change with collective energy. As they say, 'None of us is as smart as all of us', and this could not be more relevant than at the time of BoB's transformation because problems during such transformative periods are too complex to be solved by one person.

The morning meetings created an environment of esprit de corps in the ranks of the management and helped stitch together many loose ends in our policies. It invigorated and energised the top management, enforced the discipline of execution, and created accountability. More than anything, corporate management acted with responsibility and accountability, provided support to operating managers, and engaged employees in their respective functions, which improved field–corporate connect and trust across various levels. The morning meetings played a key role in implementing all the projects we had envisioned within the stipulated deadlines and in a flawless manner. It acted as a 'War Room' which processed information, reviewed strategies, and initiated action with speed and alacrity. It helped us to continually learn how to see the reality vis-à-vis our vision and strive hard to achieve our vision. It is a matter of great pride for me that not one project in our transformation deviated from its specified target date and we achieved our vision for the Bank on every single parameter. Each one surprised the rest of the group. The entire group experimented synergistically with their collective intelligence quotient (IQ) and emotional quotient (EQ) and achieved most spectacular business results and brought the Bank up from the quagmire of criticism and laggard state, in which it had entered. And even more special to me is what an executive told me:

'The morning meetings were a school of management where I learnt my lessons in management and leadership.'

Truly, the morning meetings created a new culture of team play at the top, which percolated down below. Each member of the top management energised the others, taught them, and learnt as well. They were also ready to work miracles. In fact, these meetings helped us develop and implement an ambitious first 100 days agenda and chart out several key initiatives (Table 12.1).

At a personal level, our morning meetings provided me immense learning opportunity and insights into complex banking issues and how they impacted customers. It became a laboratory for unleashing collective creative potential of our top management. It helped each one of us in the top team to rise to our fullest potential, expand our patterns of thinking, challenge our existing ways of doing things, and finally, build an architecture of intangibles to ready the Bank to take up emerging and future challenges. Much of the Bank's achievements in building its new identity can be attributed to our engaged discussions in such meetings. We, in a real sense,

TABLE 12.1   Key Decisions in Morning Meetings—Action and Review

1. Developing first 100-days' agenda:
   (a) expanding ATM network: 500 ATMs, including launch of 200 ATMs on a single day;
   (b) launch of 550 8 a.m. to 8 p.m. branches and 24-hour human banking; and
   (c) rebranding of the Bank: logo change, appointment of cricketer Rahul Dravid as brand ambassador.
2. Finalisation of Vision 2005–10 document.
3. Core Banking (anywhere–anytime) project.
4. Launching of centenary year celebrations.
5. Launch of retail loan factories and SME loan factories.
6. Joint ventures with foreign collaborations in life insurance and mutual funds.
7. Revamping international operations strategy.
8. Revamping Gujarat operations.
9. Project Parivartan: business transformation programme.
10. Various HRD initiatives.

experienced 'mindset' change as a result of collective learning process in these meetings.

Truly, morning meetings were my 'sapiental circles'.[1]

Repositioning HRD

Having rid the Bank of IR irritants that obfuscated our transformation efforts, we began our transformation journey with key focus on mobilising the collective efforts of our workforce.

Our major focus was on 'people processes', using planned interventions to develop new capabilities and awakening in the employees, a passion for re-architecting the Bank and a desire to create a new future for the Bank. I strongly believed that transformation cannot be successful if it was seen only as a 'management' play, but a joint work of management and employees. If the employees themselves are not sufficiently motivated to own the vision for transformation, there will simply be no growth, no technological development, and the organisation may fall into a drag of the past. Essentially, we had to bring radical change in our HR policies with a clear bias towards focusing on front-line employees. We strongly believed that we needed to significantly change the methodology and content of our various HRM systems to maintain our edge among PSBs. We could not allow an HR capital deficit to slow down our ambition to become a truly global bank.

As mentioned earlier, the BoB had a Board of Directors' Committee on HR. During my absence of one year at the Bank, on account of moving over to Dena Bank, it had become almost defunct. On my return, we revived the committee and developed a prioritised agenda for action in the context of Vision 2005–10. Human resources and their contributions were considered key to achieving our vision and sustaining the Bank's growth momentum. The key elements of our HR agenda included:

1. building new capabilities in our employees to cope with the demands of competition and the emerging digital environment;
2. improving performance management and developing a performance culture;

[1] The term 'sapiental circles' was first used by leading American anthropologist Margaret Mead to denote knowledge-generating groups.

3. building a leadership pipeline in the executive cadre to create leaders of the future;
4. engaging the staff and specially the front-line staff;
5. debureaucratising HR decision-making; and
6. ensuring that the HR structure, system, and processes complemented each other.

We were conscious that we needed to put in place a framework for developing new capabilities and to create a leadership pipeline to ensure that the Bank's expansion and rapid business growth were not halted for want of competent employees, managers, and business leaders. A number of initiatives had to be taken to recast HR in terms of its structure and processes, and several loose ends in our policies needed to be tightened. It was perhaps the first time after nationalisation that we had looked at our employee policies through a new lens, one that was truly developmental in its intent.

We developed an HR policy framework for the next five years to articulate a clear agenda for rejuvenating HR through employees' competency building and engagement. After much discussion and debate, the Board of Directors' Committee on HR finalised the policy, which provided multiple action points to reach out to employees and kept our unrelenting focus on building employee connect and creating among them passion for change.

For too long, the HRM function at the Bank had been overwhelmingly maintenance-driven, IR-focused, and compliance-oriented; we had lost sight of employee development. Union considerations had always weighed strongly in initiating any change and the unions had often stonewalled progressive proposals for employee development. We also had to deal with legacy problems stemming from the existing formal and informal settlements and understandings with the workmen's trade unions and the Association and build the credibility of the management in managing HR. All this required critically examining the existing HR sub-systems and introducing rigour in their operation.

It was also our aspiration now to introduce comprehensive developmental initiatives for all cadres and improve the credibility of the various

HR processes. We needed to introduce transparency and neutrality in HR decision-making. All this required a new structure and new capabilities for the HRM function across the Bank. Accordingly, the entire HR function was integrated into the HRM Department under the charge of a senior general manager for HRM. A separate HRD function was created to focus on developmental initiatives. As most of our current HR functionaries were originally recruited as personnel officers with background in IR, they needed to be inducted into the philosophy, processes, and content of HRD/organisational development practices.

I approached MDI, Gurgaon, a leading management institute, and held personal meetings with Professor Rajen Gupta, an HR/organisational development specialist, and his colleagues who helped us design a two-week-long programme for creating strategic HRD focus for our HR officers. I addressed this group of officers during the training programme, reaffirming our commitment to human processes in our transformation programme. The programme was successfully completed and I could see new enthusiasm in our HR team. We inducted some competent operational executives in HR to help HR develop strong perspective on the ground realities and the emerging context of banking. We also relocated some strong IR-oriented persons to banking operations to develop them into higher career positions. The HR officers were sent for overseas training and deputed to other HR programmes in India to give them exposure to best HR practices prevalent in other industries.

Taking care of 38,000 employees and their aspirations required special attention and could not be delegated to a department, consultants, or to trade unions. If there was any function that had received the least priority over the years in the Bank, it was HR, and if there was any function that required top priority now, it was HR. Therefore, I personally took up the task of honing our new emphasis on the HR function and inducted a bright young HR specialist in my secretariat, Prakash Ranjan, to help me directly pilot and implement our talent management and employee engagement and care programmes. With many competent colleagues on the banking operational side, I could afford to spend more time on the transformation project, which included HR transformation.

Developing a Vision for HR

A transformation programme of this magnitude covering implementation of technology, customer-centric initiatives, retail orientation, and branch facelifts needed a new culture of service and performance, new capabilities in our employees to operate in the changed environment, open and transparent communication, responsiveness at all levels, and engagement of employees in achieving the goals of the transformation. Everyone across the Bank required to understand the need for and context of the transformation and the cost of not undertaking it. Everyone needed to commit to the higher level of performance entailed in the process. In an organisation of 38,000 staff spread around 3,000 locations, this was by no means a task that could be achieved by issuing circulars, or spouting sermons, or carrying out fancy training programmes with the help of consultants. We ourselves had to take on this gargantuan challenge of reaching out to as many employees as possible, energising the management team on an almost daily basis, and taking quick action to remove internal bottlenecks that could jeopardise our new intentions to do things differently. This needed a major reorientation of our style of working. We developed a new mission for our HR: 'Creating Competence and Passion for Business Excellence'.

The real issue was to raise the level of passion by exciting our staff about the new future that we aspired to for the Bank. I strongly believed that passion is the charge within us, which drives us to achieve the ultimate thing in our focus, and when passions are raised, even impossible challenges can be achieved. Inspired by our own belief, we engaged in rebuilding the HR function with a strong focus on building employee connect.

From my field experience in Meerut and Kolkata, I had learnt the value of reaching out to employees and simultaneously maintaining a normal relationship with the unions, which paid excellent dividends. Now, as CEO, one of my principal strategies was to connect directly with the employees with a view to engaging them in the Bank's vision for the future.

It involved reaching out to as many employees as possible directly, working on their suggestions, taking empathetic action on the problems they faced, increasing career opportunities for them, building new capabilities, and using technology to ease HR administration.

Strategic Communication Initiatives

Town Hall Meetings

Throughout my years at the Bank and even during my research fieldwork, I had observed that when any major change was in the offing, the top management's chief strategy was to share its concerns with only the leaders of the Association and the workmen's unions, with the expectation that they would, in turn, communicate the message to their members and seek their involvement. Thus, the management outsourced its major responsibility to directly reach out to the employees to the Bank's officers' association/workmen's unions, who, except for symbolic gestures, leveraged this to build their own clout with the management. This was a major flaw in the Bank's HR policy that had created distance between field functionaries and the top management, and also some sort of disconnect between common employees and the top management. This was my major learning in the field and therefore, I decided to break hierarchial boundaries and reached out to operating managers and employees directly to communicate about the problems and challenges before the Bank and the need for change—adoption of new technology, innovations in product offerings, innovations in service offerings, building new capabilities, and readying the organisation to work in a technology-driven environment.

Our strategy was therefore to shift focus from IR to employee relations. I reached out to more than 15 per cent of the total Bank staff of 38,000 in the first 100 days through 10 town halls meetings at various centres. In these meetings, I spoke directly with the staff about the challenges the Bank faced, such as the slide in business, disconnect with customers, analysts' observations about the Bank, and the issues of underperformance of the Bank. I also shared our transformation agenda and Vision 2005–10, the new vision for growth and agenda for change, including the need for speedy implementation of new technology and the rebranding exercise. I understood from them the ground reality in terms of problems faced by the employees in delivery of customer service and the problems in facing the competition on ground. The staff response in these meetings was amazing, and exceeded my expectations. It was encouraging to see the commitment of our foot soldiers. I was happy to receive some excellent information and feedback about our products: what changes and modifications were required as per client need and what policies worked and what needed changes; how our competitors offered new products; what concessions they offered to customers; and how we could develop competitive advantage. Issues relating to their problems, both personal and professional, were also discussed and many doubts and apprehensions clarified on the basis of feedback in these meetings. I listened carefully to their ideas and encouraged them to share the problems they faced in discharging their duties. I sought their cooperation in going the extra mile, especially in the changeover to a technology-based system. Following these meetings, we changed many of our policies and extended coverage of our products.

These meetings provided me with useful insights about the unexplored opportunities in business. As compared to the earlier management strategy of using trade unions as the only source of field information, this direct interaction with the staff was both more authentic and refreshing.

Monthly Letters to Staff

In addition to the town hall meetings, I communicated directly with the employees on a monthly basis to keep them appraised of the various initiatives and the rationale behind them. Thus, each employee learnt about the changes directly from the CEO. Every month, I wrote a letter on my computer to each of the 38,000 staff members (thanks to facility in a computerised world), addressing each one of them by name. I personally drafted these communications because I wanted to speak to the employees from my heart. We also responded to all communications received from the employees. I reached out to the employees on all important occasions, such as initiating the core banking project, launching the new BoB logo, launching the public issue, launching customer-centric initiatives, during the recovery drive, and for special business campaigns. I also introduced a system of responding to all communications received from the employees. It was gratifying to see that these communications had a tremendous positive impact on our front-line staff.

Employee Engagement

It was my firm belief that employees must own up and develop passion for the transformation programme, which will change their own life and careers.

Thus, employee engagement was a real big challenge for the management. It meant creating emotional connect between the employees and the Bank's aspirations. This was a part of our value system. It was fundamental to our transformational process. Apart from reaching out to the employees in the ways mentioned earlier, we also reached out to them at a deep psychological level through large group events that involved talking and working together about the future vision through uniquely designed employee conclaves called 'Baroda Manthan'. The programme was woven around four key themes: building a sales and service culture; placing the customer at the centre stage; leveraging technology for business success; and moving towards a universal financial services organisation. Baroda Manthan was effectively implemented by the operating heads in collaboration with the HRM functionaries at the corporate level. The feedback from these conclaves was so overwhelmingly positive that the Bank's Gujarat Zonal Manager, G.G. Joshi, alone organised 65 Manthans, covering more than 8,000 staff. This engagement of the staff achieved excellent business results and played a key role in improving customer service and the overall image of the Bank.

Employee Care Programmes

High-performance culture can be sustained only in an environment of high compassion for the employees. While we expected employees to work beyond the call of duty for changeover to new technology-driven business transformation programme, it was equally important to give them the confidence and management commitment to stand by them during their difficult times.

Sampark

With the objective of providing instant relief to employees facing grave personal problems, a helpline called Sampark (hotline to CEO) was set up in the CEO's secretariat. As mentioned earlier, a very enthusiastic and young

HR officer, Prakash Ranjan, a PhD in HR, was inducted into the CEO's office to assist in implementing employee care and talent management programme. Cases of extreme emergency could reach us directly through a dedicated email address. I was touched by the kind of human problems, including death in employee's family and extreme sickness of parents, that came to me, and quick relief could be extended by way of transfers and so on. This brought me in touch with employees' real-life problems. We responded in most cases within 24 hours, irrespective of whether I was in India or abroad. Sampark became a potent symbol of a caring management and created tremendous goodwill for the Bank. It provided an emotional connect between employees and top management. This helped the Bank in owning its employees. This also galvanised the HR team to attend to employee problems with utmost speed and attention it deserved. It connected employees emotionally with the top management.

A woman employee suffering from cancer, after reversal of her transfer, wrote:

> Your gesture has helped me cope with the mental trauma and lengthy painful treatment that I am undergoing for this dreaded disease. I thank you for this concern for an individual employee which is unprecedented in the Bank.

Paramarsh: The Centre for Personnel Counselling

Growing complexities of life, specifically in big cities and metros, added to the pressures and strains on personal lives of employees, which had adverse repercussions on family, office colleagues, and overall work performance. There were employees who suffered from depression for various reasons— familial, work related, or psychological—which needed to be addressed with professional help.

To help them cope with these and other personal stresses, we set up a counselling service called Paramarsh in five metro centres.

The first Paramarsh service was introduced in Mumbai. A clinical psychologist was engaged to provide counselling services to employees suffering from depression, occupational stress, inner conflict, personal life problems, and tobacco, drug, and alcohol addictions.

We interacted periodically with the counsellor to learn about the psychological health of our employees. At a time of major transformation and change, many of our employees benefited hugely from Sampark and Paramarsh, which helped employees emotionally connect with the Bank. The employees responded with great enthusiasm and happily bore the brunt of the many changes that were being implemented simultaneously and helped the Bank achieve many milestones in its growth journey.

Talent Management

Khoj

With employees and officers' motivation at higher level, their career aspirations were also ignited. To achieve this, the Bank launched an innovative, organisation-wide talent identification and development programme called Khoj (discovery) on its 98th Foundation Day. To have a fair assessment of talent based on their competitive potential, we introduced a systematic methodology for talent identification in our clerical and officers' staff. An outside agency, Institute of Banking Personnel Selection, was engaged to undertake the job.

Through this mechanism, we identified talent for various functional areas, such as branch operations, sales, credit, forex, treasury, and IT. Khoj received an overwhelming response from the employees, and in the first exercise, 420 officers and 226 clerks were identified for further development. After completing the second Khoj exercise, we created a core group of 1,000 talented employees—both officers and clerical staff. These employees acted as change champions in the Bank's journey of transformation. The Khoj programme was monitored by the Directors' Committee on HR (which allocated Rs 5 million for special training programmes under Khoj).

The era of pick and choose or nominations of individuals for career opportunities and rewards lists by trade unions was replaced by this transparent and professionally conducted exercise directly monitored by the CEO. In a real sense, we moved several miles closer to our employees!

ideaonline@bankofbaroda.com

with the objective of providing a vehicle of communication to our employees to share ingenious ideas and innovative approaches on issues and matters that had direct and material relevance to the Bank's business, a new forum, known as ideaonline@bankofbaroda.com, was set up. The Bank received numerous creative and novel ideas from the employees, many of which were adopted for implementation.

All these initiatives were pioneered under my direct supervision.

Building Leadership Bench Strength

In the new competitive environment, it was imperative to build distinctive competencies in our senior executives such as strategic thinking, technology management, and emotional intelligence to organise human effort and to respond to new-age customers. Our challenge was to create a new kind of operational leadership for our branch managers to be able to effectively respond and adapt to the new technology environment. At the regional and zonal managers level, we needed to build perspective to visualise the larger picture and diagnostic skills to continuously scan the emerging environment. They needed to operate from a new mindset beyond control and compliance management. Finally, at the top, we needed to develop a holistic and collaborative mental mode to drive the futuristic agenda of the Bank. They needed better judgement calls to respond effectively to create a new architecture for their respective functions. The task was beyond a training programme and it needed a systematic grooming strategy. We hired a well-known consulting firm in HR, 'Grow Talent', which, after a rigorous and well-conceptualised strategy, developed 300 leaders through a year-long programme which included classroom training, project work, and mentoring.

The aging and superannuation profiles of executives, coupled with competency gaps in specialised and other new emerging areas of banking, created gaps in the management cadre. To meet these challenges, the Bank introduced fast-tracked promotions in order to ensure that meritorious officers are groomed quickly.

Similarly, several steps were taken in revitalising employee training and development, aligning training with emerging areas, developing a pipeline of young managers, and setting in motion continuous education programmes. We also revamped HR for overseas operations through a rigorous methodology of selection of candidates for overseas postings, territory-wise detailed competency mapping, culture training, and so on.

Simultaneous to our focus on building people processes, we took steps to consolidate the gains of IR reforms initiated earlier and institutionalised mechanisms like HR audit, prompt action on reported cases of violation of workplace discipline, initiatives to sign new settlement with workmen unions for improving productivity of staff through a pioneering settlement on transacting cheques and cash at a single counter, and clarifying on employee-related matters in a defined time period.

Demystifying HRM through Technology

One of the major irritants at the branch level was the unresolved grievances of the staff arising out of service rules on account of variations in interpretation of the rules, and this was the main fodder for union representatives to create problems and indulge in restrictive practices. In an inter-union rivalry environment, even smaller issues were escalated to a higher level.

In order to enable HR to add value to business, a comprehensive Web-enabled HRM system called Human Resource Network for Employee Services (HRnes) was conceptualised, and and it was implemented on a priority basis as one of the key projects under our technology development programme. One of our talented personnel specialists, C.V. Chandrashekhar, Deputy General Manager, HRD, piloted the HRnes project and reared it like his own baby. He spent countless long hours and late nights to install this system, which contributed to employee satisfaction at the grass-root level. The main aim of this technology intervention was to remove the day-to-day irritants at the operating unit level and to provide ease and benefits to employees as well as to decision-making authorities in various HR processes, apart from providing a technology-enabled platform for qualitative utilisation of HR. The 'HRnes' covered the entire gamut of HRM functions in the Bank, comprising about 30 modules from recruitment to retirement besides HR information system. It was a most comprehensive system to resolve the grievances of staff arising out of interpretation of service rules.

In addition, it provided online tests for promotion, overseas selection, and appraisal. Employees could view their personal data on HRnes and update or modify it. Being centrally administered, HRnes helped in the uniform implementation of policies with speed, and thus led to fewer IR problems at the branch level. Apart from being fair, open, and transparent, its implementation helped HRM functionaries to focus more on development.

Together, the above initiatives considerably reduced employee grievances on account of interpretation of service conditions and day-to-day union interference, easing the work environment in the branches. This helped the branch managers to focus on business development and customer service issues.

Thus, to sum up, some of the key decisions taken in HRM were:

1. Reviving the Board of Directors' Committee on HR and ensuring its regular meetings and critical agenda for employee development.
2. Restructuring the HRM function to respond to developmental functions in a significant way.
3. Creating an employee engagement cell in the CEO office under the direct supervision of the CEO.
4. Demystifying HR administration through technology.
5. Starting schemes for developing in-house excellence in training systems, such as:
   (a) setting up a special college for training staff in the new technologies;
   (b) grooming 500 credit officers, 100 international bankers, and 100 treasury officers; and
   (c) undertaking a large sales and service training effort for frontline staff.
6. Revamping HRM for overseas operations.
7. Introducing a new appraisal system for 13,000 officers.
8. Introducing a new appraisal system for the workmen staff.
9. Putting in place a performance improvement plan for slow pacers.
10. Setting the stage for leadership development by hiring a consultant for grooming 300 leaders for the future.
11. Initiating employee engagement and care programmes such as Sampark, Paramarsh, and Khoj.
12. Developing a pipeline of young managers.
13. Reskilling HR officers in process work and orientation to the developmental agenda.
14. Initiating executive retreats in leading management institutes to enhance learning and growth.

Industrial Relations

With many initiatives in building employee engagement through accelerated communication, employee care programmes, and talent development—an effective system of listening to the experiences and concerns of foot soldiers—a new environment of collaborative culture emerged and the influence of the trade unions was considerably diluted. After many years, the Bank was out of clutches of the trade unions and no more at their mercy to motivate employees. The management–employees connect was far better than at any other time.

The IR environment was, by and large, placid during this period, which paved the way for many reforms in HRM, including the empowerment of operating managers at all levels and the positive response of all the employees to technology implementation and other reforms to improve customer service.

Several steps were taken to ensure merit and neutrality in arriving at career decisions and to ensure that everyone had an equal opportunity to compete for the various positions. Written tests were introduced for various promotion exercises and overseas postings were based on interview results. Rigorous reference checks of each candidate were conducted with current and previous bosses to ensure as much fairness as possible in promotion decisions. This considerably improved the confidence of the officers and the executives in the management.

To enable such a huge transformation programme as we had undertaken, it was essential that our officers and executive cadres be highly motivated. Demoralisation had set in among the officers on account of pending vigilance cases in relation to credit sanctions, which, in many cases, were routine procedural lapses. Promotion exercises had been delayed in various cadres. There was despondency among the employees about the inordinate delays in promotions, which had also affected the supply chain for executive positions in a major way.

A task force was set up to examine the pending cases of vigilance, and within three weeks or so, a decision was taken on each case within the ambit of the rules. Many cases were closed, wherever there was no substantive misdemeanour. Alongside this, I also initiated a promotion exercise for all the cadres. All these steps greatly boosted the morale of the officers.

The Association's Attempts at Disruption

Initially, for about one year after my taking over, the officers' association maintained a low profile and issued circulars to its members appreciating the initiatives of the Bank. They made bold overtures to win me over by praising my leadership, a technique they often deployed with successive CEOs. A sample circular of the Association dated 20 July 2005, issued by its general secretary, read:

> ...At such a demanding time, we are benefitted with the leadership of Dr. A.K. Khandelwal as the Chairman and Managing Director of the Bank...
>
> The Chairman and the Managing Director, true to his assurances, has initiated a series of measures to get rid of fear psychosis widely prevalent possibly arising out of Staff Accountability. This will definitely facilitate decision making process. Along with this, the Chairman and Managing Director has also commenced a series of exercises for promotion from one Scale/Grade to another fulfilling the legitimate aspirations of offi- cers for career progression. Simultaneously the Chairman and Managing Director has also heralded unique facilities such as 8.00 a.m. to 8.00 p.m. banking with 24 hours banking, increase in spread of alternate delivery channels with 501 ATMs etc. which all are oriented towards enhanc- ing customer satisfaction. These innovative measures together with core banking solution in place will go a long way in putting the Bank on a fast track of growth.[2]

However, soon thereafter in its circular dated 11 November 2005, the Association, in a reversal of its earlier support for many customer-centric initiatives, exhorted that the management was indulging in issu- ing threats and intimidation of officers and mentioned about the adverse consequences of initiatives like 8.00 a.m. to 8.00 p.m. banking and 24×7 banking.[3] The real issue, as revealed in the circular, was applying pressure on the management for re-transfer of officers to their respective zones after completion of their usual tenure of inter-zonal transfers.

---

[2] Circular no. 17 of 2005 dated 20 July 2005 to all members issued by the All India Bank of Baroda Officers Association.

[3] Circular no. 24 of 2005 dated 11 November 2005 to all members issued by the All India Bank of Baroda Officers' Association.

In another circular dated 20 July 2006, on the eve of the Banks foundation day, the Association heaped praises on me. The circular said:

It is a matter of pride that at this historic moment a leader who has grown
from within the organization is at the helm of affairs of the Bank. With
this intrinsic knowledge of the strength and weaknesses, our Chairman
and Managing Director, Dr. Anil K Khandelwal sagaciously leveraged
the opportunities and faced the threats successfully to position the Bank
in the orbit of International Banking. The roller coaster initiatives starting with branding to CBS rollout have transformed the Bank as never
before successfully attempting to own and influence customers' mind
to capture the market share. From the perception of Family Banker
accepting deposits and reluctantly lending money our Bank, kudos to
Dr. Khandelwal, has positioned itself as India's International Bank with
dependability, consistency and reliability as the trademark.[4]

I was not flattered by these circulars as it was a normal strategy of the
Association to praise the CEOs, cultivate them, and build personal relations to seek favours, such as immunity from transfers for the Association
activists and office-bearers and interfering in executive careers. My research
insights had made me wiser not to fall in this trap.

At a personal level, I was, though, quite amused as the same Association
had targeted me not long back through personal vilification campaign
besmirching my professional reputation!! This volte-face by the Association
and a brazen attempt to impress me was of no particular significance to me.
My commitment to engage people in our journey of change was total and
I was not impressed by such opportunistic overtures of the Association.

Emergence of BoB Officers' Forum

A development arising out of increasing frustration amongst the officers
against the Association was the emergence of BoB Officers' Forum. This was
launched by immediate past president of the Association and in its circular,[5]
it raised several issues, such as the leadership of the general secretary of the

---

[4] Circular no. 13 dated 20 July 2006 to all members issued by All India
Bank of Baroda Officers' Association.
[5] Circular no. P/05/1, dated 9 November 2005, to all the officers of BoB
issued by the convener, BoB Officers' Forum.

Association, questioning his continuation even after retirement as a general secretary of the Association and asking him to seek fresh mandate by secret ballot to judge his acceptability, disproportionate amount collected from members as levy, non-publishing of accounts of the Association's welfare fund, and failure to attend to problems faced by the members.

The convener of the Officers' Forum approached me for extending support to this forum to enable the officers' community to replace the present general secretary who had continued in this position for about a decade. He also revealed to me as to how the general secretary had been targeting me for a long time and had been sending complaints against me to the government and various other investigative agencies. He offered to extend whole-hearted cooperation to management in its transformational endeavour. I forthrightly declined the request to support this forum and, in fact, counselled him to raise issues internally in a democratic manner, instead of complicating the IR scenario in the Bank. It was never my intent to reduce our efforts of formalisation of IR to meddle into the internal dynamics of the trade unions. The foregoing research shows the dysfunctional consequences of such a strategy by the CEOs (Chapters 4 and 5).

In the new climate of performance and enthusiasm, with so many new initiatives having been successfully implemented, and our refusal to have any informal understanding with them on important issues, the Association began building pressure on the Bank by exaggerating the issues of stress and strain being experienced by the officers as a result of the overlong hours of work that they had to put in at times. The Association leaders exaggerated a few isolated cases and used them to embarrass the management. They were worried about their fading grip over the members.

As mentioned earlier, most of the officers were against the Association because its leaders had habitually connived with the earlier managements to promote the careers of their own activists, while ignoring the genuine grievances of the rest of the officer cadre. In the new environment, the officers expected us to correct this practice. We too did not want to continue with the unfair practices of the past, so when it was time for the annual rotation of officers, we transferred some of the Association office-bearers who had stayed too long in one place.

While the general class of officers was happy about our move, the Association turned it into an issue and mobilised political pressure from the government to stall the transfers. It may be worthwhile to mention here that the Association was affiliated to the INTUC, which was the trade union wing of the Congress Party, the party in power at that time. The president of the INTUC, who was also an MP, complained against me to the finance minister and alleged that I was destroying the only Congress-affiliated union in the banking industry. Finance Minister P. Chidambaram called me to his office to understand the context of transfers of office-bearers of the Association. I explained to him my logic of transferring them as they had managed to stay in the same place in spite of promotions, against the stated government policy that all the officers were transferrable. I was able to convince the government that my decisions and actions were purely for developing a professional culture in the Bank and all such decisions were within the ambit of government guidelines.

Tough decisions on matters of principles symbolised the management determination to streamline its personnel policies to provide equitable and fair implementation of the same. The removal of immunity from transfer of hundreds of Association office-bearers was welcomed by the general mass of officers. The management, with its new policy of connecting with its officers and implementing fair and transparent systems of career advancement, promotions, and overseas postings, demonstrated its resolve to introduce a meritocratic culture in the Bank.

Frequent complaints were engineered against me and conveyed to the government and investigative agencies through anonymous letters. Political bigwigs were contacted to derail our rebranding exercise complaining that the colour of logo resembled the colour of flag of the main opposition party. I was asked by the government to withdraw the logo. But I explained to the government the logic of change and stood by my point of view. Our new identity through the new logo won us many accolades.

In this scenario of frequent complaints against me and the political pressure to go soft on the officers' association, the support of Vinod Rai, Secretary, Department of Financial Services, was a great succour and he rescued me from the usual governmental nitpicking about complaints. In fact, Rai's counsel at crucial times helped me to continue the transformation process. In the public sector, support and hand-holding by bureaucracy is very important for continuing the journey of transformation.

Workmen's Unions Maintain a Low Profile

Although the workmen staff also worked for long hours during implementation of technology and worked in 8.00 a.m. to 8.00 p.m. banking environment, it must be said to the credit of the workmen's unions that they did not make a big issue about it, except showing their concern about the new work culture which included instant actions against staff for customer mishandling, indiscipline, or insubordination of any kind. At one stage, the two major unions of workmen jointly represented against increase in number of disciplinary cases against employees. Leaders of both the workmen's unions met me and the problems of staff were sorted out. I was against any mishandling of customers, but simultaneously a strong message was sent across that legitimate grievances of employees must be solved expeditiously and all steps should be taken to create a facilitative culture. I shared my philosophy of 'Tough Love', which meant tough on performance (high standards) and compassion for people.

Our strategy in IR was quite transparent and clear to everyone. There would be no informal understandings with any union on any issue; no consultation on transfers and promotions; no favours and concessions; all unlawful facilities would cease immediately; and all facilities over and above the industry-level settlements would be withdrawn, as would any immunity from a full-day's work, except for the Federation Leader, the recognised workmen's union. The Bank maintained formal relations with the unions. Without a formalisation document, the Bank had achieved formalisation of its IR functions and of the roles each actor would play.

The Bank maintained its bipartite relations with the unions. At various levels, periodic structured meetings were held between the management and the unions to sort out issues. In these meetings, the management also raised issues relating to productivity and discipline. Some existing settlements were revised with the workmen's unions to enhance productivity of staff. The unions generally cooperated and responded to the new environment, even if grudgingly. After several decades, the management at various levels was in complete control of the IR function with clearly defined role boundaries for the unions.

While unions–management interactions at various levels continued to sort out the issues raised by them, the management exercised restraint in any informal consultations with the Association on any issue at all the levels. The management also did not seek any cooperation on business development from them and instead reached out to employees directly, and this worked with great success. The era of being dependant on officers' association for mobilising support of officers for business development was over and the direct connect between management and officers and other employees, as well as the many initiatives to engage the employees, yielded excellent results. My fieldwork during research and subsequent experience in field assignments had shown that seeking cooperation from the Association always carried a price tag in terms of negotiating more facilities and interference in management decisions on transfers and promotions for the selected few, thereby damaging the credibility of the management. Such informal understandings were essentially fragile as they had no contractual legitimacy and created more problems than they solved.

Proactive Problem-Solving

In the new environment when the Bank achieved many changes and improved its image mainly on account of its people processes, it was our endeavour to find solutions to many long-standing problems. One such issue was the regularisation of about 1,000 casual labour working since last several years against leave vacancies/permanent vacancies of subordinate staff. The issue had been raised by the trade unions several times in last couple of years but was not addressed. We looked into this issue in a humane way and developed a scheme for their absorption to the satisfaction of warring unions and signed a settlement with the recognised union about absorption of casual employees in the regular cadre.

The Federation (recognised union), in a circular dated 18 March 2008, said:

> We put on record our sincere gratitude and thanks to our Chairman and Managing Director, Dr Anil K Khandelwal, who has proved to be a Messiah for these hundreds of casuals, whose hopes were often belied in the past by the empty assurances given by his predecessors.[6]

[6] Circular dated 18 March 2008 to all members issued by All India Bank of Baroda Employees Federation.

I was convinced that it is the basic responsibility of the management to connect with the employees and respond with empathy in spite of non-cooperative attitude of the unions. Short-term approaches or bartering their interests with trade unions can only lead to long-term problems, as the Bank had already experienced in the past.

Even during the fast-paced transformation programme, we did not compromise on principles and dealt with the unions fairly without giving in to their pressure tactics or extending them any undue favours or concessions. Our core strategy was to neither mollycoddle the trade unions nor unnecessarily provoke them.

Most of our transformational initiatives, such as the technology implementation, could be implemented smoothly without any significant IR problems, except for occasional pinpricks from the Association. The management could pilot many changes by building its credibility with the employees and officers in general, in spite of hostile attitude of the trade union. Reaching out to employees was key to these achievements.

Business Outcomes

The management's strategy in focusing on building management team and extraordinary focus on building people processes helped it to achieve successful implementation of CBS and to put in place anytime–anywhere banking, the absence of which was a major handicap in retaining customers, and thereby improve business. The Bank could also introduce many new customer-centric initiatives, create new brand image, and restructure both domestic and international operation innovations. It also helped the Bank to achieve a dramatic recovery in its business. Here are some of the Bank's business as well as other achievements between April 2005 and March 2008:

1. Total business doubled from Rs 1,247.34 billion to Rs 2,587.35 billion (107 per cent growth).
2. Credit growth, a key concern of the financial analysts, grew from Rs 434 billion to Rs 1,067 billion (145 per cent growth).
3. Gross non-performing assets were reduced from 7.30 per cent to 1.84 per cent.

4. Net profit grew from Rs 6.76 billion to Rs 14.35 billion (112 per cent growth).
5. Business per employee increased from Rs 31.6 million to Rs 70.4 million.
6. Net profit per employee more than doubled from Rs 17.1 million to Rs 39 million.
7. International operations were repositioned and recorded more than 100 per cent growth. A record number of 15 new offices, including offices in new territories such as Australia, Trinidad and Tobago, Ghana, and Singapore, were opened.
8. More than 1,700 branches were put online in record time and Internet banking was introduced. Core Banking was also introduced in all foreign branches.
9. All targets under the statement of intent signed with the Government of India were achieved.
10. Eight million new customers were added.
11. New joint ventures on life insurance and mutual funds with global partners were finalised.
12. Many pioneering initiatives in rural development were taken.
13. Reorganisation of operations of two major territories, namely, Gujarat and UP, was carried out.

The major equity analysts' ratings of the Bank changed to 'Outperformers', along with 'Buy' recommendations.

Our focus on building intangibles for the stable, long-term growth of the Bank delivered excellent business results, far beyond my expectations. It was a conscious decision to sacrifice near-term growth to invest in building the basic pillars of growth, such as technology upgradation, building leadership bench strength, employee engagement, rebranding, and custom-centric innovations, because we did not contemplate that we could achieve good business results in the near term, even if we fired on all cylinders. We were proved wrong as the Bank's business started growing from the first year itself. We believed, with good reason, that when an organisation is set on transformational fire, everyone rises above their normal performance levels and this shows up collectively in extraordinary performance.

Many of the achievements, such as introduction of technology, new business initiatives, and rehashing of HR policies, could be achieved with our paradigmatic shift in IR strategies and new focus on employees. With careful oversight and occasional micro-managing, the need to listen, engage, and empower the employees was drilled into the minds of our top management and other senior operating managers. Through a variety of initiatives, as mentioned in this chapter, it can be observed that we did not tinker with an initiative here and an initiative there but transformed the entire ecosystem to build people processes. It was our shared consciousness that we could win the trust of our people by tackling delays, non-responsiveness, and internal bureaucracy, and create a more collaborative, proactive, and listening culture at all levels of management. In any large organisation, it is challenging to claim that all the employees at all times are aligned with the vision of the organisation, but there is fair reason to believe that management's sincerity and credibility in responding to employee's concerns can raise their passion, which was amply reflected in implementation of technology and remarkable business growth.

The Bank also received several accolades, including a personal honour: Lifetime Achievement Award by The Asian Banker, Singapore, for the transformation of the Bank (the only Indian banker so far to have received this honour).

Our people-driven transformation story inspired many prestigious management institutes like IIM Ahmedabad, Institute of Chartered Financial Analysts of India, and MDI, Gurgaon to write case studies on our transformation and rebranding. Academic world undertook research on our transformation, such as a case study on organizational changes in Bank of Baroda and a research on the implications of the transformation Awasthi et al. (2012). The personal reminiscences of my life and work in BOB are also recounted in my book, *Dare to Lead* (2011).

These initiatives, in fact, contributed to the long-term health of the Bank and vindicated my belief that if you focus on building intangibles, tangible outcomes follow. The Bank maintained its numero uno position even after I demitted office in 2008. It metamorphosised into a valuable brand in the banking industry. The Bank made rapid strides in technology, introducing many novel products and services benefiting the customers, all of which became possible due to a new environment facilitated by the IR reforms and HR initiatives undertaken in the recent past. During the nine-year period from 2008 to 2017, while the overall business levels and operating profits grew four times, the share price grew three times. I believe that the Bank is ready for a new dose of HR innovation and rekindling the passion of employees to meet the future challenges and maintain its prime position.

* * *

By successfully implementating various reforms in IR and restoring managerial authority at all the levels (Chapter 11), a major transformation programme, including technology-driven business transformation, was launched. My main focus was, however, to create a culture that could seamlessly facilitate transformation—a culture that was an antithesis of prevailing bureaucratic working, unresponsive to customer problems, siloed working, lack of accountability, and finding scapegoats. I was aware that it could not be achieved by pontifications but by bringing the management team together. Our initiative to start daily morning meetings was the flag-bearer of our commitment to create a team culture at the top that focused on heralding a new environment of speedy decision-making, time-bound problem-solving process, debureaucratised decision-making, smart response, and management accountability.

We also moved from an IR to an HRD paradigm by putting extraordinary focus on 'employees' in terms of building their morale, enhancing their competencies, training them for new capabilities, and creating a new mechanism in which their voice could be heard right at the top. A core element of our strategy was to build employee connect by engaging them in many transformational initiatives, especially in the implementation of technology. This was achieved through a deep HR transformation programme encompassing multiple initiatives at different levels. It also included removing hassles and irritants in HR administration through a comprehensive review of the HRM systems and processes and using technology for HR administration.

An integrated approach to HRD was introduced encompassing employee development, employee engagement, employee care, talent hunt, a fair process based on merit in career decisions, and an empowered communication mechanism. A prodigious effort, right at the CEO level, to put the employees at the centre of our HR initiatives became the hallmark of our policies. Apart from this, the major focus of our effort was aimed at creating an enabling climate for everyone to work with confidence and without any fear.

The shift in focus from a purely commercial orientation to achieve short-term results to a long-term vision of building the health of the Bank could be achieved through our overarching commitment to boosting intangibles (such as HR, leadership, governance, and technology) to lay the foundation for institution building. The dramatic growth of business and multiple new initiatives during this period, in spite of the major focus on building intangibles, vindicated my personal belief that 'it is intangibles which drive tangibles'. The successful implementation of technology, rebranding, many customer-centric initiatives, and a deep HR transformation created excellent business outcomes. We could more than double the size of business in just three years.

This could be done without any day-to-day hassles on the IR front and engagement of all the staff members, who rose to create India's International Bank (our tag line). This confirmed my personal belief that when you reach out to employees with trust and proactively attend to their problems, they can surprise you with the outcomes. There was a huge transition from the decades-old strategy that focused on union leaders only and ignored connection with the employees to now deep engagement with the employees. It was a confirmation of my belief that trade unions and employees are two separate entities and each require separate emphasis. Management can never abandon its responsibility towards employees and outsource the function to union leaders. If it does, there are dysfunctional consequences at the workplace, as we have seen during the research.

I believe that our endeavours in HRD turned out to be true value drivers that put the Bank on a fast track to both growth and excellence.

It is gratifying to note the continued growth (higher than industry average) of the Bank in the last nine years since my retirement. Our extraordinary emphasis on building leadership also created over a dozen leaders who went on to hold board-level positions in PSBs, besides one deputy governor in RBI. My proudest achievement, undoubtedly, has been the teams and the leaders I have produced. This is a true vindication of our investment in building leadership pipeline in the Bank.

The BoB story of transformation has been captured in my book *Dare to Lead* and has caught the attention of both academics and corporate world.

Some highlights of our initiatives are given in Appendix (Table A.1).

Box 12.1   From IR to HRD: Learnings from Reflection

1. Culture change is a prerequisite for transformation. Transforming organisations is not merely transplanting the new over the old. Along with cleaning the stable, the fundamental role of the CEO is to create a new culture that can absorb new thought process, adapt to new innovations, and lead enthusiastically the momentum for change.

2. The leader should stand back from day-to-day routines and foster learning about the gap between current reality and vision and how to bridge it. The main focus of his work should be on building health and long-term future of the organisation.

3. Transformation is a collaborative endeavour of management and therefore, the creation of a team of zealots of transformation is very critical for any CEO. Transformation must aim at long-term value creation and the CEO should develop this vision in his team by constantly providing a big picture.

4. For successful transformation, leaders must lead to break siloed working, debureaucratise decision-making, and create a smart, responsive culture for effective engagement with the customers.

5. Wisdom is in the field and therefore direct connect of the CEO and top management with the foot soldiers is the sine qua non for creating a vibrant organisation. This role cannot be delegated to trade unions.

6. In large organisations with geographical dispersion of business units, the real challenge is to ensure that people accept challenges of change and therefore, the major focus of the CEO has to be on engaging people by open conversations and listening to their concerns, with intention to act.

7. Transparency and communication by leaders can produce extraordinary outcomes through creation of an enabling environment for realising the full potential of employees.

8. Innovations, risk-taking, and excellence are the outcomes of teamwork and not that of a single individual.

9. During transformation, it may at times be useful for a leader to have a small nucleus focused on HR under his direct charge to pilot innovations in people area and monitor the programme of HR transformation.

10. High-performance culture can be sustained in only a high compassion culture.

11. In the context of the public sector, support from the government in general, and bureaucracy in particular, should be mobilised as this is extremely critical for successfully piloting transformation. Likewise, when necessary, skilfully protect the organisation from their undue interference.

12. The CEO is the 'Chief Employee Officer' and this responsibility is undelegable. He should build entire ecosystem of HR and not merely undertake piecemeal esoteric steps based on current fads in HR.

13. The CEOs need to hand-hold the operating managers in solving their problems and stand by them at all times. Leadership is co-leading.

Chapter 13

INFERENCES AND INSIGHTS

The journey described in this book started with my research endeavour in understanding, from a strategic perspective, the dynamics of IR in a very large and geographically dispersed PSB, the BoB. I undertook an intensive ethnographic field research study, which involved delving into the opaque world of strategy making at the top-most level of management at the Bank. My research findings exploded many myths about IR management and its impact across the organisation, with special reference to the workplace.

Circumstances so conspired that soon after my doctorate for this research, I was put into operational roles in banking, where I experienced directly the impact of top management policies in IR. Later, I was catapulted into two strategic policy-making roles, as Executive Director and CEO. In these roles, I piloted a series of unprecedented initiatives in IR and HRD, which significantly changed the whole dynamics of work at the Bank. In the post-liberalisation period, the resultant competitive environment in Indian banking allowed me to push a technologically driven business transformational agenda for the Bank at a very rapid pace.

The sequence of events that unfolded provided me a unique opportunity to apply my research inferences and insights to the practical world of executive action. In hindsight, I feel this was a rare opportunity to put research and practice together.

In this chapter, first, the key inferences and insights from my research are summarised in relation to the various IR strategies used by six different CEOs from 1956 to 1988, as also their impact on the workplace and the morale of the Bank employees. Then I share how these insights from the research provide valuable suggestions to design an integrated approach to build HR function and strategies in a large organisation to be at the centre stage to contribute to business objectives.

Some Important Insights from Research

We all know that trade unions being social organisations, their strategies and actions are fairly visible in the public domain. On the other hand, management strategies, especially in the sensitive area of IR, often go unreported and unresearched, thereby getting shrouded in a veil of mystery. The major reason for this is that researchers and academics rarely get the access needed to study the strategies of top management/CEOs in IR. This is precisely why the present study can be considered to be an important contribution to the field. I was fortunate enough to have such critical access, as a result of which I was able to gain valuable insights into managerial behaviour, actions, and strategies in this critical domain. These insights are summarised next.

The CEO as a Key Designer and Strategist in IR

Contrary to the popular belief that IR and IR strategies are largely shaped in response to demands from trade unions, my research, in fact, revealed that it is largely management strategies that shape the IR environment in the context of change in environment and in government policies. Apart from this, there are organisational variables that influence IR strategies, such as the power of the unions, management politics, the CEO's attitude and orientation towards the unions, and the immediate pressures of business. Thus, several environmental and organisational factors, in various combinations, influence managerial strategies in IR.

The research also pointed out that the CEO is the key designer of IR strategies. Although the personnel and IR functionaries may be in the forefront of negotiations, the key aspects of decision-making in IR are centralised in the CEO. Each CEO consciously shapes IR strategies in relation to the constellation of forces operating at a given point of time. The key decisions in union–management relations are shaped and orchestrated by the CEO. Such decisions include:

1. Which union should be supported?
2. What facilities and concessions should be given to unions?
3. What kind of bargaining relationships should be developed with the unions?
4. What structural rearrangements would support the strategic shifts?
5. When should unions be supported or sidelined?
6. What information should be shared with the unions?
7. What participative mechanisms should be established in IR management?

These aspects have been amply highlighted in the earlier chapters of this book.

Apart from playing a key role in the process of strategy formulation, the CEOs play an equally important role in strategy implementation. The various aspects of strategy implementation include:

1. methods used for seeking unions' cooperation;
2. methods used for confronting a union;
3. methods used for reducing the power of unions and their key leaders;
4. methods used for creating a rival union; and
5. methods used for reducing the power of unions by enlisting the support of the government.

The research also pointed out as to how centralisation of IR strategies in the CEOs constrains the development of a consistent policy and how value conflicts between the CEOs and personnel specialists can lead to delays in decision-making in personnel matters.

The increasing centralisation of strategy making in the CEO has several consequences, such as frequent changes in the strategy on account of orientation and belief system of different CEOs, apart from the environmental and organisational factors. The centralisation also enables too much discretion to the CEOs to tinker with the strategic and policy issues in IR. Unconstrained by any institutional mechanism and oversight of the board in IR matters, CEOs unbridled power to extend favours and concessions to trade unions did create long-term dysfunctional consequences for the union–management relations in the Bank. The research also revealed that CEO's decisions in IR are also influenced by the management politics at the top (Chapters 4, 6, and 7). For example, V.D. Thakkar's decision (Chapter 4) to isolate his next in command, C.P. Shah, and the personnel chief, L.B. Bhide, was guided by their good equation with the Federation leader. Similarly, Y.V.S.'s initiatives (Chapter 6) in improving the relations with the Federation were sabotaged by his Executive Director, A.C. Sheth.

The research revealed that most CEOs, with the exception of V.D. Thakkar (who made a serious attempt at formalisation of relations with unions, and in that quest gave formal recognition to the Federation and consultative status to the Coordination Committee) and R.C. Shah (who too made an unsuccessful attempt to formalise the relations with trade unions), pursued ad hoc and short-term policies in dealing with unions, with complete disregard to their impact at the workplace. The centralisation of power in CEOs also diluted the development of HR function and the contributions of HR functionaries in the Bank. On account of frequent change of CEOs, the IR function faced problems in the process of institutionalisation, with adverse consequences at the operating level.

Another feature of IR management at the Bank was oscillations in strategies from one CEO to another. Industrial relations moved from low trust to high trust, to soft-pedalling, to mollycoddling, and to complete surrender to the unions. The inconsistent, ad hoc, short-term, and patchy IR strategies practised by the different CEOs resulted in emergence of multi-unions, with the union power at the workplace leading to a chaotic workplace environment.

Exclusive Focus on Union Leaders Leads to Dysfunctional Consequences

Although the IR strategies at the Bank changed with each CEO, a common pattern is noticeable among them. The main focus of managerial strategies both in the pre-nationalisation and post-nationalisation periods was on neutralising labour militancy by extending favours and concessions to key union leaders, yielding to their pressures, and thereby ensuring industrial peace. The management's strategy to manage IR by focusing all its energies on key leaders of the unions led to a number of consequences, culminating in the creation of an adverse IR climate at the operating level.

First, the facilities and concessions extended to union leaders to neutralise union antagonism, in fact, reinforced the power of key union leaders who started demanding more favours and interfering even more in management functions. As the management found it impractical to accede to the escalating demands, the IR became more conflict-prone. The facilities and favours granted to some key union leaders were also enjoyed, without authorisation, by the rival unions as these facilities and concessions had no rationale to be offered exclusively to any one union. The IR climate was thus vitiated by claims and counter-claims by the various unions.

Second, the management's strategy of favouring the union leaders had a significant, adverse effect on the union organisation also. With extraordinary attention focused on key union leaders, the leaders began to alienate themselves from their constituents and underplay their grievances. Their need to demonstrate responsible behaviour in return for the various concessions and favours that they received overrode their concern for the genuine grievances of their constituents and in ensuring the satisfactory resolution of these grievances. Concurrently, the special status and proximity to the management acquired by the union leaders isolated them further from the members of their unions. Those who raised grievances or questioned the leaders' behaviour were punished by the leaders through their influence with the management. This process created a fissiparous tendency in the union organisation. The consequent frustration among union members was exploited either by a rival union or by a dissident group within the union, culminating in the emergence of multiple unions (Chapters 4 and 5).

Likewise, a study of trade unionism in Tata Iron and Steel Company (TISCO), a major steel behemoth in the private sector, has also revealed the apathy of workers in the affairs of trade unions on account of the unions' proximity to management, to the neglect of members (Mamkoottam, 1982).

Third, the management's IR strategies centred on the union leaders had a pernicious effect on the motivation and morale of the senior operating managers, like the zonal and regional managers. Thanks to their close relations with the top management and the concessions and favours granted to them, the leaders of the unions began to blackmail the operating managers into extending favours and concessions to their activists at the operating levels. In many cases, they were able to prevail upon the top management to get a non-cooperative manager transferred or sidelined.

Torn between their obligations on the business front and the lack of support from the top management, the operating managers made compromises at the local level and yielded to union pressures in the matters of job rotation, allotment of work, favours to union activists, and so on. In a multi-union situation, favours to one union under pressure from its leaders leads to problems with the other unions, who then continuously challenge the management's authority. This led to turbulence in IR and loss of managerial control at the operating level. The Bank management's strategy in dealing with union leaders during 1971–88 and its effect on IR at the operating level illustrates this process.

The oscillation in management strategies in dealing with the various leaders of the employee unions sent conflicting signals to the operating managers about the importance and priority accorded by the top management to dealing with the critical and sensitive issues of IR, such as discipline and productivity. In a hierarchical organisation, lower-level managers find it convenient to imitate such strategies in managing their day-to-day affairs. Interviews with management personnel at various levels suggest that oscillation in the management's IR strategy was regarded as one of the principal causes of turbulence in IR in the Bank.

Chapter 6 narrates how the operating managers neglected the issues of discipline and productivity at the branch level and allowed the branch-level union leaders to do union work during working hours, pointing out that the top management also allowed such practices at the higher levels. A survey covering 250 branch managers confirms the sense of powerlessness the managers felt in handling issues of discipline and productivity; they cited as the cause their apprehensions that they would receive no support from the higher management if a conflict situation arose out of their action. Interviews with the branch managers reveal that they adopted a cautious strategy in dealing with the unions and their leaders at the branch level to avoid trouble. A majority of the managers who were interviewed confessed that at the branch level, they managed IR by allowing the key leaders the freedom to do union work during working hours, granting them favours in matters of job rotation, and taking a lenient view of acts of indiscipline on the part of their members.

Lastly, management strategies focusing entirely on key leaders of the unions alienated the general employees as they felt that management did little to reach out to them. The inherent weakness of the strategy of concentrating on the union leaders manifested itself in the apathy of the general body of employees. It clearly proved the fallacy of the management's assumption that a happy union leader would create a happy workforce.

The natural conclusion is that merely managing union leaders is no guarantee of good employee relations; in fact, it may lead to employee alienation.

IR Based on Informal Arrangements Are Inherently Unstable

The research points out that although primary issues of wages and service conditions of employees were governed by the industry-level settlements, the IR have largely been managed by extending many concessions beyond industry-level settlement and government guidelines in return for industrial peace. Over a period of time, such informal arrangements transcended to the level of extending many concessions to the union leaders, including consultations in administrative issues and issues pertaining to the career decisions of senior management personnel. These concessions also included some unconventional favours like: promotion of some workmen union leaders to officers cadre and allowing them to represent workmen even as officers; permitting full-time union work during working hours; promotion of the general secretary of the Association and giving him senior management responsibility and perquisites; immunity from transfer to hundreds of office-bearers of the Association; and free telephone and office space at various centres to the unions and the Association (Chapters 2, 3, 4, 5, 6, and 7).

Lack of formalisation and institutionalisation of various dimensions of union–management relations, such as facilities to the unions, led to the misuse and extension of the existing facilities, claims and counter-claims in a multi-union environment, and daily conflicts at the operating level, all of which affected the productivity and smooth functioning of the branches.

Research shows the difficulty in transiting from informal relation to a formalised and institutionalised pattern due to environmental changes, with clearly defined domain areas for both the management and the unions. Chapter 4 illustrates how CEO V.D. Thakkar's (1971–74) efforts to formalise and institutionalise relations with the unions were met with resistance and counter-demands by the unions. Later, another attempt by CEO R.C. Shah to formalise relations was also unsuccessful (Chapter 5). In fact, favours and concessions, once extended, are often taken for granted and it becomes very difficult to withdraw them without inviting major conflict.

It will be useful to understand as to why the trade unions have always opposed transition to formalised pattern; how exactly 'informal relations' work in the favour of trade unions; and how they leverage them to their benefit. These informal relations are basically manifested in personal relations between the CEO and the key union leaders. Facilities and concessions beyond the industry-level agreements and sometimes in violation of government guidelines are granted to strengthen this personal bond, which carries with it informality, bonhomie, increasing visibility of the union leaders in management functions, and participation of the leaders in business meetings, task forces, and marketing efforts. All this in return for trouble-free IR, apparently for business growth. However, trade unions use their proximity to the CEO to extend, enhance, and consolidate their membership, and strengthen their influence on promotion and placement decisions. In short, they act as a 'parallel management' and interfere in all aspects of personnel administration, from discipline to vigilance management, and dilute management control in the personnel function. Thus, in a situation where union leaders enjoy direct access to the CEO, the role of personnel functionaries is often weakened. Structures and existing formal systems are bypassed to get things done. Assertive managers are replaced with the help of obliging top management and the whole administration is subverted. A few flourish at the cost of many!

Against this background, it is easy to see why the unions resisted formalisation efforts. The aim of formalisation is to create a structured framework for dealing with issues and union demands. The relationship is governed within the framework of laid-down rules and procedures, and areas of union roles and management control are clearly defined. In this arrangement, structure and processes are to be respected and adhered to, rather than being short-circuited. Union power is legitimised and clearly defined. Normally, such arrangements are more stable as parties operate within their boundaries in terms of rights and duties. For example, the Bank's decision to formalise the collective bargaining process in 1973 by providing sole bargaining rights to the majority workmen's union and consultative status to the minority union worked well for more than four decades. However, under formalised arrangements, the unions can exercise little influence in areas of management discretion and control, such as promotion and placement decisions. Their capacity to influence major changes in the organisation is constrained by the limits set by predefined roles.

From the standpoint of the management, ad hocism and too much personalisation of essentially institutional relations can lead to chaotic workplaces and loss of management control, as we have seen. They also lead to inchoate growth of the personnel function based on personalities on either side and not policies.

From the point of view of the unions, over-reliance on personal relationships weakens the union–member connect. Favours and concessions, if not formalised, are always at the mercy of the management and can be withdrawn by a new regime. It ultimately weakens the unions. My decision to streamline all informal practices and move to a new regime of formalisation (2000–08) after a bitter conflict with the unions points to the inevitability of formalisation in large organisations, especially during times of change. This formalisation in some sense was imposed as no written understanding was reached on it, and it could be achieved because we simultaneously focused on employee motivation and bringing fairness and transparency in our HR policies.

In large and geographically dispersed organisations, a well-defined policy based on formal arrangements in dealing with both majority and minority unions is likely to promote consistency in enabling all operating managers as well as union representatives to know where they stand in relation to managing the affairs of the workplace and a whole lot of issues relating to the resolution of employee grievances, articulation of employee aspirations, and the general well-being and growth of the organisation. It encourages the orderly and equitable conduct of IR by enabling the management to plan ahead by anticipating events and taking initiatives to deal with changing situations. This is not to conclude that personal relations between key actors are not important, but it cannot be the sole basis of IR management in a large organisation.

Ambiguous Role of Personnel Specialists Leads to Delays, Worsening Union–Management Relations

The research pointed out that when the role of personnel specialists in IR is ambiguous, it leads to dysfunctionality manifested in delays in decision-making, worsening of union–management relations, and accumulation of problems in the workplace. One of the key findings of this research is that the effectiveness of personnel executives was related to the level of trust they enjoyed with the CEO and the way their job was designed. When there is alignment between the CEO and the personnel executives, it leads to better planning and implementation of management strategies in IR.

Chapters 2 and 3 demonstrate a phase of complete trust between the CEO and the personnel specialist, and its impact in the form of positive IR outcomes, evident in the peaceful IR climate for a long period of time. The subsequent long period of conflict-ridden workplace IR (1974–2000), barring a short period during the tenure of S.P. Talwar, demonstrates the isolation of the personnel functionaries due to their marginalisation by the CEOs. Mostly, this lack of trust was attributable to value misalignments between the CEOs and the personnel specialists. The failure to be part of CEOs' Machiavellian tactics, and the often-questionable concessions granted to unions and shifting attitudes towards unions and their leaders, created this mistrust as the personnel specialists failed to support such tactics and rather suffered isolation. There was thus misalignment in the value system and mistrust between the CEOs and the personnel specialists (Chapters 4, 5, 6, 7, and 8).

During this long period, the management used personnel specialists mainly as advisors, without vesting them with any executive authority, but expecting them to deliver. This was a ploy of the management to frustrate the unions' attempts to find solutions to problems and reduce their influence on the personnel decision-making. The research also pointed out that the strategy of the CEOs in not vesting these specialists with any real authority in IR matters was to centralise control of personnel/IR function to manoeuvre matters like relations with the unions.

Under this system, the personnel specialists played the role of shock absorbers for the top management. In spite of these specialists maintaining a low profile, they remained at the centre of controversy and were held accountable by a majority of operating managers for all the problems the Bank faced in IR. They were torn between the expectations of the top management, who wanted to restrict them to an advisory role, and the expectations of the operating managers, who wanted them to play an executive role. The frequent change of CEO strategy in dealing with the unions and the personality clashes between the CEOs and key union leaders also diluted the role of the personnel functionaries as they had little control in responding to the frequent changes in the strategies of the CEOs.

The advisory role played by the personnel specialists also brought them into sharp conflict with their operational counterparts, who expected them to play an executive role like any other functionary of the corporate office, giving the line managers guidance and support in day-to-day IR matters. As Rice (1949: 177–84) has observed, 'the advisory function in itself is anomalous unless it is clearly defined and its authority clearly stated'. The ambiguous nature of the personnel specialists' role led to a sense of powerlessness and alienation among them, which resulted in a lack of involvement in resolving IR issues. This attitude resembles what Winkler (1974) has termed as anti-concern. This anti-concern was not an unintended consequence of organisation, but was built intentionally into the management strategy on IR. The ambiguous role of the personnel functionaries led to bureaucratisation of personnel decision-making, loss of corporate control over the personnel function, inconsistencies in rule implementation, rise of union power at the operating level, disempowerment of operating managers, and overall, to ineffectiveness of the IR function. There was ample evidence of this during my fieldwork at the Mumbai corporate and zonal offices (Chapter 8).

This brings to the fore the need for clarity in defining the personnel function in terms of its structure, authority for decision-making, support in times of crisis, and competency building to play the role effectively.

Events during 2000–08 amply demonstrate how trust in personnel specialists helped the Bank pilot many reforms in IR and lay the foundation for integrated HRD.

Lack of Integrated HR Policies Leads to Chaotic Work Environment

The research shows that barring the period when N.M. Choksi was the CEO (1956–68), the entire focus of the HR function was on managing IR. It shows that the management's connect with the employees, their aspirations, their grievances, and their day-to-day problems was very marginal. The obsessive focus of the management in managing the key leaders of the unions underlines the assumption that this would perhaps automatically improve the satisfaction of the employees, as if there is some pass-through mechanism. In a service industry like a bank, the management has to ensure that the front-line staff is motivated, competent, and shares the vision of the Bank to ensure good customer service and business growth. However, the Bank's strategy of developing a narrow focus on IR led to the alienation of the employees and apathy among the front-line staff. An integrated framework of employee relations would mean looking at employees as a talent resource, and proactive action on the part of the management to bring within its policy framework issues of employee engagement, compassion, open communication, and expeditious resolution of grievances.

In large and geographically dispersed organisations like banks, which deal with customers though millions of face-to-face transactions every day, it is encumbent upon the management to install a system of open communication to get feedback from employees about customers and their level of satisfaction with the Bank, take measures to ensure the quickest possible way of handling employee grievances, implement employee care programmes, and meet career aspirations to ensure their fullest engagement with the Bank. Outsourcing these functions to unions shows a narrow understanding by the management about its role in employee relations. The major transformation of the Bank with spectacular business growth during 2005–08 was a consequence of its focus on employee engagement, employee care, and employee capacity building.

Industry-level Institutional Mechanisms for Wage Settlement Alone Cannot Create Better IR

The findings of the research dispute the common belief of bank managements that industry-level agreements on wages and service conditions act as a deterrent in motivating the staff as the management is constrained in offering any financial incentives for performance. The research indicates that in spite of the industry-wide character of wage payments in banking, the top management in an individual bank has considerable discretion in motivating the staff through non-financial incentives, such as listening to their concerns, career path planning, training and development, and an open and transparent process for grievance resolution. The research shows that IR at the enterprise level are governed by the relationship that exists between the management and the trade unions on the one hand, and between the management and the employees on the other. It shows that IR at the enterprise level are governed by a host of factors such as the initiatives taken by the management in seeking the involvement of the unions and the employees in work-related problems, information sharing on vital issues concerning the bank's growth and development, working of institutions of collective bargaining for problem-solving, the working of mechanisms for the management of grievances or disputes, and the structure of the personnel function.

The research also shows that despite stabilisation of IR through the bipartite mechanism at the industry level, the enterprise-level IR can be turbulent on account of a variety of factors as industry-level agreements rarely encompass the whole spectrum of IR. Hence, there is considerable discretion available to individual managements in structuring IR. Industry-level agreements may constrain management initiatives in IR to a certain extent, but the internal climate of industrial peace and tranquillity in an organisation largely depends on the managerial initiative in installing structures, systems, and processes that are conducive to building general trust and collaboration between the management, unions, and employees. Thus, it may be hypothesised that the quality of IR in an organisation is primarily determined by the forces within the organisation, and external factors operate merely as a constraint. Against this background, the management has a critical role to play in shaping the IR climate.

Oscillating Managerial Strategies: A Plausible Explanation

When one looks at the management strategies followed by the different CEOs of BoB from 1956 to 2000, one is struck by the absence of any consistent policy framework to manage IR. The strategies at different points of time have shifted quite drastically from being humanistic to accommodative, combative, back to accommodative, to acquiescence and soft-pedalling, and so on. One may also notice that during the same period, the Bank's commercial performance also shifted from being good to stagnant, declining to rising. Oscillations between different approaches to IR undermine stability and continuity and more specifically, place major limitations on the extent to which trust can be generated and maintained. There is no simplistic correlation between the different IR strategies and their various outcomes. Nor is the search for a direct correlation a wise one, as Schein (2003: 243) noted in his study of Digital Equipment Corporation over a period of 30 years:

> There are obvious lessons [from the story of DEC] to be learned that are fairly clear based on events, but, more important, there are subtle lessons to be learned by trying to explain why the obvious events occurred. Second, the events of history are highly interactive. The search for a root cause is flawed because it implies that there is a root cause, when, in fact, the events may have occurred for a multiplicity of reasons.

However, just as Schein reflects on the situation he studied and attempts plausible explanations from the perspective of culture, it seems worthwhile to look for the major factors that may help us understand the shifting IR strategies employed by the Bank's CEOs based on environmental and organisational imperatives.

Bank of Baroda is one of the foremost public sector enterprises in a democratic society. A PSB in India is expected to perform well on all business parameters and conduct itself efficiently and consistently. The top management can expect to be judged by the Bank's achievement of positive business outcomes as well as the concomitant social objectives. This twin responsibility makes the task of the CEO of a bank quite challenging.

However, as Simon (1997) has pointed out, due to 'bounded rationality', executives are rarely able to work towards optimal work solutions to organisational problems and end up mainly focusing their attention on selected aspects of the situation.

In the context of BoB, it can be seen that all the CEOs prior to me came from the banking stream and were accomplished dyed-in-the-wool bankers. The period after the nationalisation of banks was specially challenging on account of many government-mandated programmes in rural and semi-urban areas, which required rapid expansion in those areas. Simultaneously, there was a resurgence of the trade union movement in the banking industry, BoB being no exception. Under the circumstances, it makes eminent sense to imagine that the CEOs focused their attention on achieving the commercial growth objectives, which demanded their undivided attention. So far as the rising IR and HR challenges were concerned, they ended up adopting a satisficing[1] (Simon) approach.

This meant that the CEO's main objective was to somehow contain any visible signs of discord which could either prevent the meeting of pressing commercial challenges or attract the punitive eye of the government. This commercial logic combined with the pro-labour proclivities of the government led the CEOs to choose the easier options. The only exception to this can be seen in the case of R.C. Shah (1975–81), who took a decisive step to change the prevailing IR scenario, but he did so after mobilising government support at the highest level.

It may be worth pointing out that IR based on such considerations moves from crisis to crisis. Eventually, the people in the organisation become dominated by events and reactiveness. The operating managers move from one crisis to another and develop deep cynicism and find themselves to be hapless victims of such oscillating policies. Often, in order to buy peace from unions, operating managers give in to union pressures. The research amply demonstrates the impact of managerial strategies leading to conflict-ridden workplaces.

---

[1] According to Herbert Simon, people tend to make decisions by satisficing (a combination of sufficing and satisfying) rather than optimising (Simon, 1956). Decisions are often simply good enough in light of the costs and constraints involved. As a heuristic, satisficing individuals will choose options that meet basic decision criteria. A focus on satisficing can be used by choice architects when decision-makers are prone to procrastination (Johnson et al., 2012).

It is baffling that successive CEOs in the post-nationalisation period till the year 2000 looked at IR from the narrow lenses of managing trade unions only and consequently the focus on the operating managers, employees, and the workplace remained ambiguous. This ambivalence predictably contributed to workplaces remaining in perpetual situation of conflict.

While it is for researchers to explore such apathy in general at the top towards the HR function, my exploration of the problem suggests that the Bank's management was too scared to touch this sensitive subject and preferred to 'let sleeping dogs lie'. It could also be because of the *Après moi, le déluge* (After me, the deluge) attitude of the infamous King Louis XV of the French Revolution!

Role of the CEO in HR/IR: Reflection and Strategies

Modern organisations are becoming increasingly complex on account of rapidity of changes as a result of the process of globalisation, technological disruptions, and ever-increasing competitive pressures. Additionally, organisations are also undergoing immense challenges on account of rapid intergenerational issues, gender diversity, and other forms of change. The forces of these changes are especially exacerbated in public sector organisations, which have a larger social purpose, and are additionally affected by governmental pressures and democratic accountability. Contrary to their private sector and multinational counterparts, public sector organisations, by their very raison d'être, have to be open and transparent in their policies and programmes. An environment of multiple unions, including officers' organisations, and their political affiliations and proclivities, often adds to the problems. Management of HR in such organisations poses special challenges. The role of the CEO in IR and HRD, thus, is of strategic significance.

Any short-term or myopic approach to managing HR issues can be problematic. The research has amply brought out how at different points of time, the short-term policies of the CEOs at BoB have contributed to long-term problems in the organisation, especially in taking the organisation forward through transformational initiatives. It must be noted that effective IR/HR management defies a single-step solution. Rather it requires a whole range of action steps encompassing an entire ecosystem of HRM.

Using this insight, my exclusive experience of reforming IR (Chapter 11) and moving on to initiate a wider programme of engaging and developing employees (Chapter 12) points to a multitude of actions that created a desirable HR climate, which has withstood the test of time, as demonstrated by the Bank's sustained prime position in the industry. In order to ensure a balance between the achievement of organisational goals and employee welfare and customer satisfaction, the CEO needs to consciously develop strategies on multiple fronts, or else face turbulence on the employee front, as demonstrated by the research documented in Part I of this book.

The modern organisations are also ever-grappling with myriad challenges on account of changes in the business landscape, competitive pressures, technological disruptions, and the ever-changing regulations. All this calls for availability of critical capabilities and rehashing the existing ones. To respond to these challenges and adjust to the emerging workplace culture, CEOs will need to give prominence to their HR role and bring it centre stage. However, sometimes, if not often, the pressure to achieve results blinds the CEO to the need for building an architecture of HR and leadership, till the dissatisfaction and alienation levels in the organisation are heightened and begin to get manifested in union action and reaction and through industrial conflict in various forms. In the last few decades, as Kochan (2012) rightly points out in the American context:

> That it [America] has become a financial driven economy…the view of shareholder value as corporations' primary objective has dominated since the 1980s. That motivation—to get short-term shareholder returns—then pushes to lower priority all the other things we used to think about as a social contract.

Such a myopic focus on business can no doubt help achieve business goals in the short term, but it can also adversely affect organisational health, which can inhibit its sustainability and its propensity to address future challenges.

In this context, it may not be imprudent to say that the 'business of the CEO is not to do business alone' but to also take foundational steps in building other intangibles, such as technological readiness, corporate social responsibility leadership, governance and ethical architecture, customer-centricity, and most importantly, employee relations and development. Many socially inspired CEOs today seem to defy their traditional roles of only creating shareholder value and are going much beyond short-term profit considerations to create social impact. Unilever's Paul Polman (2009) is one such CEO who is pursuing the company's target to double its size, while reducing its overall environmental footprint and improving its social impact through its sustainable living plan. Polman has argued that in a volatile world of finite resources, running a business sustainably is vital for long-term growth in emerging markets and it also mitigates risk and reduces cost.

Given the ambiguity and the complexity of IR environment in the large public sector organisations, the role of key actors in management also ends up being fuzzy and poorly defined and understood. Hence, it becomes imperative to achieve a certain level of role clarity in regard to key functionaries like CEO, HR managers, and line managers. There is also a need for synergistic understanding amongst these roles. Accordingly, in the public sector, issues of employee relations are often expected to be handled by the HR functionaries and the unions. Usually, the CEO steps in only when relations with the unions have escalated to a level where they threaten to disrupt the functioning of the organisation. The normal trend is to contain the conflict and manage the union expectations through expedient methods such as concessions and compromises, which may have long-term deleterious consequences for the organisation, as seen in this research. Hence, the need for proactive and methodical understanding of evolving or emerging employee expectations, industry patterns, and other relevant considerations must guide against any short-term, ad hoc measures. Experience suggests that temporary and Band-Aid solutions for complex problems increase their potential to recur and lead to major disruptions. More specifically, the CEO must engage with:

1. *Policy formulation in HRM*: Specify key dimensions of policy in relation to various sub-systems of HR, expectations, deliverables, and accountability of HR function. Like any other business function, HR policy document should be developed after wide-ranging discussions in the organisation. The document should clearly outline policy on employee development, leadership development, succession planning, rewards and recognitions, organisational justice mechanism, and so on.

2. *Upgrade and support the role of HRM function*: Ensure that there is no ambiguity in the role of HRM functionaries. The research has pointed

out that mere advisory nature of the role of HR creates several dys-functionalities in the conduct of this function. My executive experience suggests that a hybrid role combining executive and advisory components is best suited in the context of managing this function in a large organisation. It needs to play the advisory role in the area of policy-making and strategy formulation and executive role in ensuring effective decision-making and guiding operating managers in problem-solving process. The CEOs need to show respect for the knowledge of HR functionaries and trust them to be able to successfully respond to emerging HR challenges.

3. *Invest in innovative HR policies*: Like every other area of business, HR gets its share of new technologies and practices and HR and senior line functionaries should always show keen interest in adopting such practices (Ulrich, 1990).

4. *Developing operating managers*: To have an appreciation of the big picture about the consequences of their actions and inculcate in them necessary soft skills to manage conflicts, build teams, and productively engage them. Successful line managers are the best source of creating future leadership pipeline.

5. *Developing appropriate structure*: To put in place an appropriate organisational structure in HR that is non-bureaucratic, tech-savvy with minimum hierarchies, and in tune with high-speed decision response to respond to people issues.

Obviously, the challenge is to provide resources and learning infra-structure to continuously provide professional expertise in adequate measure to deliver on the plan and achieve the desired future value positioning of the organisation. This calls for professionalisation of HR function. In a government report of PSBs (Khandelwal Committee, 2010), it was pointed out that HR function has still not attained specialised status in PSBs. Barring very few exceptions, most banks, large and small, do not have qualified HR professionals who can provide continuity and expert knowledge in regard to methodology for talent and leadership development. The HR functionaries in most PSBs end up busying them-selves with routine administration, such as union–management relations, transfers and placements, and handling appraisal and promotion process. Rarely do banks adopt modern methodologies in selection and internal promotions, talent and leadership development, or undertake HR climate surveys, or HR audit to plan systematic interventions in HR area. One of the key roles of the CEO is to build HR competencies of the highest standards, appropriate structure and subsystems of HR, and mechanisms to ensure professional approach in HRM and link it to business goals. The other roles of CEO in IR/HRD are given next.

IR–HR Integration

Both in academic literature as well as in organisations, IR and HRD are kept separate, almost as if HRD was the sacred and IR profane. This dichotomy in an essentially people-related function works to cross-purposes. In an IR environment which may be distrustful, leading to mutual suspicion, HRD overtures which claim to promote an open and trustful culture would not only prove to be ineffective but also create cynicism. It was interesting to note during the research that overtures to involve unions in business development in an otherwise mistrustful IR environment could not be sustained. Similarly, the creation of an HRD Department in an overwhelmingly IR-driven environment could not receive the support of the IR functionaries (Chapter 5). Reflecting on my journey of research and executive life in handling IR and HR, certain thoughts reverberate in my mind:

1. Is IR all about conflict, confrontation, disruption, machinations, manipulations, deceit, and compromises?
2. Is HRD about superficial and esoteric concern for employees?
3. Is an integration of IR and HRD possible?
4. Is an integration of the two at all a practical proposition for a corporate CEO?

One does not often observe many examples of an organic integration of the two functions of IR and HRD. However, such a view of the two does injustice to the foundations of both. If one goes back into the historical development of the ideas of IR and HRD, one would get a more optimistic view of them. The development of the ideas and practices of IR is rooted in the gross injustice done to workers in the initial stages of the Industrial Revolution. The theory and practice of IR was to ensure 'fairness and organisational justice' to all employees. Over time, this degenerated into a power game between the union and the management of an enterprise at times, and into a cosy, collusive relationship between the two at others.

Similarly, the foundations of the HRD movement lie in the development of a humanistic perspective exemplified in the human relations and HR movements. These movements aimed to create healthy workplaces where human beings could flourish through their engagement with the enterprise. Here again, soon enough, the original intent was replaced by a superficial and esoteric perspective of viewing human beings as mere instrumentalities for achieving commercial interests. As a result, HRD efforts became peripheral. A well-meaning CEO needs to be aware of this dilution of the foundations of IR and HRD and would do well to reflect on the myopic nature of such an approach to manage HR. In my view and based on my efforts in recapturing the spirit of original movement in IR and HRD, it will be imperative to integrate IR and HRD and ensure that both functions have an organic linkage in terms of philosophy about people, respect for processes, long-term orientation, and commitment to build a sound work culture. This will require reskilling of HR functionaries and rehash of the HR function itself. It is important that the HR functionaries be a creative set of individuals, professionally competent, and fired with the imagination and commitment to building people. Creating an HR team that has both competence and a passion for people development is crucial for building leadership. To develop the credibility of the HR function and also demonstrate the impact of HR competence in delivering business outcomes, it may be useful to offer opportunities to HR functionaries to work in business/operational roles. Until I worked in operational roles in Meerut and Kolkata, I remained a half-baked HR specialist! I could reach my full potential only after successfully working in business roles, eventually reaching a position in which I could lead the organisation.

Based on this insight, when I became CEO, I took several steps to integrate IR and HRD. These steps included:

1. Reorienting the personnel and IR functionaries to the HRD philosophy and practices through a well-planned training programme. This programme had a special component to develop human process sensitivity through sensitivity training.
2. Rotating personnel functionaries in IR and HR roles.
3. Bringing some senior line managers to HR and IR roles and sending some HR and IR functionaries to senior line positions.
4. Setting up joint task forces for planning and problem-solving in IR and HRD.
5. Continuous review to ensure successful integration and take corrective action as and when needed.

One of the key issues in integration is that while IR problems require deeper engagement of the functionaries in resolving live issues and problems which can sometimes be personally fatiguing, HRD, as generally practised, tends to be driven by current fads and methodologies which fail to go to the root of the problems that cause tension for operating managers and employees. Eventually, such accumulated tensions at the workplace become fodder for industrial conflict. Therefore, in the true sense, the integration of IR and HRD should result in a better relationship, better problem-solving mechanisms, better grievance redressal, better conflict resolution mechanisms, and eventually, better workplaces. Some such efforts are illustrated in Chapters 9 and 10, which took place during my tenures as zonal manager in Meerut and Kolkata, and later as Executive Director and CEO (Chapters 11 and 12).

Engaging Employees

The twenty-first century world is increasingly service-driven and therefore, only those organisations that can ensure consistent and extraordinary levels of service to ever-demanding customers can survive in the competitive marketplace. Discerning and demanding customers can besmirch the reputation of organisations on social media in minutes. Therefore, increasing the sensitisation of employees to operate in this environment, their emotional connect with their work and the organisation, and their accountability to new performance benchmarks has to be an unrelenting endeavour.

This is a task that the CEO cannot delegate. The CEO has to put in place systems and processes, monitor the outcomes of efforts, and constantly engage with HR and line functionaries to ensure that the employees are engaged with the work, both intellectually and emotionally, and that their feedback about products, services, or any personal problem are available online to take prompt corrective action. Periodic customer and employee surveys, corrective actions, both structural and procedural, and constantly reviewing internal mechanisms for problem-solving can help in employee engagement. Open and transparent communication lines from the field staff to the top management, and vice versa, and extensive use of technology for facilitating this two-way communication should, in fact, help get field insights to the top and likewise, the agenda and aspirations of the top to the lower-level staff.

The research (Part I) demonstrates the increasing sense of alienation and disillusionment experienced by both operating managers and employees as a result of the top management's failure to reach out to them, instead practically outsourcing this function to the union leaders. We have seen the pitfalls of such a strategy. Ironically, this kind of disengagement of the top management with the front-line operating managers and employees goes contrary to the very logic of the service industry. Engagement crisis is highlighted by a Gallup survey (2014) which pointed out that a staggering 87 per cent of employee's worldwide are not engaged. It also points out that companies with highly engaged staff outperform their peers by 147 per cent in earning/share. Further, going by purely business logic, in this volatility, uncertainty, complexity, ambiguity (VUCA) environment, it would be preposterous to conclude that only top-end senior management can drive business results without the engagement of lower-level functionaries. In spite of the well-intentioned employee surveys undertaken by some organisations, the lack of follow-up action can result in disengaged staff. More often than not, managements do not follow through on the survey findings with credible actions on the ground to improve engagement, apparently due to business overload. This is where the CEOs have to break the trap.

My experience (Chapter 12) in piloting a major transformational programme for the Bank, mainly through an integrated HR policy framework and its implementation, confirms the critical role HR can play in business success. I personally piloted many employee engagement programmes, like 'Manthan' (Chapter 12) and a direct hotline for employees to reach out to me.

Creating Culture

One of the most important roles of the CEO is to drive and shape corporate culture. Culture is an important aspect of competitive advantage. However, it is the most difficult piece of CEO's job. Researchers such as former Harvard Business School professors, John Kotter and James Haskett, have also found consistent co-relation between robust, engaged cultures and high-performance business results (Kotter and Haskett, 1992).

Most vision statements mention service, transparency, and many other similar objectives as the core values, but the challenge for CEOs is: how to create these values and make them a way of life? From the standpoint of HRD, how does a CEO create a culture of team spirit, initiative, risk-taking, service, collaboration, learning, and innovations?

One key way to develop the open and supportive culture is also to look for the positive initiatives taken by the managers in the middle, support them, and appreciate and popularise them. The CEOs need to believe in 'Reverse Inspiration' (Chapter 10) and create a culture to promote this.

It may be pertinent to mention that today's successful and popular CEOs' major preoccupation is to build culture in their organisation. For example, Jeff Bezos, CEO of Amazon, was asked about his role these days and he said:

> My main job today: I work hard at helping to maintain the culture. A culture of high standards of operational excellence, of inventiveness, of willingness to fail, willingness to make bold experiments.... Many of the traits that make Amazon unusual are now deeply ingrained in the culture. In fact, I wanted to change them, I couldn't. The cultures are self-reinforcing, and that's a good thing.[2]

---

[2] https://www.businessinsider.in/When-I-Asked-Jeff-Bezos-The-Tough-Questions-No-Profits-The-Book-Controversies-The-Phone-Flop-He-Proved-Why-Hes-A-Genius-CEO/articleshow/45507079.cms (accessed on 10 December 2017).

Chapter 12 elaborately describes as to how we can prioritise on building a facilitative culture as a precursor to our transformation programme and how our efforts to drill that culture into the organisation can deliver spectacular results.

The CEO's main work is to focus on building a facilitative culture that will keep the organisation's future fit.

Empowering Operating Managers

Operating managers are the fulcrum of any organisation, and they carry the major responsibility of managing the organisation's business and achieving its goals. In this context, the role of the top management is to facilitate and create an environment through proactive policies, a stout support system, and open communication, so that it can understand problems and provide quick solutions to operating managers. A major constraining force in large organisations, and more so in public sector enterprises, is the internal bureaucracy, which is often stifling. Lack of coordination, silo-style work-ing, and lack of accountability at the top are often bigger reasons for lack of performance than the pressures of the external environment. One of the key roles of the CEO is to uproot the internal bureaucracy and to deal with problems of internal coordination and accountability with bold moves. In public enterprises, including PSBs, the HR function is highly centralised, administration-driven, and remains largely on the periphery of the organ-isation. To address the issue of empowering operating managers, the CEO needs to decentralise the HR function in the various business verticals. It is important for the CEO to empower functional heads to develop their own teams, succession, and leadership in their functions with the support of a central HR team. Lack of ownership of HR by the majority of top line managers can prove to be dysfunctional in building the leadership bench strength across functions. It is imperative for the CEO to build ownership and accountability in the top team for HR.

Dealing with Collectives

Trade unions, especially officers' unions in the public sector, pose special challenge to respond to their concerns as their members are at centre of developing business and delivering service. Besides multiple trade unions of workmen, one has to deal with SC/ST welfare associations, which more or less demand same treatment and facilities as accorded to trade unions, notwithstanding the fact that they are not trade unions.

Multi-unionism and political affiliations/patronage to trade unions complicate the environment. Generally, policies in dealing with unions are not codified and even where codified, the managements, at their discretion, extend many new facilities under pressure from unions as a quid pro quo for their support for smooth conduct of business. Short-tenured CEOs, in their anxiety to buy peace, often succumb to trade unions tactics to interfere in areas which are beyond their domains. Trade unions also capitalise on acts of commission and omission of top management and in this process, take full advantage of management vulnerabilities. Thus, some organisations develop a whole range of uncodified informal understandings on various issues. Attempts to subsequently formalise the same result in a disruptive environment.

Chapters 11 and 12 show as to how difficult it is to streamline IR from an indulgency culture to structured pattern.

The CEOs, therefore, need to understand the consequences of their action in the long term and should use their discretions with prudence and caution. They should also develop a perspective in their top team and operating managers about IR issues. A system of structured meetings, open and transparent dialogue on various issues of the organisation, and a policy of non-discrimination and fairness can help better union–management relations. Pampering or mollycoddling trade unions can have long-term deleterious consequences.

Identifying and Developing Talent

The CEOs today rank talent management among their top priorities. According to a KPMG survey (2016), 99 per cent of CEOs report the need for developing future talent to meet the significant transformation plans and rapidly advancing technology in organisations. There is a war for talent globally. The CEOs in public enterprises increasingly complain about talent deficit to meet the requirements of these competitive times, and yet it is observed that very little planned attention is paid to the issue of building a leadership talent pipeline. As mentioned elsewhere in this chapter, there are very few innovations in the performance management systems, talent identification, and various processes of HR development. Often, there is a tendency to blame the government and its policies for standardised HR systems.

In spite of having a well-structured training system, in many public sector undertakings, the coupling between training and operations is weak. Therefore, the issues of identification, development, and nurturing of talent in various areas are of crucial importance in achieving organisational aims. Talent and HR gaps in the case of PSBs have been cited as new risks in the risk management matrix by the Khandelwal Committee (2010) and yet, there is very little initiative either by the government or by individual banks to take any substantive steps in this regard.

Chapter 12 articulates the range of initiatives I undertook to use HRD as the main lever of transformation with extraordinary business outcomes.

Crusader for Diversity and Inclusiveness

Diversity and inclusiveness are the two pillars on which the credibility of the organisation rests. The CEOs have a huge role to play in taking proactive steps to ensure respect for people irrespective of gender, religion, caste, and colour, and in taking special measures to protect the interests of those who feel discriminated against. Public enterprises in India are given a statutory mandate for reservation in the recruitment of socially disadvantaged and physically handicapped categories. Similarly, increasing the intake of women employees puts responsibility on the organisation to ensure equal opportunity and lack of discrimination. It is also encumbent upon the organisation to devise special HRD policies to unleash the potential in all these groups. The CEOs have to put in place a zero-tolerance policy in dealing with issues of gender discrimination and sexual harassment cases and lead by example.

Concern for Institutionalisation

Institutionalisation is the process of creating consistency and uniformity across the organisation in regard to applying its policies. In the 'People' domain, any inconsistency in application of rules creates potential for grievances and likely trade union problem.

It is therefore imperative that CEOs ensure uniform application of rules across their organisations and fix accountability for violations. Lack of fairness on this count not only reduces credibility of the management but could also result in a perpetual conflict-prone environment. Discretion in HR area has to be used with prudence and for legitimate reasons.

HR Governance

Human resources governance includes the internal oversight and management of an organisation's HR strategy, programmes, practices, and outcomes, through clearly defined roles, responsibilities, and accountabilities across the enterprise. The board needs to ensure that there is an effective internal HR framework and it understands various HR risks facing the organisation. It should also be satisfied that management priorities, policies, and practices effectively respond to strategic, regulatory, and operational needs (Cullwick, 2011).

This is one area which has received minimum attention of the boards of organisations in India. In public sector organisations, industry-level wage agreements and government guidelines on HR issues have led to standardisation of policies, with little scope to link wages and incentive with performance of the individual banks. This apart, many areas in HR, especially in developing people and improving productivity, have not received due attention. The HR governance requires initiatives at board and CEO level to ensure that there is continuous supply of leadership at various levels and the policies and programmes in HR are in alignment with business priorities. In a highly competitive scenario, HR is a new risk for the public enterprises in general, and PSBs in particular. The CEOs thus have a very critical role in designing strategies and policies in both the sub-systems of HR, namely, IR and HRD, to respond to the new wave of digital and new workforce. They need to take multiple steps internally to create a new culture of transparency and open communication in HR matters and lift the veil of secrecy from the HR issues.

Personal Integrity

Companies, especially in the public sector, by their very nature, meaning, and purpose, are accountable to the state for their performance and conduct. They are supposed to operate within the framework of rules, regulations, and a governance structure, often with much greater sensitivity than the private sector because of their parliamentary accountability. Apart from this, they are expected to work with greater transparency, fairness, and good conduct in dealing with employees, customers, and other stakeholders. They are open to close scrutiny in business as well as personnel decision-making through investigative agencies such as the Central Vigilance Commission, the Central Bureau of Investigation, and the Comptroller and Auditor General of India. They also come under the purview of the Right to Information Act. This imposes very high demands and expectations on the role of public sector executives, and the CEO in particular. Apart from technical skills, the CEO needs to set an example of highest level of personal integrity for himself and the people of his organisation. Abuse of official position in any way by those in authority can be very demoralising and send wrong signals across the organisation. This is basic to the credibility of the leader.

* * *

In my experience as the CEO of a large bank, bringing about reforms in the domain in IR/HR was a crucial prerequisite for laying the foundation for multi-pronged transformation of the organisation in the emerging competitive landscape.

It leads me to even suggest that it may not be inappropriate to expand the acronym CEO as 'Chief Employee Officer'. It is more so in organisations committed to national priorities and social purpose. Notwithstanding the importance of disruptive impact of technology, the people in such organisations have a central role in serving the superordinate goals of such organisations, besides operating as a sustainable business organisation. It must however be conceded that the issues related to IR/HRD are not as simple as they may appear to be, or be looked at as mere constraints bordering on nuisance which need to be contained, or delegated to the HR Department.

Even when there are no major problems, the challenge to develop people and organisations requires deep commitment, rigour, and engagement of the CEO, supported by the HR professionals. Simply, the CEO needs to have a systemic understanding of 'people strategies' and their interconnectedness to other aspects like technology, culture, and business.

Chapter 14

CEO—CHESS MASTER OR GARDENER?

My research—documented in the first part of the book—indicates that often on account of environmental and organisational changes, the CEOs ended up being trapped in win-lose game with the trade unions, failing to see their duty towards the employees. In some ways, they could not grasp the long-term consequences of their myopic strategies on the motivation of employees and operating managers. As mentioned in Chapters 11 and 12, because of my insights from research, I chose to deal with the people domain with a systemic perspective and led a major reform process in dealing with the legacy issues in IR. This was later followed by major technology-driven business transformation programme, with deep involvement and professional rigour, by undertaking multi-fold changes in HR domain.

In hindsight, the shift from what I saw during my research and what I undertook with significant success evokes the metaphor of CEO as 'Chess Master or Gardener', as enunciated by Stanley McChrystal et al. in the book *Team of Teams* (2015). My experience actually enriches the usefulness of these metaphors and extends the metaphor of leader as a gardener in a significant way.

Leaders as Chess Masters

This book is about IR/HR strategies of CEOs. The IR management in the Bank during the research phase appeared more akin to a chess master's role played by the CEOs (with the exception of Choksi; Chapter 2) from time to time, by meddling in the internal dynamics of the trade unions, buying their support and concessions, pampering them by splurging favours and concessions to contain labour militancy, reducing the power of individual leaders, and supporting rival groups in the unions. These moves and counter-moves of the CEOs were able to contain union militancy; and at other times, it was reduced to rather highly personalised win-lose game. This would fall into the classical game of chess playing in which there are victors and vanquished. While it is not disputed that the circumstances prevailing during the tenures of the respective CEOs would have prompted them to target individual union leaders, the important issue is that in this process, the leaders failed to craft any long-term strategies for structuring union–management relations. Their short-term actions led to chaotic IR at the operational levels and demoralisation of employees.

The management actions or inactions can be seen as moves and counter-moves mainly to either strengthen its own power or weaken the power of the trade union leaders. It became less between two institutions, namely, management and trade union, to settle issues of principles and more between the CEO and the leaders of the unions at the personal level, staking the fate of the organisation. This resembles the typical game of chess between two opponents, each one trying to defeat the other. In order for one to win, the other must lose. It is a highly personalised game, mainly to experience the sense of power over the opponent. This hunger for emotional gratification and power is human. Sometimes, this need overpowers an individual and becomes an end in itself, causing immense harm to self and others. It is not rare to find great sportsmen and politicians becoming victims of such a syndrome and harming themselves and their vocations.

It is not claimed here that organisations operate in an ideal setting, or that conflicts can always be avoided. The issue, however, is that we need to distinguish between actors resolving conflicts within the institutional framework and boundaries to guard their respective principles/ values and the strategies and moves to annihilate the other, irrespective of its consequences. Strategic moves to hold one's values or principles is not chess mastering, but moves to defeat someone to get personal gratification is. For example, strategic moves and counter-moves to defend national boundaries is not chess mastering but an act based on principles. Thus, strategic moves with a purpose to weed out a dysfunctional culture, or even against individuals to weed out their disruptive potential, are not chess mastering. The core of chess mastering is defeating someone for personal survival or gratification.

My initiatives and actions for IR reforms (Chapter 11) involved a number of strategic moves to reduce the power of trade unions and restore the authority of operating managers. All this was successfully achieved (winning) but in doing so, the purpose was to carve out a hassle-free path for going ahead with new technology and a new future for the sustainable development of the Bank post liberalisation. The core purpose of our strategies was development and growth of the organisation.

Leaders as Gardeners

Typically, the four most important steps in gardening are the process of weeding, preparing the soil, planting the seedlings, and nurturing the plants. Let us analyse each of these processes in the context of a leader's role as a gardener in a live organisation.

Step 1: Weeding

One of the most important and critical processes in gardening is weeding out the unwanted plants from the ground. However, in the case of organisations, weeding out has largely remained an unattended concern. It essentially involves challenging and removing the accumulated attitudes, dysfunctional processes, overriding bureaucracy, and a status quoist mindset. Questioning some of these issues means moving people out of their comfort zone. Any attempt to tackle this makes the leader open to intense criticism, making even his personal reputation vulnerable. On account of such inherent risks, leading becomes a risky business (Heifetz and Linsky, 2002).

Most leadership efforts tend to focus only on the softer side, such as promoting organisation-wide communication, engagement, and employee development. The problem is only half tackled, especially in those organisations where the existing culture puts barriers on the new initiatives to flourish. In an old culture, new initiatives, howsoever well intentioned, have a tendency to fail. The reasons are not far to seek. In a culture where employees have flourished without any demands on their productivity or workplace behaviour, the leadership overtures have a high probability of failure unless steps are taken to weed out such attitudes and tackle the culture that has supported such behaviour. Similarly, if for years an organisation had not demonstrated its commitment to service, grand pontifications of leaders on the value of service might fall on deaf ears. Therefore, in any journey of transformation undertaken by a leader, weeding out becomes the starting point and the most significant part of the gardener-leaders role in an organisation. In fact, the success of undertaking weeding out process would really prepare the leader to undertake other steps in the ecosystem.

Weeding out process is a precursor to a major transformation initiative. In our specific context, such weeding out involved debureaucratisation of decision-making across the Bank, tackling non-responsiveness to customer issues, remedying workplace indiscipline and restrictive practices, shifting balance of power from trade unions to management, and breaking siloed working at the top.

This was the most fundamental challenge before commencing any worthwhile transformational exercise. All these issues related to an existing culture developed over a long period of time. Such culture change, despite appreciation of the same at the intellectual level, is always pain-producing to those who have to adjust to new ways of working. Culture change cannot be affected by sermons, entreaties, exhortations, or by emails. It requires prodigious efforts in streamlining many existing legacy-based systems, drilling new attitudes, and initiating new processes in the organisation.

It may be relevant to mention how I faced the pain and trauma of weeding out the union attitudes in reforming IR (Chapter 11) and how our transformation programme was disrupted for about three years. However, once the resistance of the unions was tackled successfully, we could undertake many changes without much hassle and achieve a new culture of productivity, leading to spectacular all-round growth in the business and propensity of the Bank to undertake many innovative steps. It is gratifying to note that the Bank continues to maintain its prime position and making rapid strides even after over a decade of the weeding out process.

Step 2: Preparing the Soil

Preparing the soil would involve readying the ground for planting. In the organisational context, this would mean preparing the organisation to absorb new initiatives and innovations without hassle. It calls for building internal support systems and creating a facilitative environment in which people are encouraged to give their best. It also essentially requires extraordinary efforts on the part of gardener-leaders to unleash the collective potential of the workforce, empower critical managers for change agentry roles, build accountability across the organisation, foster an open communication system, and work towards continuous development of people.

I endeavoured to prepare a conducive climate for transformation by initiating several steps that involved a very powerful system of recognising the employee as the unique focus of all endeavours (in place of trade union leaders), reaching out to individuals through town hall meetings, monthly communication to individual employees, establishing a direct hotline with employees, as also encouraging innovations and ideas from employees. In sum, the entire focus was on effective communication—listening intently to employee concerns with a view to addressing them.

Likewise, the introduction of daily morning meetings among the members of the top management created a highly effective mechanism to bring the top team together to discuss, debate, and implement the cherished vision of the Bank. As noted earlier (Chapter 12), the morning meetings became an effective vehicle for propelling change and transformation, eventually laying the foundation for many innovations and remarkable business growth. Thus, through persistent efforts we could, to a great degree, create a team at the top, mobilise employees, improve their attitudes, and create a culture of speedy implementation of our transformational agenda. These became my most effective leadership tools to change the existing culture.

Step 3: Planting the Seedlings

This would essentially mean that the soil is ready for planting. In the organisational context, this would mean readiness to innovate products, processes, services, and systems. Such innovations would cover both employee-centric and customer-centric initiatives. It would also mean laying the foundation for effective policy initiatives in HR area to ensure that the organisation is able to provide an uninterrupted flow of talent at various levels through meritocratic processes of selection, placement, promotion, and training.

In this endeavour, I focused on creating a culture of high performance and high compassion, which flowed out of my conviction that high-performance orientation cannot be sustained without equal emphasis on developing a compassionate organisation. A number of initiatives for talent building, like 'Khoj' (talent hunting exercise), grooming 300 leaders project, and revamping the training system, exemplified our employee-centric initiatives.

Similarly, a number of customer-centric initiatives, such as introduction of 8 a.m. to 8 p.m. banking, 24-hours human banking, happy hour banking, Sunday banking, retail loan factories, SME loan factories, gen-next branches, ATM expansion, and introduction of anytime–anywhere banking, symbolised our new emphasis on customers.

Step 4: Nurturance

Finally, it is in the caring of the plants that the garden blooms. In the words of McChrystal et al. (2015: 229):

> Gardeners plant and harvest but more than anything, they *tend*…. Regular visits by good gardeners are not pro-forma gestures of concern—they leave the crop stronger. So it is with leaders. (emphasis added)

As for organisations, this process of nurturing holds the key to maintaining the organisation in good health for successful transcendence to the next orbit. This process of nurturing holds key in maintaining the morale and confidence level of employees. The human beings who are at the core of organisations require constant motivation, encouragement, and emotional support to maintain their level of efficiency and commitment. It is the job of gardener-leaders to mentor, encourage, and hand-hold the employees during work, and at times to protect them from unnecessary external interference or unfair treatment. It is also the leader's role to give employees new perspectives of the emerging issues and problems and help them respond positively. As the gardener walks around his garden, the smallest thing becomes a matter of concern for him.

Through constant pruning and shaping like a gardener, the leaders have to continuously nurture their organisations through several steps, such as inculcating new perspectives in the people, broadening their depth and breadth of knowledge and experience, challenging the existing ways of thinking and doing things, developing their competencies and new capabilities, external orientation, innovation and learning culture, recognising talent, and providing opportunity for personal growth and renewal.

Caring by senior leaders is the essence of the nurturing process. Nurturance is key to creating an environment in which people can flourish with their own leadership talent and align their organisations to ever-increasing challenges. In our transformation story, this was amply reflected in our three unique programmes, namely, 'Sampark', 'Khoj', and 'Paramarsh' (Chapter 12), all aimed at nurturing the employees through caring, support, and development.

What Gardener-Leaders Do or Need to Do?

These leaders:

1. Need to be clear about their priorities and redefine role and behaviour to transcend from overwhelmingly 'business mindset' to 'people and organisation mindset'. Also, they need to delegate their day-to-day temptation to engage with business and elevate themselves to leadership and culture crafting work.
2. Constantly work on structure, systems, processes, and people to create an enabling culture for work and help individuals to give their best and rise to their full potential.
3. Act as 'live-in coach' on the job to next-generation leaders, making their knowledge, experience, and wisdom available to them, stand by them during any crisis, and provide meaning in their lives.
4. Foster learning by encouraging creativity, engagement, and personal growth.
5. Guide their teams on the priorities of the organisation and ensure that the execution machinery remains in motion impeccably.
6. Encourage team excellence, which alone can maintain momentum for business.

The challenge before twenty-first century performance-maniac organisations is to create the breed of gardener-leaders. The challenge is a real daunting one to the leaders who are shaping the future of their organisations and want their organisations to flourish without jerks. Building leadership is not a choice but a part of their duty to create long-term future for their organisations. Leadership development is far more challenging than what is normally thought of. Leaders will need to foster intergenerational and intercultural teamwork. To be able to build competitive strength to face the ever-growing challenges, leaders will have to strengthen leadership inside their organisation. In fact, the organisation will be in great peril if today's leaders abandon this role. They must constantly lead their organisations and push them uphill. If they fail to do so, the slide backward would be catastrophic. Leadership development in an organisation is as important as the need for a robust fire system in a multi-storeyed building. But the question is: how do people become such leaders? Peter Senge (1990: 359), the author of the classic, *The Fifth Discipline*, observes:

> Such people are not made to order. They make themselves that way.... The ability of such people to be natural leaders... is the by-product of a life time of effort to develop conceptual and communication skills, to reflect on personal values and to align personal behaviour with values, to learn how to listen and to appreciate others and other's ideas. In the absence of such efforts, personal charisma is style without substance. It leaves those affected less able to think for themselves and less able to make wise choices.

The relevance of gardener-leaders is far more today than ever, and herein lies the responsibility of the individuals to embark upon this ardous journey early in their career.

APPENDIX

TABLE A.1 The BoB's Transformation Exercise

No.	Intangibles	Focus	Mechanism
1.	**Compelling vision**	Conceptualising and building a vision for the future.	• Draft vision document arrived at in the morning meeting sessions. • Sharing the vision across the Bank through structured communication. • Developing accountability at all levels for execution.
2.	**Employee-centric initiatives**	Engagement through caring and listening.	• Employee conclaves. • Monthly letters individually addressed to employees. • Hotline to CEO (Sampark); professional counselling services (Paramarsh). • Town hall meetings. • idea@bankofbaroda.com
3.	**Customer-centric initiatives**	Listening to customer issues.	• Hotline for customer grievances; customer meets at all levels.
		Innovations in retail and SME.	• Retail Loan Factory, SME Loan Factory. • Time deadlines for sanction of loans. • Operationalising over 500 branches from 8 a.m. to 8 p.m.

(Cont'd)

TABLE **A.1** *(Cont'd)*

		Innovation in service level.	• 24-hour banking, Gen-next branches.
4.	**Communication culture**	Building a communication culture across the Bank.	• Guaranteed reply to any communication from employees. • Regular communication with customers and all other stakeholders.
5.	**Leadership pipeline**	To create operational business and strategic leadership.	• Project for development of 300 leaders for the future. • Consultants hired to undertake and implement the project.
6.	**Speed**	Challenging timelines.	• 500 ATMs in first 100 days, including launch of 200 ATMs on a single day. • Record opening of 12 overseas offices in a single year. • Rollout of first CBS branch in less than nine months.
		Creative destruction of delay-producing processes and creating new mindsets.	• Restructuring of Credit Department. • Reduced layers in credit sanctions. • Setting deadlines for decision-making.
7.	**Leveraging technology**	To set in motion all processes for implementing the technology project, including CBS.	• Commenced CBS implementation. • Operationalised 1,700 branches with CBS. • Trained more than 15,000 staff. • Set up specialised IT training centre.

8. **Building human resources**	Capability building in the new environment.	• Massive training effort to create digital literacy across the organisation. • Marketing and selling skills for front line. • Khoj (talent hunting exercise).
	Performance management system (PMS)	• New PMS for officers and workmen.
	Debureaucratising HRM.	• Introduction of single Web-enabled HRM system.
	Structure and systems of HR.	• A new organisational structure for HRM. • Reinvigoration of the Board of Directors' Committee on HR.
9. **Leadership excellence**	Promoting strategic thinking, emotional intelligence, and reflective ability.	• Daily morning meetings with strong focus on 'processes' to build depth and breadth of thinking. • Forum of collective reflection.
	Behavioural competencies and marketing skills.	• Comprehensive leadership development.
	Developing young leadership.	• Identification of different stages of leadership development. • Implementation.
10. **Ethics and governance**	Creating an architecture of ethical functioning.	• Quick action in cases of reports of incidents of unethical working; training in preventive vigilance.

(Cont'd)

TABLE A.1   *(Cont'd)*

	Zero tolerance for ethical violations.	• Introduction of whistle-blower mechanism. • Anti-Sexual Harassment Committee set up.
11. **Branding**	Building new image and repositioning as India's international Bank.	• Rebranding of Bank involving logo change and appointment of youth icon and cricketer Rahul Dravid as brand ambassador.

BIBLIOGRAPHY

Argyris, C. and D. Schön. 1974. *Theory in Practice*. San Francisco, CA: Jossey-Bass.

Awasthi, Richa et al. 2012. 'Organizational Changes in Bank of Baroda', *Asian Case Research Journal*, 16(1): 65–92.

Blake, R.R. and J.S. Mouton. 1976. *Diary of an OD Man*. Book Division, Gulf Publishing.

Brown, Eric. 2014. 'The Role of the CEO—Driving Corporate Culture', available at www.ericbrown.com/role-ceo-driving-corporate-culture.htm.

Business Journal—January 7, 2016, available at http://www.gallup.com/services/190118/engaged-workplace.aspx.

Cullwick, Ian. 2011. 'HR Governance: A Deloitte Point of View', available at http://irc.queensu.ca/articles/hr-governance-deloitte-point-view.

Dalton, M. 1961. 'In Union Management Relations Research', Comments on an article about local union–management relationship by Milton Derby *et al.*, *Industrial and Labour Relations Review*, XIV: 456.

Ghoshal, S. 2005. 'Bad Management Theories Are Destroying Good Management Practices', *Academy of Management Learning & Education*, 4(1): 75–91.

Flanders, A. 1970. *Management and Unions: The Theory and Reforms of Industrial Relations*. London: Faber and Faber.

Fox, A. 1974. Beyond Contract: Work, Power and Trust Relations. London: Faber and Faber.

Govindarajan, V., N.R. Sheth, and T.V. Rao. 1979. *Management Control in Bank of Baroda*. Indian Institute of Management Ahmedabad.

Gallup. 2014. http://www.gallup.com/services/190118/engagedworkplace.aspx (accessed on 10 December 2017).

Heifetz, Ronald A. and Marty Linsky. 2002. *Leadership on the Line: Staying Alive through the Dangers of Leading*. Harvard Business School Press.

Johnson, E.J., S.B. Shu, B.G.C. Dellaert, C.R. Fox, D.G. Goldstein, G. Häubl, R.P. Larrick, J.W. Payne, E. Peters, D. Schkade, B. Wansink, and E.U. Weber. 2012. 'Beyond Nudges: Tools of a Choice Architecture', *Marketing Letters*, 23: 487–504.

Khandelwal, Anil K. 2011. *Dare to Lead: The Transformation of Bank of Baroda*. New Delhi: Sage.

―――. 2016. 'Transformation in a Large Organisation: How Intangibles Drive Tangibles', in T.V. Rao and Anil K. Khandelwal (eds), *HRD, OD and Institutional Building*. New Delhi: Sage.

Khandelwal Committee. 2010. *Report of the Committee on HR Issues of Public Sector Banks*. New Delhi: Ministry of Finance, Government of India (available on the website of Department of Financial Services, Government of India).

Kochan, Thomas. 2012. 'Can America Compete? An Interview', *Harvard Magazine*, September–October, available at http://harvardmagazine. com/2012/09/the-workforce.

Kotter, John and James Haskett. 1992. *Corporate Culture and Performance*. Free Press.

KPMG. 'Now or Never: 2016 Global CEO Outlook'. https://home.kpmg.com/ xx/en/home/insights/2016/06/despite-new-challenges-ceos-confident-in-growth-through-transformation.html (accessed on 10 December 2017).

Lawler, E.E., S.A. Mohrman, G.E. Ledford, T.G. Cummings, and Associates. 1999. *Doing Research That Is Useful for Theory and Practice*, 2nd edition. Lanham, MD: Lexington Books.

Lindblom, C.E. and D.K. Cohen. 1979. *Usable Knowledge*. New Haven, CT: Yale University Press.

Lupton, T. 1983. *Management and Social Sciences*, 2nd edition. Harmonds-worth: Penguin.

Mamkoottam, Kuriakose. 1982. *Trade Unionism, Myth and Reality: Unionism in the Tata Iron and Steel Company*. Oxford University Press

McChrystal, Stanley and others. 2015. *Team of Teams: New Rules of Engagement for a Complex World*. USA: Portfolio, Penguin.

Narasimham Committee. 1991. *Report on Banking Sector Reforms*. Reserve Bank of India.

Parker, P., W. Hawes, A. Lumb, and W. McCarthy. 1971. 'The Reform of Collective Bargaining at Plant and Company Level', Manpower Paper No. 5, Department of Employment, *Her Majesty's Stationery Office*, London.

Paul Polman. 2009. https://www.oneyoungworld.com/counsellors/paul-polman (accessed on 10 December 2017).

Pettigrew, Andrew. 1985. *The Awakening Giant: Continuity and Change in ICI.* Oxford: Basil Blackwell.

Purcell, J. 1981. *Good Industrial Relations.* London: McMillan, p. 66.

————. 1983. 'The Management of Industrial Relations in the Modern Corporation: Agenda for Research', *British Journal of Industrial Relations,* XXI(1): 1–15.

Reserve Bank of India. 2017. *Report on Trend and Progress of Banking in India 2015–16,* p. 9.

Rice, A.K. 1949. 'The Role of the Specialists in the Community: An Illustrative Study of the Relations between Personnel and Executive Managers', *Human Relations,* pp. 177–84.

Rynes, S.L., T.L. Giluk, and K.G. Brown. 2007. 'The Very Separate Worlds of Academic and Practitioner Periodicals in Human Resource Management: Implications for Evidence Based Management', *Academy of Management Journal,* 50(5): 987–1008.

Schein, Edgar H. 2003. *DEC Is Dead, Long Live DEC: The Lasting Legacy of Digital Equipment Corporation.* San Francisco, CA: Berrett-Koehler Publishers.

Senge, Peter M. 1990. *The Fifth Discipline: The Art and Practice of the Learning Organization.* New York: Currency/Doubleday.

Shapiro, I. and J. Wagner DeCew (eds). 1995. *Theory and Practice.* New York: New York University Press.

Sheth, N.R. 1968. *Social Framework of an Indian Factory.* Manchester: Manchester University Press.

Simon, H.A. 1956. 'Rational Choice and the Structure of the Environment', *Psychological Review,* 63(2): 129–38.

————. 1997. *Administrative Behavior,* 4th edition. New York: MacMillan.

Tripathi, Dwijendra. 2007. *The Dynamics of Ascent: A Centenary History of Bank of Baroda.* New Delhi: Oxford University Press.

Tushman, M. and C. O'Reilly. 2007. 'Research and Relevance Implications of Pasteur's Quadrant for Doctoral Programs and Faculty Development', *Academy of Management Journal,* 50(4): 769–74.

Ulrich, Dave (ed.). 1990. *Delivering Results: A New Mandate for Human Resources Professionals.* Harvard Business Review Book.

Uyterhoeven, Hugo. 1989. 'General Managers in the Middle', *Harvard Business Review,* September–October.

Van de Ven, A.H. 2007. *Engaged Scholarships: A Guide for Organizational and Social Research.* New York: Oxford University Press.

Walton, R. and R. McKersie. 1965. *A Behavioural Theory of Labour Negotiation.* New York: McGraw Hill.

Winkler, J. 1974. 'The Ghost at the Bargaining Table: Directors and Industrial Relations', *British Journal of Industrial Relations*, XXII(2): 191–212.

INDEX

ABOUT THE AUTHOR

Anil K. Khandelwal, PhD in management, is former Chairman and Managing Director of Bank of Baroda and Dena Bank. He can be counted as one of the top transformation leaders of India. Under his dynamic leadership, Bank of Baroda became a prime brand in the banking sector in India. As the Chairman and Managing Director of Dena Bank, he was successful in turning around the Bank which was struggling for survival. His brand of leadership focuses on human resources, customer-centric processes, technology, and branding.

His three decades in banking, especially his leadership style, are now legendary. Some periodicals, namely, *Harvard Business Review* and *Human Resource Development International*, and the book, *The India Way* (2010), by Wharton professors, have featured his story, focusing on how he transformed the Bank of Baroda. A multi-awarded Chief Executive Officer (CEO), he is the only banker in India to have been honoured with the Lifetime Achievement Award in Financial Services by The Asian Banker, Singapore. He is also the recipient of the Lifetime Achievement Award from the National HRD Network for his contribution to the profession of human resource development (HRD) in India. He has captured the transformation of Bank of Baroda in his bestselling book, *Dare to Lead* (2011). He is an international keynote speaker and a sought-after leadership trainer. He has chaired the Government of India-appointed committee on HRD for public sector banks (PSBs) and his report has given a push to human resource reforms in the banking sector.

Currently, he is a member of Banks Board Bureau, a high-powered body appointed by the Government of India to select full-time board members for PSBs and to suggest reforms in the banking sector. He is also a Senior Strategic Advisor with the KPMG in India.